D0618846

Confessions of a
Chatroom Freak

Confessions of a Chatroom Freak

Mr Biffo

FRIDAY
BOOKS

First published in Great Britain in 2007 by Friday Books

An imprint of The Friday Project Limited

83 Victoria Street, London SW1H OHW

www.thefridayproject.co.uk
www.fridaybooks.co.uk

Text and photographs © Mr Biffo

ISBN – 978-1-905548-51-4

All rights reserved. No part of this publication may be reproduced or transmitted in any form or by any means, electronically or mechanically, including photocopying, recording or any information storage or retrieval system, without either prior permission in writing from the publisher or a licence permitting restricted copying. In the United Kingdom such licences are issued by the Copyright Licensing Agency, 90 Tottenham Court Road, London W1T 4LP.

British Library Cataloguing in Publication Data

A catalogue record for this book is available from the British Library

Cover and Internal Design by Snowbooks Design
www.snowbooksdesign.com

Printed by MPG Books Ltd

The Publisher's policy is to use paper manufactured from sustainable sources

Foreword

The intanet is a SMASHING thing, and one day I hope to physically own one myself. In the meantime you could do no better/do no worse than to physically read this book, which, as far as I understand, is made up of a number of electronified mail messages sent between one person (whose name is on the cover I think) and others (too many for the cover probably).

The result (of the reading of) is a very funny and severely enjoyable one, and I hope and PRAY that you too will have as much PLEASURE from the time you spend (or are about to spend) reading this book.

So – what are you waiting for?!!!!!!!!!!!!!!!!!!!!!

Happy reading!

All the billy best,

Robin Cooper
Author of The Timewaster Letters

Introduction

I stumbled across the following transcripts while rooting around in a skip for a new pair of trousers. Beneath a pile of rusting segs and ruptured harps I found a discarded laptop. Upon taking it home and powering it up I was confronted with the footprints of an online life: emails, blog extracts, and these remarkable chat sessions.

A series of dialogues between LoopyLisa – animal-obsessed, toilet business-fixated, schoolteacher, special constable and amateur psychic – and a succession of would-be suitors; it seemed somehow wrong to keep them to myself. Indeed, they paint a better picture of our electronically saturated world, and the dank, unspoken reality of online socialising, than any thesis.

Stripped of special requirements, Lisa's admirers reveal themselves to be, by turns, aroused, bigoted and lonely. Judge for yourself whether this is the stark truth lurking beneath the skin of our friends, loved ones, and colleagues.

We can but speculate upon the identity of the real LoopyLisa, though I am confident that she is all woman (probably).

Everything you read in this book is real. Only names have been changed to spare the blushes.

Mr Biffo

LOOPYLISA'S BLOG

Monday, January 09

Hello, loves, and welcome to this: my first ever blog post!

For this first post I'd like to greet you with a list of my top five (8) broad things:

1. Broad beans
2. Broadmoor Hospital
3. Broadcasting
4. Eamon Holmes (broad/fat)
5. "Broads" (women – not in "that" way please)
6. Holidays a-broad
7. Broad Henry (a fictional character I have just thought up)
8. Broadband

In retrospect, the list is nonsense. I have a near-lethal allergy to broad beans, Broadmoor Hospital is full to the rafters with lunatics (and not even the funny kind), I don't really have an opinion on Eamon Holmes, and I've only ever been a-broad twice – and on one of those occasions I was blindfolded.

However, I can assure you that the list isn't a total waste of time. You see, number 8 really is one of my favourite broad-things, because we've just had it "piped" into the living room. Yes, I am now on the Internet literally "2-4-7", and I'm looking forward to making lots of new friends!

You see, if the Internet has taught me one thing, it's that everyone is very friendly.

If it has taught me two things it's that everyone is very friendly, and I should never have clicked on the link to www. dwarfparty.com that my friend Craig sent me.

POSTED BY LOOPYLISA AT 11:30

<<NEW CHAT SESSION STARTED

VWXman: hey there

LoopyLisa21f: Hello, dear

VWXman: so wot do u do then?? work, play, student, mummy, housewife??

LoopyLisa21f: I'm training to be a school teacher, and at weekends I work at a garden centre. We have a special offer on leaves at the moment. "ALL LEAVES: 4% off. ALSO: BUY ONE FROND GET ONE FROND FREE".

VWXman: frond?

LoopyLisa21f: Yes. We sell fronds. In fact, the centre's mascot is a big fern called Frondzie. Sometimes they let me dress up as him. I have to walk around the centre giving the thumbs-up to customers, and saying "Heyyyyy. Buy me and get one free. Heyyyyy".

VWXman: sounds weird

LoopyLisa21f: "Heyyyyy".

LoopyLisa21f: And what do you do, dear?

VWXman: studying IT at mo. mature student

LoopyLisa21f: "IT"? The little brown alien guy?

VWXman: information technology

LoopyLisa21f: Oh!

LoopyLisa21f: So, what do you want to be when you grow up?

VWXman: i am grown up

VWXman: 33

VWXman: tut

LoopyLisa21f: Sorry. You must really hate me now.

VWXman: its ok hun, so u got pic plzzzzzzzzzz?

LoopyLisa21f: Give me some time to take one. I want to look my freshest for you. You don't want to be given one of my mouldy old "snaps".

VWXman: ok

LoopyLisa21f: So, tell me, what are your five favourite smells?

VWXman: what do u mean?

LoopyLisa21f: Exactly that; I want to know your most appreciated stenches.

VWXman: I don't do smells bye

LoopyLisa21f: Wait! Where are you going now?

VWXman: sorry hun its just that a bit of a weird thing 2 ask

LoopyLisa21f: Come on – what are your five favourite smells?

VWXman: er not sure

LoopyLisa21f: Do you want to know mine?

VWXman: not really brb

LoopyLisa21f: "brb"?

VWXman: be right bak

LoopyLisa21f: Hmm. Where are you going?

VWXman: 2 mins

LoopyLisa21f: Please come back. I'm really lonely, and scared. I'm all alone in the house, and I think I can hear a spider.

VWXman: back

LoopyLisa21f: Were you in the lavvy? Were you having a number one or a number two? One time, I accidentally did a number four. You really don't want to know what that's like! Oh man!

LoopyLisa21f: Please ... please tell me where you went.

VWXman: someone at my door

LoopyLisa21f: Was he selling stuff?

VWXman: yeah

LoopyLisa21f: Can we play a game where I try and guess what he was selling?

VWXman: no, i just want u to tell me bout urself hun

LoopyLisa21f: Please let me play that game. It's my favourite game of all time.

VWXman: go on then

LoopyLisa21f: Was he selling tea towels?

VWXman: nope

LoopyLisa21f: Pins (bowling pins)?

VWXman: nope

LoopyLisa21f: Bread?

VWXman: nope

LoopyLisa21f: Cakes of soap?

VWXman: no

LoopyLisa21f: Was he selling Shinola?

VWXman: no wat is that?

LoopyLisa21f: I give up. You tell me what he was selling.

VWXman: dvd's

LoopyLisa21f: Really? Were they illegal ones?

VWXman: yep

LoopyLisa21f: Did you buy any?

VWXman: nope nothing there i wanted

LoopyLisa21f: Have you bought illegal DVDs before? My friend Craig bought a copy of The Grinch once, and The Grinch wasn't even on there – it was just a home video of some people sort of prancing around a field. At one point, one of the people threw a wooden mallet over a fence, and they all ran for it because it landed on a sheep. It really wasn't as good as it sounds.

VWXman: never knocked at my door b4 they usually in pubs

LoopyLisa21f: Yes. In my local pub a man comes round selling pirate clothes.

VWXman: yeh we have that at market like louis vuitton and nike stuff but it got raided

LoopyLisa21f: No! Pirate clothes. You know: velvet breeches, tricorn hats, eyepatches …

VWXman: so wheres this pic then??

LoopyLisa21f: One second.

VWXman: ok

LoopyLisa21f: Sent.

LoopyLisa21f: Did you get it?

<IMAGE SENT – lisa4.jpg>

VWXman: ur a bloke

LoopyLisa21f: What do you mean?

VWXman: well less u sent rong pic ur a bloke

LoopyLisa21f: I don't think I sent the wrong one.

LoopyLisa21f: Let me try again.

LoopyLisa21f: There you go.

<IMAGE SENT – lisa5.jpg>

VWXman: fucking puff piss off

LoopyLisa21f: Well, that's not very nice.

>>VWXman SIGNED OFF AT 12:46

"

LOOPYLISA'S BLOG

Wednesday, January 11

While I finish my teaching degree I've taken a new job working in a garden centre called Riverbank Garden Supplies (Incorporating Riverbank Dung Services PLC., and Gee Eff Kee Dung Accessories Ltd.).

During my interview they seemed keen on my suggestion that they hold an open day, and invite the main, plant-themed celebrities. Ie: Robert Plant, Fern Britten, Stamen Hargreaves, Stem Petal etc.

With the extra money I get from my garden centre work I'm hoping I can save enough to move out of my dad's flat, and into my own home. I want a place where I can have friends over without worrying that my dad is going to walk in wearing nothing but a stained bib and spatz, and try to straddle the dog.

POSTED BY LOOPYLISA AT 14:43

<<NEW CHAT SESSION STARTED

BernieC: hi there

LoopyLisa21f: Good afternoon, dear.

LoopyLisa21f: How are you?

BernieC: i am good hun. bored shitless. u?

LoopyLisa21f: I just had some very bad news – my mum just rang to tell me that my old cat has died.

LoopyLisa21f: He was about 20 years of age, which is about 904 in cat years. I cried so hard that my neck swelled up. It

7

looked like I had a pink tumble dryer tube wrapped around my throat.

BernieC: sorry about that hun

LoopyLisa21f: He didn't even go peacefully. Apparently, he choked to death on a battery.

BernieC: : -(

LoopyLisa21f: You'd think that would have made him more lively, not less.

BernieC: lol

LoopyLisa21f: It was a big one, as well. A 'D' battery. He somehow managed to get the battery compartment off a travel hairdryer, and swallowed the battery in a single gulp. Mum said she watched the whole thing from beginning to end, so I've no idea why she didn't intervene.

LoopyLisa21f: She says she was waiting to see what would happen, but before she realised what was happening it was simply too late to prevent it.

LoopyLisa21f: She was going to try and fish the battery out using a magnet glued to a pencil, but by the time she'd found such a thing the cat was already sneezing up blood, and rolling around on the rug, making a sort of distorted honking sound …

LoopyLisa21f: My dad says the battery probably got lodged in the cat's thorax.

LoopyLisa21f: I dunno how he'd come to that conclusion though – he wasn't even there.

BernieC: : -(

LoopyLisa21f: Him and mum don't live together anymore, you see. Not after she had an affair with Mr Who, who worked in Lidl.

BernieC: the swine

LoopyLisa21f: But the good news is: Mr Who is also dead, having recently frozen to death in a launderette! Anyway – you probably don't want to hear about that.

BernieC: i would rather know about our affair

LoopyLisa21f: Mmmm? Whaaaaa?

BernieC: the one we are gonna have

LoopyLisa21f: Doesn't one of us have to be married in order for that to work?

BernieC: yes

LoopyLisa21f: I've never been married, but one time Craig did ask me to marry him.

BernieC: who is Craig?

LoopyLisa21f: My friend. I don't think he was being serious. He'd drunk two and half a bottles of Peardrax, and could barely stand up. He was so drunk he even pulled down his pants, and tried to do a blow off on a bowl of ice cream! What a mess. What a terrible, unnecessary mess … Are you married, Bernie?

BernieC: yes

LoopyLisa21f: Is your wife nice?

BernieC: lovely

LoopyLisa21f: She can't be that lovely if you want an affair. I'm thinking she maybe does stuff you don't like so much. Does she bite you in the night? I could never marry someone who gave me "night-bites".

BernieC: she is lovely. nothing wrong with some fun though

LoopyLisa21f: Craig said I was lovely when he was drunk on that alcoholic pear drink. He really was very drunk that night. He kept putting peas and stuff in the bottle.

LoopyLisa21f: That was the only time he ever said anything nice about me, actually ...

LoopyLisa21f: What sort of fun do you like?

BernieC: the naughty kind

LoopyLisa21f: Craig was always being naughty. One time he threw a banger out of my car, and it hit an old lady in the neck. It went went off just as it hit her, and she dropped her bread.

LoopyLisa21f: Craig felt really bad, actually. He spent a week in church after that, until he had an argument with the caretaker, because he dropped a bottle of cider in the the font, and it cracked the font.

BernieC: i meant naughty more like you sucking my cock

LoopyLisa21f: Whaaaaa?

LoopyLisa21f: Oh god. I'm just going to open a window.

LoopyLisa21f: The dog's emitted an air biscuit. Hang on.

LoopyLisa21f: Right. Back now. God, what a stench. I swear he's been eating from the toilet again.

LoopyLisa21f: Anyway, what were we talking about? Fireworks? Oh yeah – yeah, fireworks can be really dangerous, so I prefer to go to displays. At least then you know they're mostly always going to take the correct precautions. That said, I was at a display once, and a rocket fell off its shooter, and it shot along the ground, and set fire to a little trumpet.

LoopyLisa21f: Another time, we had some fireworks in Craig's back garden, and he tied a carrot to a rocket! He said it was Carrot Aldrin, even though that wasn't a very good pun. He should've strapped some "fuzz" to a certain brand of "ginger beer", and called it "Fuzz Idris"!

BernieC: I mean naughty in the playing with my cock way

LoopyLisa21f: Oh. Oh, ok.

LoopyLisa21f: what do you want me to do?

BernieC: tell me what u would do with my cock

LoopyLisa21f: Uh ... wash it?

BernieC: i mean suck it wank it

LoopyLisa21f: I dunno about this. I've not ever really done this sort of thing before.

BernieC: first time for everything

LoopyLisa21f: Ok, well, against my better judgement I've kicked things off this end, but I'm really not sure if I'm doing it right. It's making my elbow hurt, and my eyes water.

BernieC: just tell what u would do if i were there

LoopyLisa21f: Alright. Here I go. Are you ready?

LoopyLisa21f: Initially, I would slide into the wardrobe ...

LoopyLisa21f: And then ...

BernieC: ok

LoopyLisa21f: ... And then I would burst out, making a high-pitched squawking sound, like some insane, prehistoric bird.

LoopyLisa21f: Then I would start smashing things up with my fists and feet. Lashing out! Smashing up! Bashing around!

LoopyLisa21f: First I would smash up a photo of my mother.

LoopyLisa21f: Then I would knock the photo of my father off the dressing table, and grind it into the carpet with my heel.

LoopyLisa21f: Then I would stab a photograph of my geography teacher, while making a distressing hissing sound. It is the most unusual sound ever heard by human ears.

BernieC: what about me ?

LoopyLisa21f: I don't have any photos of you.

BernieC: whilst you were doing this i got my cock out

LoopyLisa21f: Ok. Well, you can leave that there for a minute, and watch what I do next.

LoopyLisa21f: This is what I do: I go back into the wardrobe, and I wait there for anything up to five minutes whilst I calm down.

LoopyLisa21f: When I re-emerge, I have become a golden butterfly.

LoopyLisa21f: You open the window for me, and I soar away into the sky, ever higher, until I have disappeared entirely from view.

LoopyLisa21f: It is the most erotic thing you have ever seen.

LoopyLisa21f: What are you doing?

BernieC: waiting for you to be normal

LoopyLisa21f: But I'm speaking in erotic metaphors.

BernieC: and i am wanting you fuck me

LoopyLisa21f: Ok. Well, you have to be patient. It's just that I have never done this kind of thing before. I really haven't. And I fear that things this end have taken a turn for the worse.

BernieC: ok

LoopyLisa21f: I'm trying to "enjoy myself", and normally I like to read erotic poetry, you see.

BernieC: well i am thinking of lying there with you

LoopyLisa21f: Ok. I'll try and picture the scene …

LoopyLisa21f: Is one of us reading a book of erotic poetry?

BernieC: no

LoopyLisa21f: Are we reading a book of normal poetry?

BernieC: no

LoopyLisa21f: Are we reading a book of limericks?

BernieC: no you are rubbing my cock

LoopyLisa21f: With a book of poetry?

BernieC: with your hands

LoopyLisa21f: But I have to hold the book with my hands.

BernieC: the book is gone

LoopyLisa21f: Where did it go?

BernieC: in the bin

LoopyLisa21f: Hmm. Well, I don't know how that would've happened. I would never throw a book away. When I've finished a book I take it to Scope. Though one time they got a bit cross with me, because I took a cookery book in there, and I hadn't realised that Craig had drawn a willy in it, and he'd done it so that it looked like the willy was coming out of a casserole. If you've thrown the book away I really won't be very happy.

LoopyLisa21f: Anyway, let's soldier on.

BernieC: well your rubbing my cock

LoopyLisa21f: Why am I doing that? Is it sore?

BernieC: it will be

LoopyLisa21f: Please can I get the book out of the bin?

BernieC: no

BernieC: because now its in your mouth

LoopyLisa21f: Why is the book in my mouth?

LoopyLisa21f: What am I doing with the book? Am I trying to eat it?

BernieC: nope you are sucking my cock

LoopyLisa21f: I can't do that and have the poetry book in my mouth at the same time. It's quite a large book, because it's full of colour illustrations by Jane Sparrow.

LoopyLisa21f: You know what? I've heard about this sort of thing, and expected it to be quite a lot different to this.

LoopyLisa21f: Don't get me wrong – I'm having fun, but I expected there to be more metaphors.

LoopyLisa21f: Have I disappointed you?

LoopyLisa21f: Hello?

>>BernieC SIGNED OFF AT 15:34

LOOPYLISA'S BLOG

Thursday, February 02

I have mixed feelings over the recent death of my mother's cat. On the one hand it's sad when things (people, animals) die, as our dog did recently when my father straddled him a bit too vigorously. On the other hand, it was a truly horrible cat, and in some ways it probably deserved to die.

Craig said he once caught the cat trying to drown next door's guinea pig, and another time I think I saw the cat smoking a cigarette and pulling a tough face.

Also, its hair was always falling out, and in its bald patches my mother had got the cat tattooed with pictures of her favourite pop stars; Elvis, and that man out of Keane who has a giant baby's head.

POSTED BY LOOPYLISA AT 19:53

<<NEW CHAT SESSION STARTED

Poddm24: hi babe were u from

LoopyLisa21f: Hello, dear. I'm from London.

Poddm24: kewl

LoopyLisa21f: Where are you from, dear?

Poddm24: bristol

LoopyLisa21f: I love those special "Bristol Cakes" you have there.

15

LoopyLisa21f: You ever had those?

Poddm24: no

LoopyLisa21f: They have raisins in them, I think. Do you like raisins?

Poddm24: yep

LoopyLisa21f: What's the difference between "raisins" and currants?

Poddm24: nowt

LoopyLisa21f: What's the difference between currants and "currents"?

Poddm24: wot?

LoopyLisa21f: Currants are the black ones, right … and "currents" are the little green electric ones?

Poddm24: yeh

LoopyLisa21f: You don't really know, do you?

Poddm24: nope

LoopyLisa21f: So, what sort of stuff do you like, dear?

Poddm24: sex drinkin goin tv music girlz

LoopyLisa21f: What do you like drinking?

Poddm24: vodka

LoopyLisa21f: I like squash and cocktails. Actually, I suppose squash is a bit like a cocktail. You know: a cocktail comprised of water and a fruit-flavoured concentrate. I also like drinking Minted Sminnies. Have you ever had one of those?

Poddm24: nope

LoopyLisa21f: They're really minty. I call them 'Sminties' for short. The recipe is as follows: two parts water, three parts ice, and four parts sugar free gum. You put it all in a big glass and just drink it, guy!

Poddm24: ok

Poddm24: r u horny ?

LoopyLisa21f: Not sure. Probably. What do you mean?

Poddm24: u know

LoopyLisa21f: I should warn you that I'm covered in Germolene at the moment. I had a bit of a rough night, if you know what I mean. I had a VERY distressing dream that I was being chased by Patrick Swayze, who was driving this sort of motorised tepee thing. I woke up drenched in sweat, and I must've been thrashing around like an epileptic at a strobe festival, because this morning my skin was utterly shredded.

Poddm24: wot r u wearin

LoopyLisa21f: I'm wearing a pair of leather chaps, and a t-shirt which has a picture of a crab on it, and the words "Das Crab".

Poddm24: kewl r u playin wid ya self

LoopyLisa21f: Not yet! Would you like me to?

Poddm24: yea

LoopyLisa21f: I'll start in a moment. In around 64 seconds, if that's ok.

Poddm24: ok u lik fone sex ?

LoopyLisa21f: I can't do that.

LoopyLisa21f: I'm too hoarse you see. I spent the morning shouting at a hairdresser. I went to get a perm, and fell asleep in the chair, and when I woke up he'd woven tiny little bones into my hair (I think they were cat bones). When I confronted him about it he denied he even worked there, and when I pressed him on the matter he simply curled up beneath a sink, and started crying, and puffing up his cheeks.

Poddm24: ok

LoopyLisa21f: Right. I've started doing that thing you've told me to do.

Poddm24: wot finger your pussy?

LoopyLisa21f: It feels kind of strange. I don't think I'm doing it right.

Poddm24: i wud do it 4 u

LoopyLisa21f: Is it supposed to smell so bad?

LoopyLisa21f: Stuff is coming out.

Poddm24: wot tha stuff look lik

LoopyLisa21f: I dunno ... I don't want to look at it. But it smells awful. It's ... it's wafting up.

Poddm24: is it white and runney

LoopyLisa21f: Shall I look at it?

Poddm24: yeah

LoopyLisa21f: Well ... I've wiped some off with a tissue, and looked at the tissue.

LoopyLisa21f: I probably shouldn't have done that.

Poddm24: wot do it look lik

LoopyLisa21f: It's sort of a beige/brown colour.

Poddm24: cum

LoopyLisa21f: Pardon?

Poddm24: it was cum

LoopyLisa21f: I don't know anything about that.

LoopyLisa21f: It stinks terribly. I'm not sure what it is.

Poddm24: u was fingering your pussy yea?

LoopyLisa21f: What?

Poddm24: was u fingering ya pussy ?

LoopyLisa21f: I was touching my bottom area.

LoopyLisa21f: That is right, yes?

Poddm24: u r meant 2 finger your pussy

LoopyLisa21f: Oh ... oh no. What have I done?!?!

LoopyLisa21f: This is awful.

Poddm24: wot ?

LoopyLisa21f: It's going everywhere. It's just all coming out. Oh no. It's like I've pulled out a plug of compacted matter, and now it's all belching out everywhere. Huge waves of the stuff.

Poddm24: wot is it??

LoopyLisa21f: God ... This is so horrible. It's the worst thing I've ever experienced.

Poddm24: wotz ya number ?

LoopyLisa21f: I can't talk on the phone ... not now ... not after this ... it's such a terrible mess ... all over the chair ... my socks, and wellies ...

LoopyLisa21f: This is awful ... I'm so embarrassed and distressed ...

LoopyLisa21f: What should I do?

LoopyLisa21f: Please, dear – what should I do?!

Poddm24: clean tha shit up

LoopyLisa21f: I am ...

LoopyLisa21f: God ...

LoopyLisa21f: It has literally gone everywhere. I'm using a towel to clean it up. And now I'm having to use another towel.

LoopyLisa21f: Most of it is gone, but the smell lingers on!

LoopyLisa21f: I've never experienced this kind of thing before.

LoopyLisa21f: Are you cross with me?

Poddm24: no just let me fone u

LoopyLisa21f: But I'm in a terrible state now.

LoopyLisa21f: I'm shakin' all over. I feel drained, and headachey.

LoopyLisa21f: Plus: I'm chronically dehydrated, and I feel like someone has thrown a handful of pebbledash at my lower areas.

LoopyLisa21f: How do I explain this to my doctor and colleagues?

Poddm24: just let me fone u

Poddm24: wotz ya number ?

LoopyLisa21f: If I let you call me, will you talk me through the correct procedure to prevent this event from ever occurring again?

Poddm24: yep

LoopyLisa21f: Should I just bung it up with some tissue?

Poddm24: no

LoopyLisa21f: Would a sponge do? I could block up the affected passage with a sponge.

Poddm24: numba

LoopyLisa21f: It's not numb as such. It just smells.

Poddm24: wotz your number?

LoopyLisa21f: I'm scared you'll make fun of me.

Poddm24: i wont

LoopyLisa21f: Oh! Oh, wait ... oh, god ...

LoopyLisa21f: it's started up again

Poddm24: number

LoopyLisa21f: I can't. I need to go and attend to this. It's coming out all sticky and black, like molasses. What HAVE I done?!? Should I call the emergency services?

LoopyLisa21f: It's pulsing out in a sort of sticky foam ...

Poddm24: fone me

LoopyLisa21f: There's more here than you could possibly imagine.

LoopyLisa21f: My entire lap area is covered in grey and black, glutinous suds.

LoopyLisa21f: And it's making a popping noise. Pop-pop ... thrrrrsssss-blubb-blubbb-blubb ... That's how it's going.

Poddm24: gross

LoopyLisa21f: I should go and attend to this. I'll use a loofah, I think.

LoopyLisa21f: Thanks for all your help!

LoopyLisa21f: I love you!

>>LoopyLisa21f SIGNED OFF AT 21:40   **" "**

LOOPYLISA'S BLOG

Saturday, February 04

I had a dream last night that I was a bad angel. I'm not normally a violent person, but I spent most of my dream strutting around Heaven being disruptive, and punching the other angels in the throat.

Eventually, I got hauled up before the Archangel Gabriel, and asked to explain my actions, which included – but were not limited to – forcing an angel to eat his own halo (raw), defacing the Pearly Gates with a marker pen, setting fire to a special henhouse, and making fun of the ghost of James Brown's hair (to be honest, I was surprised to see him up there).

By way of punishment I had to drink an entire trough of penicillin.

POSTED BY LOOPYLISA AT 08:01

 <<NEW CHAT SESSION STARTED

LuvHerts: Hola Lisa

LoopyLisa21f: Hello, dear. Who are you please?

LuvHerts: Ian

LuvHerts: just saying hello

LoopyLisa21f: Yes. Hello, dear. Now tell me something: how are you?

LuvHerts: talented and handsome thanks

LuvHerts: but also single and desperate lol

LoopyLisa21f: I'm sorry to hear that news. I'm so sorry that "it" literally "hurts" my "face".

LuvHerts: it was just an attempt at humour

LoopyLisa21f: Was it? I absolutely LOVE humour! It's so funny! Hoo!

LoopyLisa21f: I especially love the sound of laughter. Unless that laugher ends in tears, or if it's sarcastic laughter, or cruel laughter, like when some guy is laughing to himself because he thinks it's funny to mash up a cat.

LuvHerts: ok.

LoopyLisa21f: I know someone who once laughed until he was sick. It was an awful scene, Ian. You see, he "barfed" all over an insurance claim form. And here's the rub: it was a form for claiming on a vomit-stained pouffe!

LuvHerts: ok lol tell me about yourself

LoopyLisa21f: Well, I would do that, but I don't know exactly what it is that you want to know.

LuvHerts: your likes and dislikes

LoopyLisa21f: This is going to sound a bit whacked-out, but I really like the unicycle I got for Christmas.

LoopyLisa21f: And here's the rub: though I like my unicycle, I dislike my father's tricycle. Sometimes he just sits on it in the corner of the room, parping on his cornet!

LoopyLisa21f: Sometimes I think he likes that trike more than he likes me and Craig. He wrote on the fridge that he did, so I suppose he must. So, y'know ... well ... never mind!!!!!!!!?

LoopyLisa21f: Anyway, dear – tell me the sort of things you enjoy.

LuvHerts: chat, music, games, swapping movies

23

LuvHerts: meeting new people

LoopyLisa21f: I literally LOVE the movies!

LoopyLisa21f: Have you seen The Pilot and the Passenger?

LuvHerts: no is it good?

LoopyLisa21f: Yes. It's about a pilot and a passenger. I don't really remember what happened in it though.

LoopyLisa21f: I think at the start it begins with an inciting incident, which serves as a catalyst for the remainder of the movie.

LuvHerts: I have clearly caught you in a patronising vein

LoopyLisa21f: I'm not being patronising. What makes you think I'm being like that? That's actually really quite upsetting that you think that. I hate that you think I'm being patronising. That's literally beyond comprehension.

LuvHerts: how can I atone for my assumption?

LoopyLisa21f: Shall we start again?

LuvHerts: why not

LuvHerts: I have all the oscar nominated movies on dvd

LoopyLisa21f: All of them? How is that even possible? There isn't a house built that could hold them all! I reckon the only building on earth which could possibly hold that many DVDs is Balmoral, the world's biggest house. But half of that is already stuffed to the rafters with "Royal Bisto", and "Cif".

LuvHerts: I have contacts

LuvHerts: we swap dvds

LuvHerts: I got King Kong two months early

LuvHerts: it was from a negative, cut privately

LoopyLisa21f: Is that even legal?

LuvHerts: do you agree with all laws Lisa?

LoopyLisa21f: Actually, I don't think laws are tough enough. I think criminals should be put in prison regardless of whether or not they've committed a crime.

LoopyLisa21f: Also, I think the punishment should fit the crime. Say if someone has stolen some bread, I reckon they should be made to open a bakery, and then have all their bread stolen, so that they know what it feels like.

LuvHerts: you've never seen a bootleg dvd?

LoopyLisa21f: I did once, but I didn't like it. There were these people doing things to animals.

LoopyLisa21f: There was a scary man wearing a mask inside-out, and he punted a pig up a vent, and bunged up the vent with gloves. And then another man clogged up a cow's udder with Shreddies.

LuvHerts: if you really are a movie fan I can send my lists

LoopyLisa21f: Yes please. Would you like to see my list?

LuvHerts: sigh, go on

LoopyLisa21f:

1. Harris Ford.
2. Greg Peck.
3. Mars.
4. M/A/R/R/S
5. Solar power.
6. Cern.

LuvHerts: what is that a list of?

LoopyLisa21f: I'm not sure. It's just a general list of things I've been thinking about recently.

LuvHerts: one always needs lists

LoopyLisa21f: I guess so. Normally I only make lists of things I need to buy. For example: 1. Courgettes 2. Snails. 3. Nails. 4. Sails etc.

LuvHerts: you like to cook?

LoopyLisa21f: Yes. Yes, I do.

LuvHerts: or train snails with courgettes?

LoopyLisa21f: What are courgettes anyway?

LoopyLisa21f: My dad has always said they were actually dog eye stems, but I've doubted that for some time now.

LoopyLisa21f: Hello? Ian? Ian, have you gone?

LoopyLisa21f: Ian?

>>LuvHerts SIGNED OFF AT 19:47

"

LOOPYLISA'S BLOG

Monday, February 20

I've been given a new cat (I say new, but it is actually over six months old) by one of my neighbour's friends. It is a yellow and orange cat, and it is 18 inches long. Having had 12 or so pets die in the past year alone I was in two minds about taking on another, but I'm pretty confident that this cat is impervious to harm. I don't know why I think that – I just do.

Despite owning many pets over the years, I haven't actually been into a pet shop since I was seven years old. On my birthday that year, my dad had promised me a trip to a pet shop to buy a tortoise, but he actually took me to a local butcher's shop as a joke. When we went inside he told me that the pet shop owner had gone mad, and killed all the pets.

It was even worse than the time he took me to "Alton Towers" (a rundown rendering plant on the outskirts of Daventry).

POSTED BY LOOPYLISA AT 17:15

<<NEW CHAT SESSION STARTED

Swanvester1975: are you really Loopy?

LoopyLisa21f: I don't know about that, but I'm certainly quite itchy! My cat has fleas, you see.

Swanvester1975: ok not fun

LoopyLisa21f: I've scratched a hole in my t-shirt already, and I'm practically through to the bone on my ankles. That isn't even a lie!

LoopyLisa21f: What's good for flea-bites – other than rubbing your shins against a flea-ridden cat, that is? Ha ha. Ha. <COUGH>

Swanvester1975: vineger

LoopyLisa21f: Urrgh! I'm not drinking that!

LoopyLisa21f: I could mix it with some orange squash, I suppose.

Swanvester1975: are you mad!?!!

LoopyLisa21f: You're the one who told me to drink vinegar. It isn't my idea.

LoopyLisa21f: It might taste better if it has ice cubes in. Hang on.

LoopyLisa21f: I'm going to find out. One moment please.

LoopyLisa21f: …

Swanvester1975: hello ??

LoopyLisa21f: OK! Back now.

LoopyLisa21f: I have to say – that is the most DISGUSTING drink I've ever had.

LoopyLisa21f: I took two big mouthfuls, but most of it came out again – through my nose and bottom.

Swanvester1975: jesus

LoopyLisa21f: That is the most revolting thing I have EVER tasted. Worse even than the time Craig made me eat a bit of mud he'd pickled.

LoopyLisa21f: I can really taste the vinegar through the squash and the ice. I thought it would be disguised more than that, but it isn't at all.

Swanvester1975: u off ur trolly. took your mind off the bites though

LoopyLisa21f: Yes, but now I'm thinking about doing some vomiting.

LoopyLisa21f: Do you want some advice?

Swanvester1975: yes

LoopyLisa21f: Don't ever dilute orange squash with vinegar and try to drink it. It's horrible. You see – it will make you want to vomit.

Swanvester1975: advice taken. so what do u look like?

LoopyLisa21f: You first. Be warned – I'm still fighting my gag reflex. So if you're hideously deformed in some way I really don't want to know.

Swanvester1975: I am 6ft1 very athletic build with brown eyes.

LoopyLisa21f: Wow! You sound like a movie star! You know: like "Rock Cracksie", or Sir Ian McKellen.

LoopyLisa21f: I really do want to vomit, you know.

Swanvester1975: what do u look like tho?

LoopyLisa21f: I'm 12' 5".

Swanvester1975: babes

LoopyLisa21f: Yes, dear?

Swanvester1975: have you a pic?

LoopyLisa21f: Yes. Yes I do. Unfortunately it isn't the sort of pic you can see with the naked eye. It's on microfiche.

LoopyLisa21f: Do you know anything about refrigerators, incidentally?

Swanvester1975: yes why?

LoopyLisa21f: I think mine is broken. Earlier it started leaking some sort of gas out the back, and it has made me feel all dizzy.

Swanvester1975: switch it off

LoopyLisa21f: I have. I took the plug out, but the stuff is still coming out. It's making my eyes water. Also: it is starting to defrost!

Swanvester1975: can you not cover it wih something and open the windows?

LoopyLisa21f: I opened a top window, and put a tea towel over it, but that hasn't helped a great deal. There really is quite a lot of stuff coming out now. It's sort of billowing out the back, and covering the floor of the entire flat. It would be a cool effect if I wasn't so worried about it being hazardous to my health. It's like a scene from The Matrix, or Ocean's 11!

LoopyLisa21f: It's making me feel even more sick than I was already.

LoopyLisa21f: It isn't bothering the cat, at least. He went to sleep.

Swanvester1975: can you not take the fridge outdoors?

LoopyLisa21f: Not on my own.

LoopyLisa21f: It's a big one. It's a Zanussi "Icebandit".

LoopyLisa21f: I don't think it would fit on the balcony anyway. I could push it over the balcony, but there are cars below. Cars, children … a fat goth in a wheelchair …

LoopyLisa21f: Actually, I just thought of something: should I put the cat somewhere else?

LoopyLisa21f: His bed is right by the fridge, see.

Swanvester1975: nah it will be ok

LoopyLisa21f: Ok. I think the gaseous barf is thinning at last. Or the clouds are taking on more of a sort of blue tinge, anyway.

LoopyLisa21f: I've opened another window. God, I do feel ill. Vinegar and fridge-fumes: the worst combination of badness known to man.

LoopyLisa21f: Shall I check the cat?

Swanvester1975: if you like

LoopyLisa21f: One moment please.

LoopyLisa21f: ...

LoopyLisa21f: The cat won't wake up.

Swanvester1975: ha ha

LoopyLisa21f: It's not funny. I'm not joking. I've shaken it really hard, and it's gone all limp. I shook it, and tried to shock it out of its bed by banging a ladle on the floor, but it wouldn't move. What shall I do?

LoopyLisa21f: It's still breathing, but not very hard. Very shallow breaths. It's taking gulps of air in its sleep. This is YOUR fault.

LoopyLisa21f: You told me not to ruddy move her. I asked whether I should move her, and YOU told me not to. If she dies I'll sue you.

Swanvester1975: wtf? don't have go at me

LoopyLisa21f: First you make me feel sick by making me drink your stupid "invisibility potion", and then you kill my cat. What am I supposed to do!? I don't even know you, yet you deliberately and maliciously set out to ruin my afternoon. What DO I do NOW, you spiteful malcontent?!

Swanvester1975: throw the cat out the window

Swanvester1975: and then jump out yourself

LoopyLisa21f: I have to say I don't think that's a very polite or helpful attitude to have towards a complete stranger like myself.

Swanvester1975: fuck ur mental!

>>Swanvester1975 SIGNED OFF AT 13:43

LOOPYLISA'S BLOG

Saturday, March 04

Well, the "new" cat didn't last very long. According to the vet, fumes from my leaking fridge caused the cat to develop the worst case of lockjaw he had seen in thirty-seven years. In fact, the cat's jaws were so tightly locked together that they had actually created their own gravity field.

The vet demonstrated this by dropping paperclips near the cat's head. Sure enough, the paperclips landed on the cat's face as if they were space capsules landing on a small, furry moon (admittedly, the cat's head may have been magnetic, rather than gravitational, but I only thought of this later).

As odd as the paperclip thing was, my main concern was how to feed the cat. The vet tried pouring soup down the cat's nose, but this just made the cat die even faster.

POSTED BY LOOPYLISA AT 18:18

<<NEW CHAT SESSION STARTED

HoDoYouDo2000: hi Lisa. have you a picture of yourself ?

LoopyLisa21f: Yes I do.

HoDoYouDo2000: bet ur sexy

LoopyLisa21f: Well, I don't know about that. Nobody has ever really said that before. Oh, goodness – I'm such a terrible blusher. I'm blushing so hard that I've burst a blood vessel in my eye: Pow!

LoopyLisa21f: There goes another one: Ka-ka-ta-pow!

HoDoYouDo2000: whatever

LoopyLisa21f: It's like there's a party in my eyes, and the following people are invited: Iris Brown, Chris Astigmatism, and Reginald (Retinal) Bleeding.

HoDoYouDo2000: ok

LoopyLisa21f: Actually, seeing as you asked so nicely I will send you a picture of myself.

HoDoYouDo2000: have you a web cam ??

LoopyLisa21f: Yes I do! In fact, I've just this second used it to "snap myself", and send you something a little cheeky. Check your emails.

HoDoYouDo2000: ok

<IMAGE SENT – lisa11.jpg>

LoopyLisa21f: Do you like it?

HoDoYouDo2000: can i have a clearer one please?

LoopyLisa21f: One moment please.

HoDoYouDo2000: what you doin ???

LoopyLisa21f: Just taking one now. Have patience.

HoDoYouDo2000: ok. sweet

LoopyLisa21f: There you go, dear …

LoopyLisa21f: Do you have it yet? Can you see me in all my glory?

<IMAGE SENT – lisa7.jpg>

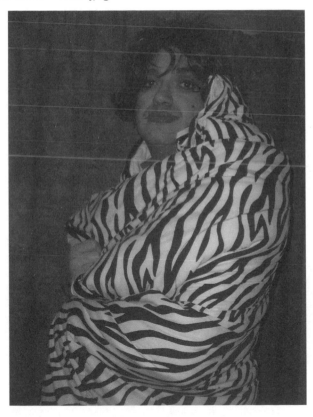

HoDoYouDo2000: take a sexier one

LoopyLisa21f: So you'd like to see me being even sexier than THAT??!

HoDoYouDo2000: yes please

LoopyLisa21f: I don't know if that's even physically possible. I'll try though.

LoopyLisa21f: ...

LoopyLisa21f: Ok. That was pretty exhausting, but I think I got myself looking moderately sexy.

LoopyLisa21f: Do you want to see it?

HoDoYouDo2000: please

<IMAGE SENT – lisa10.jpg>

HoDoYouDo2000: thats a bloke

LoopyLisa21f: That's me.

HoDoYouDo2000: looks like a bloke

LoopyLisa21f: That's an awful thing to say. I'm really hurt.

LoopyLisa21f: I've done a big smile for you and everything.

HoDoYouDo2000: bloke

LoopyLisa21f: What? What do you mean? Please – please tell me what I have to do to make myself look sexy enough for you.

HoDoYouDo2000: bloke

HoDoYouDo2000: bloke

LoopyLisa21f: Why are you being so nasty to me?

HoDoYouDo2000: bloke

HoDoYouDo2000: bloke

LoopyLisa21f: I'm not a bloke. I've never been so hurt as this. I've never done anything bad to anyone, and this is what I get?

LoopyLisa21f: I'll even show you a photocopy of my actual bra if proof is what you need.

HoDoYouDo2000: no thanks it is a bloke

LoopyLisa21f: Please stop hurting my feelings. I don't have a "John Thomas", or anything.

HoDoYouDo2000: fuck off

LoopyLisa21f: If I turn up dead on the news it'll be YOUR fault you know.

HoDoYouDo2000: fuck off

>>HoDoYouDo2000 SIGNED OFF AT 20:21

LOOPYLISA'S BLOG

Tuesday, March 07

I have to say, I'm a little taken aback by some of the reactions I've received whilst chatting to people online. Not everyone is quite as friendly as I'd hoped they'd be.

Yesterday, I arranged to meet up with one of my new friends for a coffee, but he seemed to take great offence at my appearance. When I tried to kiss him hello he forced me backwards over a table, violently rubbed a handful of brown sugar into the top of my head, and stomped out of the coffee shop.

It's a shame, because he runs a party accessories shop, and when we spoke online he'd promised to help me fulfil a long-held dream I've had of working in my own joke shop.

According to his inventory sheet, he sells the following novelty items: Black-Face Golf Balls, Electric-shock Cuttlefish, Dribble-Me-Do Toilet Seats, a new type of Big-Mouth Billy Bass which functions only intermittently, and over four types of whimsical belt.

POSTED BY LOOPYLISA AT 11:22

<<NEW CHAT SESSION STARTED

seasideuser: hi where r u? u doing good?

LoopyLisa21f: I'm doing good in London! Where are you?

seasideuser: Weymouth by the sea

LoopyLisa21f: I know Weymouth! That's where they have that massive whale sanctuary.

LoopyLisa21f: Have you been?

seasideuser: dont know bout any whales i would have spotted them

LoopyLisa21f: It's a big sanctuary a little way down the coast from you.

LoopyLisa21f: They have all sorts of whales there. They take care of injured whales, sick whales, endangered whales, whales with stuff jammed down their blowholes. I think one time they had a whale brought in which had half a bicycle stuck up its ruddy arse crack! They had to employ a giant electromagnet to get it out.

LoopyLisa21f: They keep the whales in a big warehouse, and you can go and watch them put on shows.

LoopyLisa21f: They have a man there who rides the blue whale. He actually climbs inside the blowhole, while it drags itself around a stage making this mournful lowing, and the man waves to the crowd!

LoopyLisa21f: He only wears a little cropped t-shirt while he does it. It's cool. Also, for some reason I keep wondering where he bought the t-shirt …

LoopyLisa21f: Anyway, I've never been, but Craig said it was the third best thing he'd ever seen, after his dog swallowing a bee, and a Billy Joel concert he went to in 1988. Joel fell off the stage and crushed an admin assistant!

LoopyLisa21f: Apparently, the whale sanctuary also has this whale called Gerhart Clank, who had a stroke. He keeps listing to the right, and just goes round and round his tank all day, scraping against the side. It's so sad. "Gerhart Clank: he lists in his tank!" – that's what it says on the sign.

seasideuser: we are talking weymouth not california for whales. monkey sanctuary maybe

seasideuser: u type 2 fast! cant keep up

LoopyLisa21f: So, they have a monkey sanctuary in Weighmouth too?

seasideuser: and donkeys

LoopyLisa21f: And donkeys! Are the monkeys and donkeys in the same sanctuary?

LoopyLisa21f: That would be cool! I hope the monkeys ride the donkeys. They could dress them like jockeys! If they were spider monkeys, and the donkeys themselves were on the small size, the whole thing would be at a scale relative to human/horse racing.

LoopyLisa21f: Craig says when he was in Thailand he ate a proboscis monkey's nose.

LoopyLisa21f: He said he put it in a bap with some poupon. Do you think he was lying?

LoopyLisa21f: It wouldn't be the first time.

seasideuser: Who is craig r u sure he came to the south coast ?

LoopyLisa21f: Craig is my friend. One time he told me Eamon Holmes was in my back garden, and he wasn't.

seasideuser: no ?

LoopyLisa21f: Nope!

LoopyLisa21f: Craig said I was really gullible to believe him, but if someone told you something like that, you'd still go and have a look wouldn't you? Craig had said he was just standing there, all alone.

LoopyLisa21f: But by the time I'd got back from the shop he was gone. I wish I'd seen him …

seasideuser: not good having some fat irish bloke in your garden annoying the neighbours

LoopyLisa21f: Well ... he wouldn't really be annoying anyone if he was just standing there. At worst he'd be trespassing.

seasideuser: what with a film crew ?

LoopyLisa21f: No, on his own.

LoopyLisa21f: Craig told me he was standing there looking really sad, and staring at his hands.

seasideuser: probably didnt like the garden

LoopyLisa21f: But he wasn't there when I got back. Do you think Craig lied to me? Perhaps he didn't lie, but the whole thing seems pretty unlikely.

seasideuser: eammon prob saw u not there so buggered off got a programme to make

LoopyLisa21f: I guess so. It's a bit sad if it really was him, and he's just wandering around, ending up in people's back gardens.

LoopyLisa21f: I hope he's ok.

seasideuser: hope he doesnt come to mine

LoopyLisa21f: Please don't be too mean to him if he does, though.

seasideuser: what music do you like?

LoopyLisa21f: I like Yorkie Peters.

seasideuser: who??

LoopyLisa21f: He's a singer.

LoopyLisa21f: Do you not know him?

LoopyLisa21f: He sung that song – 'Knickers For Sale'.

seasideuser: yorkie peters?

LoopyLisa21f: Yup!

LoopyLisa21f: You remember it?

seasideuser: no! tryin to find a pic of him online

LoopyLisa21f: The song went "I've put your knickers on sale … I don't want to see them on my bedroom floor no more … I've taken them down the car boot sale … I hope to get four pounds or more".

seasideuser: lol!

LoopyLisa21f: So what "music" do you like specifically, please?

seasideuser: anything a bit sensual

LoopyLisa21f: Pardon?

seasideuser: theres is more to life than just a quicky

LoopyLisa21f: A quicky?

seasideuser: sex

LoopyLisa21f: Oh!

LoopyLisa21f: I understand.

LoopyLisa21f: Yes. I understand now. Here we go.

seasideuser: just jumping quick into bed is such a waste of something that could last and enjoy for hours

LoopyLisa21f: My mum told me that if you have too much sex you get thrush.

seasideuser: I wish I got thrush that way

LoopyLisa21f: No you don't. I had it once, and had to spoon yoghurt down my trousers until it went. It burnt so bad one day that out of sheer, tear-stained frustration I smashed myself between the legs with a Cornetto.

seasideuser: really??

seasideuser: well,, at least you had lots of sex

LoopyLisa21f: My mum accused me of having done so.

LoopyLisa21f: But it just wasn't true. To be honest, I'm glad she's terminally ill.

seasideuser: oh

seasideuser: well it proves that you dont have to have lots of sex to get it

seasideuser: often is a conbination of things

LoopyLisa21f: Yeah. She said it was because I'd done too much rudies, or I'd been putting, you know, things where they shouldn't go. I guess she means like that time I put my gonks in the fridge. She really had a go at me for that, because I got gonk hair in the butter.

LoopyLisa21f: Never mind! The thrush is mostly gone now! No more itchies.

seasideuser: no.. often you only have to have sex with someone who`s lacking in hygiene

LoopyLisa21f: I know all about that. Craig used to eat pickled onion Monster Munch, and then try and kiss me.

seasideuser: personaly,, I do like sex like evreyone else, but I do like the extras

LoopyLisa21f: Like pickled onion Monster Munch?

seasideuser: no way !!! like gentle kissing ...the sensual touch ... the feeling ...

LoopyLisa21f: Another time Craig had got piccalilli all down his t-shirt, and he'd wiped Marmite on the front of his pants, and came into the living room, and started dancing – even though there wasn't any music. For a while I thought he'd been sick and dirtied himself, and not cleaned it up.

seasideuser: one should never eat anything spicy b4 you get near your partner seasideuser: Would spoil the love making

LoopyLisa21f: Well, I guess. It's just not very nice in general life either, though.

seasideuser: so.. you have a b`fiend?

LoopyLisa21f: No, I don't go out with Craig anymore. He's just a friend now. One time I was kissing Craig and he moved my hand to his bottom, and broke wind! I couldn't stand him doing that sort of thing. He made me smell my hand afterwards.

seasideuser: aaaggghh!!

seasideuser: where is the romance ??

LoopyLisa21f: We eventually broke up when he contracted Sifflesons Contagion.

seasideuser: thats why now so many girls go with older men

LoopyLisa21f: Why?

LoopyLisa21f: Because they have Sifflesons?

seasideuser: more romance into it for a start

seasideuser: and more sensable

LoopyLisa21f: Sifflesons isn't very romantic.

seasideuser: I know ...

LoopyLisa21f: When he got it he was always wetting himself, and falling off patios.

seasideuser: i wasnt talking about that

LoopyLisa21f: And he would make that horrible clicking sound as his head lolled around, and his mouth flapped open.

LoopyLisa21f: And it freaked me out the way he was able to change the channel on "TV" just by doing the clicking really fast.

seasideuser: yo better off without him

LoopyLisa21f: Yeah, but he still makes me laugh.

LoopyLisa21f: He's always doing crazy stuff!

LoopyLisa21f: One time we were in a model village, and he kicked a church over a fence, and emptied his pockets all over Trafalgar Square!

seasideuser: and you r looking for romance?

LoopyLisa21f: I don't mind – romance is fun!

seasideuser: my name is Luis by the way

LoopyLisa21f: Hello Luis! That's an unusual name. I guess people are always saying stuff to you like "The Luis blocked because Luis put too much toilet paper down it again", and "Luis has gone down the shops to buy a tightening strap because his trousers are too Luis".

seasideuser: spanish name

LoopyLisa21f: Excellent! So you must know El Denizio.

seasideuser: whats that?

LoopyLisa21f: He makes the best Yorkshire Puddings in Spain.

seasideuser: you are kidding?!

LoopyLisa21f: No! I went there on holiday, and he owned this little restaurant, and they were doing Yorkshire puddings. Yorkshire Puddings full of crab paste and roast perrins.

LoopyLisa21f: Oh! Oh, I have to go.

seasideuser: oh nooo..

LoopyLisa21f: My dad just came in and threw a load of paint over me.

LoopyLisa21f: He told me to get off the net in case his auntie calls to tell him about her parrot's rash.

seasideuser: ok,,, coud we chat again?

    LoopyLisa21f: Yes please, Ellis!

    LoopyLisa21f: Goodbye!

seasideuser: its Luis

seasideuser: xxxx

>>LoopyLisa21f SIGNED OFF AT 13:45   **"**

LOOPYLISA'S BLOG

Sunday, March 12

I had a dream last night that I had a job labelling quantities of sodium benzoate, putting them in small, plastic boxes, and mailing them to research companies up and down the country. Doing that took up most of the morning, then after lunch it was my task to separate combined acids from their base components using a centrifuge.

Once the components were separated they were channelled into a silicone block, and studied beneath an infra red microscope. The initial reaction rates, measured by the rate of oxygen uptake, and the yields of terephthalic acid, were used to compare the effectiveness of acid additives. The autoxidation reaction increased with the Mn(OAc) concentration. This was confirmed by studying the reaction between Mn(OAc) and p-xylene in the presence of trifluoroacetic acid.

POSTED BY LOOPYLISA AT 16:56

<<NEW CHAT SESSION STARTED

RobbieRaxman23: hi there sorry to bother you but do you fancy a natter ?

LoopyLisa21f: I do, actually.

RobbieRaxman23: cool i was hoping for an awncer along those lines

RobbieRaxman23: hows you n your day going thus far ?

LoopyLisa21f: I'm having a really weird day.

RobbieRaxman23: oh whys that ?

LoopyLisa21f: I had to call out an ambulance this morning.

LoopyLisa21f: I went out to pick up the milk, and there was a dying tramp in my front garden.

RobbieRaxman23: shit thats bad

LoopyLisa21f: I called an ambulance, and they took him away.

RobbieRaxman23: do you know if he is ok now ?

LoopyLisa21f: I don't know. The ambulance men just told me he was dying because he'd probably eaten some bad tramp food. You know: out of a bin, or a toilet.

RobbieRaxman23: i can see why your day is a bit strange so far

LoopyLisa21f: That's not all.

RobbieRaxman23: do go on

RobbieRaxman23: dose it get weirder lol ?

LoopyLisa21f: I asked if they were going to take him to a hospital to, y'know, somehow prevent him from dying, but they just shook their head, tapped the sides of their noses, winked, and then laughed.

LoopyLisa21f: It creeped the hell out of me.

RobbieRaxman23: what ???????????????????

RobbieRaxman23: why did they do that?

LoopyLisa21f: I've no idea. Maybe they have somewhere special for dying tramps to go. A sort of tramp abattoir. Or maybe they take tramps off to a basement somewhere, and hold special tramp Olympics, and the tramp who gets the gold gets to have some medicine. Or some gin.

RobbieRaxman23: are you winding me up with that one ?

LoopyLisa21f: I've no idea if I am or not. It just really freaked me out. I felt somehow complicit in whatever it was that they were planning to do.

LoopyLisa21f: I'm really shaken up by it.

RobbieRaxman23: thats well fucked up pardon my french

LoopyLisa21f: I don't mind finding dead animals in my garden (we've had them all – badgers, magpies, rabbits, foals …), but not a big, human tramp.

LoopyLisa21f: Have you ever seen a dead animal?

RobbieRaxman23: yer i have

RobbieRaxman23: i went with my mum n dad to have 3 of our dogs put down and a few years ago i hit a deer with my car

LoopyLisa21f: We had to have one of our dogs put down. He ate some of the keys off my dad's piano, and got one stuck in its throat, and it restricted the air to his brain, and gave him dog-brain damage.

RobbieRaxman23: thats not good

LoopyLisa21f: If you consider that dogs are already pretty stupid you can imagine what a brain-damaged one is like.

RobbieRaxman23: yer

LoopyLisa21f: Afterwards, he could only bark backwards. "Foow! Foow! F'toom!"

LoopyLisa21f: Do you want to play truth or dare?

RobbieRaxman23: yer go on then but it will just be truth cos internet dare aint no fun is it lol

LoopyLisa21f: No. No, I suppose not. I played it on here with someone once, and he dared me to lick a piece of raw chicken, and I did, but he didn't believe me. It gave me a chicken virus, and everything. I had to spend three weeks in a hospital coop.

RobbieRaxman23: truth or truth sounds more achivable

LoopyLisa21f: Ok. Let's do that. You ask me first.

RobbieRaxman23: no no ladys first

LoopyLisa21f: Ok. Which would you rather eat – a dog, or a cat?

RobbieRaxman23: errrrr a dog i think i hate cats

LoopyLisa21f: What? You hate the taste of cats?

RobbieRaxman23: no just in general

LoopyLisa21f: But if you like dogs, why would you want to eat one?

RobbieRaxman23: more meat i guess

RobbieRaxman23: what a strange question

LoopyLisa21f: Ok. Your turn to ask.

RobbieRaxman23: rite here goes

LoopyLisa21f: Ok.

RobbieRaxman23: sorry brb phone ?

LoopyLisa21f: I don't understand the question.

RobbieRaxman23: ok ok miss funny

LoopyLisa21f: Mm? But I really don't understand it.

RobbieRaxman23: sorry about that back now

RobbieRaxman23: do you know what … that first question has totaly put me off track

LoopyLisa21f: Why?

RobbieRaxman23: why did you even ask that as a question ?

LoopyLisa21f: I just wanted to know the answer. It's something I'm really interested to know.

RobbieRaxman23: just a very random thing to ask

LoopyLisa21f: Not really.

RobbieRaxman23: ok did you realy see a dying tramp?

LoopyLisa21f: Yes.

RobbieRaxman23: whot about the stuff with the tramp abbattoir?

LoopyLisa21f: That was me extrapolating from the evidence at hand. I can't be sure such a place exists. Nobody can be sure of that. Not unless they've been there in person, and I've only been there in my imagination.

RobbieRaxman23: sure. go on your turn

LoopyLisa21f: Ok.

LoopyLisa21f: How much money would you have to be paid to eat an entire beehive full of wasps?

RobbieRaxman23: there is not enough money you could pay me to eat 1 wasp let alone a full bee hive of them

LoopyLisa21f: Everyone has their price.

RobbieRaxman23: nope im unbuyable on that one

LoopyLisa21f: What about a beehive full of bees?

RobbieRaxman23: no

LoopyLisa21f: Would you do it for £12 billion?

RobbieRaxman23: nope sorry no deal

LoopyLisa21f: That's a real big shame.

RobbieRaxman23: i think id die from the stings

LoopyLisa21f: Not if you ate them over the course of the rest of your life —one every couple of weeks.

RobbieRaxman23: but that will be no good to you then will it because you would get paid as you eat the last one and what good is all that money when you are dead ?????

LoopyLisa21f: That's a very good point. I haven't thought this through, have I?

LoopyLisa21f: You could have the money in instalments, I suppose.

LoopyLisa21f: £100 per wasp.

RobbieRaxman23: thats not a bad deal

RobbieRaxman23: but i think there is some kinks to iron out

LoopyLisa21f: So you're coming around to the idea?

LoopyLisa21f: What about a beehive full of baby porcupines?

RobbieRaxman23: your now moving the gole posts to suit you own rules lol

LoopyLisa21f: The rules haven't changed, I'm just making it easier for you to accept the terms of what is, essentially, a bizarre deal.

RobbieRaxman23: i need not accept it i wouldnt do it lol

LoopyLisa21f: Ok. Your turn to ask.

RobbieRaxman23: i cant think im sorry im totaly stunned by these questions

LoopyLisa21f: Why?

LoopyLisa21f: What's the beef here, son?

RobbieRaxman23: theyre so randon

RobbieRaxman23: good but random

RobbieRaxman23: ok ok i got one would you drink you own wee wee ?

LoopyLisa21f: Under what circumstances?

RobbieRaxman23: thats all i can think of along this weird line of questions. i saw a thing on telly about people who do so it stuck in my mind

RobbieRaxman23: just as a thing to drink ?

LoopyLisa21f: Well, no. Never just as a thing to drink.

LoopyLisa21f: Maybe if my life depended on it I might have a sip.

LoopyLisa21f: Or to wash out the taste of the wasps.

LoopyLisa21f: Would I be allowed to drink it out of a cup? Or would I have to go to the source (as it were)?

RobbieRaxman23: pardon???

RobbieRaxman23: some people think is good for them and just drink it as a drink

LoopyLisa21f: Yes, but those people are disgusting idiots. I mean, they drink wee wee, for heaven's sake! What must their breath smell like?!

LoopyLisa21f: Like a toilet, I'd imagine. I wonder what they eat …

RobbieRaxman23: go on your go

LoopyLisa21f: Ok.

RobbieRaxman23: ok ok

LoopyLisa21f: What would you rather be stuck on a desert island with – one gorilla, or your worst enemy?

RobbieRaxman23: my worst enemy

LoopyLisa21f: What if your worst enemy was a gorilla?

RobbieRaxman23: how wud that be possible?

LoopyLisa21f: Maybe you ran over his bride. Maybe you laughed at him in a zoo, and it really hurt his feelings, and he has never forgotten about it.

LoopyLisa21f: I love monkeys. They're nature's funny guys!

RobbieRaxman23: but gorillas are not monkeys

LoopyLisa21f: Yes they are. Of course they are.

RobbieRaxman23: ok if you were on a desert island would you rather have a gun with one bullit or 1 pork pie ?

LoopyLisa21f: I would have one gun, please. Then I could use it to shoot down a coconut (I don't really like pork pies). Also, I would use the gun to dig a hole, and I would sleep in the hole at night, so that I was below the horizon.

RobbieRaxman23: h aha ok

RobbieRaxman23: off you pop hit me with it

LoopyLisa21f: How much money would you need to be paid to change your name to "Rory Anus"?

RobbieRaxman23: not a lot i think thats a lovely name then my son could be called little anus lol

LoopyLisa21f: Do you have a son?

RobbieRaxman23: no but it a thought for the future

LoopyLisa21f: Yes. Good. Your turn.

RobbieRaxman23: ok i got a silly one for you

RobbieRaxman23: if you went in to space a went for a walk about in a space suit what would you rather do – fart or be sick ??

LoopyLisa21f: Oh, fart. The fart will probably be cleared away in time by the suit's air system. Don't you think? Or are you thinking of a different sort of fart? You know: the sort of fart which has both a physical, as well as an aural and smellial composition.

RobbieRaxman23: you are a forward thinker i like you

RobbieRaxman23: ok shoot

LoopyLisa21f: Right. If you could go back in time, when and where would you go?

RobbieRaxman23: the wild west cos it looks real fun on back to the future

LoopyLisa21f: I'd like to go back and watch some really early episodes of Only Fools And Horses.

RobbieRaxman23: but you can get then on dvd

RobbieRaxman23: derrrrr brain

LoopyLisa21f: Yeah, but the DVDs are really expensive.

RobbieRaxman23: theyre on UK Gold all the time

LoopyLisa21f: I don't have cable.

LoopyLisa21f: I know! I'd like to go back in time, and meet the Queen!

RobbieRaxman23: hello?!? u can meet the queen now. She is still alive!!!!

LoopyLisa21f: I must go shortly.

LoopyLisa21f: I have to pick up my friend Craig from the doctor.

RobbieRaxman23: oh ok

LoopyLisa21f: Last night he kept rubbing his face up against the radiator, and rubbed off his eyebrows. He just wanted to check that they'll grow back.

RobbieRaxman23: oh i see

LoopyLisa21f: Anyway. Must dash. Nice talking to you.

RobbieRaxman23: and you take care

>>LoopyLisa21f SIGNED OFF AT 19:34

LOOPYLISA'S BLOG

Friday, March 24

I've noticed that I've been putting on a bit of weight recently, so I decided that it was long overdue that I did some exercise. To this end, I signed up for some local flamenco dancing lessons, but realised upon arrival that I'd misread the advert, and had actually signed up for FLAMINGO dancing lessons.

As you might expect, this is a special sort of dancing that people do with flamingos. Unfortunately, flamingos are fairly hard to come by in this country, and so we all had to IMAGINE we were dancing with flamingos.

Some of the people were really getting into it, muttering things to their imaginary flamingos, like *"You're a really good bird"*, and *"I like pink birds like you"*, and *"What sort of food do you like best – is it seeds? Or something else?"*.

I decided to leave when the dance instructor rang a bell, and announced that it was time for the dirty flamingo dancing to begin.

POSTED BY LOOPYLISA AT 11:31

<<NEW CHAT SESSION STARTED

welshguy: hi

LoopyLisa21f: Hello, love. So, are "you" really Welsh?

welshguy: yes

LoopyLisa21f: And how are you today, dear?

welshguy: im ok thnx

LoopyLisa21f: I think you're feeling good!

LoopyLisa21f: Where in Wales are you?

welshguy: near cardiff

LoopyLisa21f: I know that place; that's where they have Ferret World!

welshguy: never seen that place

LoopyLisa21f: It's cool. It's like a special knacker's yard for ferrets/theme park for people who have an interest in ferrets. I like ferrets; they're sort of like self-propelling scarves!

welshguy: oh right lol

LoopyLisa21f: Some of the ferrets at Ferret World are quite old. But the last time I was there they had some babies too.

welshguy: ok

LoopyLisa21f: I was going to offer to sponsor them, but Craig said they were probably just being bred as food for the older ones.

welshguy: ok

LoopyLisa21f: I thought it was a bit sick, personally, but he said it was just The Circle of Life in action. You know; the way elephants only have babies in order to eat them.

LoopyLisa21f: I saw an elephant eating a baby elephant on a documentary once. It was sick. You could hear it crunching the baby one's bones and then shooting them out of its trunk – right over a wall! I'd have thought everyone in Cardiff would know Ferret World.

welshguy: ok cant say id know

LoopyLisa21f: It's the Capital City of Ferrets. It says so on the leaflets. I have one here. It says: "Ferrets big and ferrets small, ferrets old – we have them all! Over 400 acres of ferreting fun! You're guaranteed to go mad ferret (for it)" welshguy: ok

LoopyLisa21f: And there's a map of the place, and it's divided up into four kingdoms; Ferrets of Tomorrow, Ferrets in History, Ferret Town, and Ferret Creek. And you can ride around the place in a little electric cart called The Grand Conveyor, and they have the "Ferris (Ferret) Wheel", which is a big wheel that you can ride upon with a ferret. You choose your ferret as you're going on – they're all on a shelf near the entrance, sealed into plastic tubes numbered from 1 to 16.

welshguy: as i said never heard of the place

LoopyLisa21f: Hmm. I'm not sure whether to believe you.

welshguy: why not?

LoopyLisa21f: Do you like zoos?

welshguy: ye, nearest 1 is bristol though

LoopyLisa21f: I know that one!

LoopyLisa21f: They've got a marmoset in a jar there!

LoopyLisa21f: It was the funniest thing I'd ever seen.

welshguy: ok

welshguy: havent been since i was like 10

LoopyLisa21f: The jar had some sort of speaker attached to it, so you could hear the noises he makes. I shouldn't laugh, because the marmoset is clearly in a state of considerable discomfort.

LoopyLisa21f: While I was in the zoo toilets, Craig said he held a stick of rock up against the side of the glass, and the marmoset tried to lick it!

welshguy: ok

welshguy: so wot u normally talk about on here

LoopyLisa21f: I dunno. Just stuff. You know: ferrets and marmosets.

welshguy: ever sex

LoopyLisa21f: I used to like that singer; David Eversex. He was gonna make me a star, apparently.

welshguy: essex

LoopyLisa21f: Never been there.

welshguy: david essex

LoopyLisa21f: Never heard of him.

welshguy: u got a bf?

LoopyLisa21f: Pardon, dear?

welshguy: boyfriend

LoopyLisa21f: Oh. I was seeing someone a couple of weeks ago, but he smelled of meat all the time.

LoopyLisa21f: He was an apprentice butcher, see.

LoopyLisa21f: One time I was petting him, and I touched the back of his neck, and there was a bit of liver beneath his collar.

welshguy: did u have sex

LoopyLisa21f: Why would you want to know that? That's like asking someone whether they wipe their bottom or not.

welshguy: sorry. u got ne pics

LoopyLisa21f: Yes, but they're not very flattering. I have chronic water retention in one of them, and my neck has swollen up to the diameter of a 12 inch vinyl record. First, shall I tell you a joke?

welshguy: k den

LoopyLisa21f: Question: What do you get if you cross a pig with a saddle, a saddle with a brake, and a brake with a path?

welshguy: i dunno

LoopyLisa21f: Answer: Pig-ston!

LoopyLisa21f: Ha ha ha!

welshguy: very funny

LoopyLisa21f: I know!!!! It's HILARIOUS!!!!

welshguy: u found dat pic yet

LoopyLisa21f: Not yet, dear.

welshguy: u wan cyba neway

LoopyLisa21f: What's that?

welshguy: talkin dirty

LoopyLisa21f: What ... what's going on?

welshguy: u start

LoopyLisa21f: Wait – what is it you want me to do?

welshguy: take advantage of me

LoopyLisa21f: Ok ... Um ... You want me to borrow fifty pounds, and not give it back? Stuff like that?

welshguy: no sexual

LoopyLisa21f: Oh ...

LoopyLisa21f: What shall I say?

welshguy: dunno wateva jus make it really dirty

LoopyLisa21f: Hmm ... Ok.

welshguy: n kinky

LoopyLisa21f: Ok. I know what to say.

LoopyLisa21f: Can I look up your bottom please? Can I kick you in the bottom until it swells up, please?

LoopyLisa21f: That sort of thing?

welshguy: ur takin da piss

LoopyLisa21f: Is that too kinky?

LoopyLisa21f: Or is it not kinky enough?

welshguy: no tie me up n take advantage of me really tease me

LoopyLisa21f: Ok.

LoopyLisa21f: Imagine you're tied up.

welshguy: yeh n .....

LoopyLisa21f: I start taking advantage of you by really teasing you.

LoopyLisa21f: First I make fun of your ears.

LoopyLisa21f: And then say you have a big nose.

LoopyLisa21f: And then I tickle you under the chin. And then I open my mouth. Somehow, I emit a burst of electronic static. You start to realise that I'm not entirely human ...

welshguy: cant we jus get down 2 action

LoopyLisa21f: You start. I don't think I really know what I'm doing.

LoopyLisa21f: You demonstrate for me, please.

welshguy: k my hands slowly move down ur body

LoopyLisa21f: Ok.

welshguy: teasin ya circlin round ur clit

LoopyLisa21f: I understand.

welshguy: wat u doin ?

LoopyLisa21f: I'm squatting down.

welshguy: n ....

LoopyLisa21f: I'm bending my knees, and as I'm bending them, they're moving outwards from my body, and I'm making a noise like a tractor. I do this faster ... faster ... And then the tractor crashes into a tree, and I make the following noise: "hubbada hubbada hubbada-pooooh".

welshguy: wat u wearin

LoopyLisa21f: I'm wearing a pair of dungaree shorts, which is fastened at the back using pencils that have been forced through the fabric. I have around my head a rubber chin strap.

LoopyLisa21f: I am also wearing a metal bra.

welshguy: sounds nice

welshguy: keep goin babes cant say much so hard having to type wid 1 hand

LoopyLisa21f: The bra is studded, and on one of the cups is a red letter "A", and on the other a red letter "P" – the initials of the Associated Press.

LoopyLisa21f: I am now swinging from the ceiling on a monster truck tire.

LoopyLisa21f: I can feel the tire cutting into the top of my thighs, making them a bit sweaty and sore.

LoopyLisa21f: Are you enjoying me?

LoopyLisa21f: Love?

LoopyLisa21f: Hello, love?

LoopyLisa21f: Have you "gone off", love? Hello? Did I get it wrong?

>>welshguy SIGNED OFF AT 19:44

"

LOOPYLISA'S BLOG

Friday, March 31

Only six months until my next birthday. My best present was a trumpet, which my dad gave me. He said that it used to be his lucky trumpet, and he's had it since he was little.

I never knew this, but it turns out my dad was orphaned at quite a young age, and adopted by the members of a brass band. This might sound like the ultimate experience for a young lad, but the brass band was apparently quite cruel. For a while things were ok, but one day the bandmembers started making my dad sleep in a drum, and sometimes they would hit the drum while my dad was still inside.

One time, the band leader – Ricki Nuu – made my dad eat a clarinet reed, and part of a xylophone. Every night my dad would rub his trumpet, hoping that a genie would come out of the bell-shaped end, and teleport him to somewhere else. Sadly, this never happened.

Eventually, the brass band was investigated by Social Services, and my dad was sent away to live with a wealthy chamber orchestra.

POSTED BY LOOPYLISA AT 19:08

<<NEW CHAT SESSION STARTED

benreeko: hi … …..how are you sexy

benreeko: have you got a pic

LoopyLisa21f: Sorry – I'm currently a bit confused.

benreeko: about what hun ?

LoopyLisa21f: It's awful …

LoopyLisa21f: Something awful has happened

benreeko: what is ?

LoopyLisa21f: Was I talking to you earlier?

benreeko: no

benreeko: too much to drink … … …or talking to too many men?

LoopyLisa21f: No, it's not that. My dad came in and hit me around the head and neck with a wet towel. He accused me of putting a little shell in his milkshake for a joke, and then just started flicking me with the towel. I think I blacked out for a while, because when I woke up my dad was gone, as if he'd never existed, but taped to my computer was a Polaroid photo of him shaking his fist at the camera. He looked so angry …

LoopyLisa21f: And now my head is throbbing, and I just don't know what's going on.

benreeko: not nice

benreeko: tell me a something about yourself

LoopyLisa21f: Ok. Well, I have large, unsightly welts around my head and neck …

benreeko: 'welts' …?

LoopyLisa21f: Yes. A series of purple welts.

benreeko: ??????

LoopyLisa21f: You know: welts from my dad's attack.

benreeko: ????

LoopyLisa21f: Welts. Bruises. Sores. Abrasions. Boo-boos.

benreeko: ok tell me something more attractive

benreeko: want to hear all about you

LoopyLisa21f: One moment please. I'm applying some ice to the damaged areas.

benreeko: ok

LoopyLisa21f: There we are. I've also covered up the worst of it with a shawl.

LoopyLisa21f: So, where were we? Ah, yes. All about ME. Well, my legs are pretty good. They're not too beaten up, and I have the minimum of cigarette burns, and fairly dry skin.

benreeko: sexy ... .

benreeko: are you tall ?

LoopyLisa21f: I'm fairly tall. However, the higher up you go, the flakier my skin gets.

benreeko: sound hot lisa

LoopyLisa21f: I am. I'm all hot and clammy like you wouldn't believe.

benreeko: we need a cold shower ... . making me feel sexy

LoopyLisa21f: I'm feeling sexy too! This is a real sexy chat! Possibly the sexiest chat I've ever had!

benreeko: if you send me a pic i will send you a photo of anything you ask i have a camera here ... ...for you. first the face and then the ....!!!!

LoopyLisa21f: Ok!

LoopyLisa21f: Here comes my first pic.

benreeko: ok

LoopyLisa21f: there you go

<IMAGE SENT – lisa15.jpg>

benreeko: u r very sexxus

    LoopyLisa21f: Thanks! I'm blushing now

    LoopyLisa21f: I've literally gone "the wrong side of purple".

benreeko: dont be shy

benreeko: bet u have nice chest

    LoopyLisa21f: I do have a nice chest. I keep my felt tips and colouring set in it.

benreeko: ????????

benreeko: are you really 21?

benreeko: just seen pic again n think you should leave

benreeko: sorry

    LoopyLisa21f: Leave my house?

    LoopyLisa21f: To come and find you?

benreeko: not funny ... ...you r sick

LoopyLisa21f: Whaaa? Why am I sick?

LoopyLisa21f: Am I still sexxus?

LoopyLisa21f: Sexxus?

LoopyLisa21f: Is sexxus happening still?

LoopyLisa21f: Sexxus?

LoopyLisa21f: Why has sexxus stopped?

LoopyLisa21f: Sexxus? What has happened to all the sexxus?

LoopyLisa21f: Hello, Sexxus?

LoopyLisa21f: Time for sexxus?

LoopyLisa21f: Sexxus please

LoopyLisa21f: Attention. Attention, Mr Sexxus.

LoopyLisa21f: Sexxus?

LoopyLisa21f: Sexxus?

LoopyLisa21f: Sexxus?

LoopyLisa21f: Earth to sexxus?

LoopyLisa21f: Hello, sexxus.

LoopyLisa21f: Hello.

LoopyLisa21f: Sexxus?

LoopyLisa21f: Goodnight, sexxus.

LoopyLisa21f: I miss you!

LoopyLisa21f: Sexxus?

benreeko: sick

LoopyLisa21f: Goodnight, sexxus

>>benreeko SIGNED OFF AT 20:25

"

LOOPYLISA'S BLOG

Sunday, April 02

I got quite a shock last night when Craig told me that he's been diagnosed with St Vitus's Dance. This explains a lot of things, including why Craig keeps winning body-popping competitions, despite not actually entering any.

POSTED BY LOOPYLISA AT 17:54

    <<NEW CHAT SESSION STARTED
HotShaft: hi lisa

LoopyLisa21f: Hullo, "Shafty".

HotShaft: lol

LoopyLisa21f: Pretty funny the way I altered your name there, huh?

HotShaft: yup wot u up too

LoopyLisa21f: I'm looking up the symptoms of a type of palsy.

HotShaft: y u sufferin

LoopyLisa21f: My ex boyfriend has it.

HotShaft: k, been ther hun not nice

LoopyLisa21f: Have you? Did you have it too?

HotShaft: yea

HotShaft: scary

LoopyLisa21f: Craig used to vibrate the spoon out of the bowl when he had his pudding. Sometimes when he was having his pudding he vibrated so fast you could barely see him. He was a total blur. You could just hear the legs of his chair banging against the floor, and the spoon clicking against his teeth.

HotShaft: I had paralised left side of face

LoopyLisa21f: Oh no! So you couldn't eat pudding at all?

HotShaft: no

HotShaft: drink wit straw

HotShaft: couldnt use contact lenses

LoopyLisa21f: What sort of work do you do?

HotShaft: own business

LoopyLisa21f: What sort of "business"?

HotShaft: internet based home shoppin

LoopyLisa21f: I once bought something off one of those "Internet" sites.

LoopyLisa21f: You know those new type of magnets?

HotShaft: yea

LoopyLisa21f: The ones that can attract ferric metals? That's what I bought. It featured a rubber grip so that it didn't turn the user into one big magnet. Unfortunately it didn't work particularly well, and I broke Craig's helper robot with it. I dragged it in through the kitchen window from the garden, and it "split in two", so to speak.

HotShaft: so wot do u do

LoopyLisa21f: I occasionally work for Ellis Metals Ltd, in the accounts department, in Sheffield.

LoopyLisa21f: It's cool. My duty manager is called Eric Lensman, and his favourite food is paella.

HotShaft: gud u enjoy then

LoopyLisa21f: Have you heard of Ellis Metals Ltd?

HotShaft: no

LoopyLisa21f: Have you seen Lord of the Rings?

HotShaft: yea

LoopyLisa21f: Well ... can I ask you something about that film?

HotShaft: only saw 1st one, n got lousy memory but fire away

LoopyLisa21f: Well ... I just wondered whether you might know what sort of metal that ring was made out of.

HotShaft: no soz

LoopyLisa21f: I was just wondering whether there was any chance that it was a magnetic metal. Do you know some of the things that are made in Sheffield though?

LoopyLisa21f: Here's one of them: pen knives!

HotShaft: i no its a major steel city

LoopyLisa21f: Yeah, but they also manufacture stuff with a variety of other metals, including – wait for it! – zinc, aluminium, and tin!

LoopyLisa21f: Have you ever eaten beans directly from the tin?

HotShaft: yea

LoopyLisa21f: Were the beans cold?

HotShaft: yea

LoopyLisa21f: That's crazy!! What other mad stuff have you done?

HotShaft: u dont wanna no hun lol

LoopyLisa21f: Do you know what the maddest thing I ever did was?

HotShaft: go on

LoopyLisa21f: I once threw a dart at a teacher!

HotShaft: bulls eye i hope

LoopyLisa21f: It's ok though – I'm not totally insane.

LoopyLisa21f: It was a velcro dart.

LoopyLisa21f: It stuck to his big, fat ... BUM!!!! Ha ha.

LoopyLisa21f: It was there all afternoon. And when he sat down during maths, he had this weird look on his face, as if he kind of liked it, but wasn't totally sure what it was that he was enjoying.

HotShaft: lolololol

LoopyLisa21f: Talking of other crazy things, one time I was on the toilet, and Craig just walked in!

HotShaft: oops

LoopyLisa21f: I said ... "Craig, what are you doing?"

LoopyLisa21f: And he stood in the corner jabbering, and jerking around ...

LoopyLisa21f: And it turns out his palsy had come back!

HotShaft: mine never came back

HotShaft: never fully recovered tho

LoopyLisa21f: Craig has never really been the same.

LoopyLisa21f: Sometimes you'll be talking to him, and his head would tilt back, and he'd just suddenly stick his tongue out through his nose.

LoopyLisa21f: It'll come out like ... pop! And then go back in again!

LoopyLisa21f: Pop! Pop!

LoopyLisa21f: Thppp!

HotShaft: lol

> LoopyLisa21f: Sometimes you'd be in the shed, or down the bottom of the garden, and you'd hear this popping sound coming from round the side.

> LoopyLisa21f: Can you guess what it was?

> LoopyLisa21f: That's right – it was Craig!

HotShaft: god u had fun lol

> LoopyLisa21f: Yeah! His parents had built this really mad swing in the back garden.

> LoopyLisa21f: It was in a tree.

> LoopyLisa21f: One time his dad was sitting on it, and he was swinging back and forth, and it shook about eight apples out of the tree …

> LoopyLisa21f: And one of them hit his dad in the bum!

> LoopyLisa21f: At least, I think that's what happened. I wasn't actually there.

HotShaft: lol

HotShaft: so how old r u hun

> LoopyLisa21f: 21. You?

> LoopyLisa21f: YOU?

HotShaft: ur a little babe lol

HotShaft: dont mind chattin to an old get do u

> LoopyLisa21f: Not really.

HotShaft: gudddddddddddddd

HotShaft: so wot u like

> LoopyLisa21f: With regard to what?

HotShaft: look like

LoopyLisa21f: Craig says I look like that woman off the telly.

HotShaft: which one hun

LoopyLisa21f: Oh, I dunno.

LoopyLisa21f: The one who does that thing, where she bends over backwards, and makes a hissing sound into a paper tube.

HotShaft: not seen her

LoopyLisa21f: Oh. Nor have I – I'm just going on what he says. There's someone else I look like, though. Do you know who it is?

HotShaft: explain

LoopyLisa21f: Well … perhaps you know a little lady by the name of Dame Edna Everard?

LoopyLisa21f: He said I also looked like her.

HotShaft: lol, u got a pic

LoopyLisa21f: Not as such. Tell me, please, what was the biggest surprise you ever had?

HotShaft: flight tickets to vegas lol

LoopyLisa21f: Did you find them in the street?

LoopyLisa21f: I once found a parrot's head in the street.

LoopyLisa21f: It was awful …

HotShaft: lol

LoopyLisa21f: I'm not kidding either.

LoopyLisa21f: I bent over to pick it up, and something terrible happened.

LoopyLisa21f: Two things happened, actually … No – three things.

LoopyLisa21f: 1) Craig threw a slipper at my bum.

LoopyLisa21f: 2) I fell onto a pebble and cracked a tooth.

LoopyLisa21f: 3) I did a blow off!

HotShaft: lolololol

LoopyLisa21f: I suppose from anyone else's point of view these events appeared to occur simultaneously.

HotShaft: lol

LoopyLisa21f: Has that ever happened to you?

HotShaft: na

LoopyLisa21f: Don't get me wrong – I don't think anybody heard me.

LoopyLisa21f: It just came out like …. spppthhhhhh

HotShaft: lol

LoopyLisa21f: You know the sort of blow-off I mean?

HotShaft: o yea

LoopyLisa21f: We all like those, huh?

HotShaft: huh huh

LoopyLisa21f: But you can't be too careful with those ones.

LoopyLisa21f: You know what I mean?

LoopyLisa21f: We've all been there.

HotShaft: o yea

LoopyLisa21f: One time I cracked one off in Sunday school … oh man!

LoopyLisa21f: Everyone knew what had happened.

HotShaft: the smell

LoopyLisa21f: Well … the smell was just the start.

HotShaft: o u didnt follow thro

LoopyLisa21f: Well … almost.

LoopyLisa21f: I pursed my bits, and it went back in.

HotShaft: lol

HotShaft: funny

LoopyLisa21f: I'm not kidding, though …

HotShaft: bet ur not

HotShaft: do i get to c ur pic

LoopyLisa21f: Well … perhaps … I'm very shy.

LoopyLisa21f: At Sunday school I had to wear a cushioned sheath over my upper body.

LoopyLisa21f: My mother knitted it for me.

HotShaft: lol

LoopyLisa21f: I used to cover it with badges.

LoopyLisa21f: And tinsel.

HotShaft: lol

LoopyLisa21f: I met Craig at Sunday school.

LoopyLisa21f: The first time I saw him he was reading a passage from Job.

LoopyLisa21f: Specifically, the passage where Job finds a parrot head in the street. Do you know the one I mean?

HotShaft: sorry no

LoopyLisa21f: Have you ever read the Bible?

HotShaft: years ago hun

LoopyLisa21f: I like Chapter 4 best.

LoopyLisa21f: Who's your favourite character?

HotShaft: god

LoopyLisa21f: My favourite Bible character is Fanny Wyman.

LoopyLisa21f: Get a load of this: my friend Craig once broke a swan's neck!

LoopyLisa21f: He was trying to feed it a KFC hot wing, and it went for him, and because he was still getting over the palsy Craig just sort of juddered, and somehow his arm hit the swan, and the next thing we knew it was dead with a busted neck.

LoopyLisa21f: We just punted it into a bush and went home.

HotShaft: oops

HotShaft: protected arnt they?

LoopyLisa21f: I've got to go.

LoopyLisa21f: I think my prowler has come back.

LoopyLisa21f: I can hear someone down the alley rattling a tin. It sounds like him.

HotShaft: so do i get to c ur pic before u go

LoopyLisa21f: No time – the rattling is getting louder.

LoopyLisa21f: And more rhythmic, and intense!

LoopyLisa21f: Bye, Gary!

HotShaft: gary?

LoopyLisa21f: I love you, Gary!

LoopyLisa21f: xxx

HotShaft: bye luv u

HotShaft: xxxxxxx

>>LoopyLisa 21f SIGNED OFF AT 20:43   **"**

LOOPYLISA'S BLOG

Tuesday, April 04

I'm thinking about calling an exorcist, because I'm convinced there's something spooky going on in my flat. This is quite a turnaround for me, as I never used to believe in ghosts. However, I had my scepticism banished the weekend I stayed at Craig's aunt's house, which is literally filled with ghosts.

There are four ghosts living in her house: Princess, Apple Blossom, Sunshine, and Sugar Lump.

As you might have guessed from their names these aren't your typical ghosts – they're the ghosts of four homosexuals.

POSTED BY LOOPYLISA AT 09:20

<<NEW CHAT SESSION STARTED

OrcaSpain2: hi lisa

LoopyLisa21f: Hello, OrcaSpain2.

OrcaSpain2: hope u are fine today?

LoopyLisa21f: Sort of. I've been having a traumatic few weeks. Do you believe in ghosts, by any chance?

OrcaSpain2: ya i do

LoopyLisa21f: Phew! Finally! Everyone thinks I'm going mad. I've tried talking about this with everyone, but they think I'm overreacting, and losing the plot.

OrcaSpain2: no,you are not mad

OrcaSpain2: have seen a ghost?

> LoopyLisa21f: Yes. I think my flat is haunted by a "something from beyond". Specifically: I think it's haunted by the ghost of a pig. Not any old pig, though; a pig who wants revenge because I ate part of it in the form of a bacon roll.

OrcaSpain2: where are u from if i may ask?

> LoopyLisa21f: I am from London. That's where my haunted flat is.

OrcaSpain2: so how do u want to deal with the ghost?

> LoopyLisa21f: You are taking this seriously, aren't you? I don't want you poking fun at me. I swear there's been a pig ghost in here the last few weeks.

> LoopyLisa21f: Have you ever seen a ghost? Porcine or otherwise?

OrcaSpain2: yes a lot of time

OrcaSpain2: there are good and bad ghost, depending

> LoopyLisa21f: Tell me more. What do the bad ghosts do? Do they just blow raspberries against the stomachs of the living, or is it more serious than that?

OrcaSpain2: first the liv is stronger than dead, do u belive?

> LoopyLisa21f: I think so. To be honest, I'm not sure I understand everything that you're saying. Something about the living being stronger than the dead, yes?

OrcaSpain2: yes it is this

> LoopyLisa21f: Surely that's fairly obvious, though. Even weedy living people are stronger than the strongest dead people. If World's Strongest Man Geoff Capes dropped dead tomorrow I'm sure I'd be stronger than him, relatively speaking. I guess you could pile more stuff on top of his corpse than you could pile on top of me … but that's partly because I'd complain about what

you were doing. The late Geoff Capes, on the other hand ...
he'd just lay there.

OrcaSpain2: yes is true

LoopyLisa21f: What does that have to do with my phantom
sow?

OrcaSpain2: so no matter the ghost, u have the right to deal
ghost it is they way u like

OrcaSpain2: bad ghost can be very funny,and stuborn

OrcaSpain2: can u tell about the one in ur flat

LoopyLisa21f: I have to make friends with the ghost? Is that
what you're trying to say? To be honest, a lot of what you're
saying is coming across quite garbled. Also: I've already told
you that the ghost in my flat is the ghost of a pig. Either that,
or it's the ghost of a small, fat man, who crawls around naked,
and has two rows of rather prominent teats running along
his torso. How is any of what you're saying helping with
this traumatic situation, dear? It's one step away from utter
nonsense.

OrcaSpain2: that's why i said is depending on ur
commitment

OrcaSpain2: cos the dead and the living don't have any
contect

LoopyLisa21f: I assure you that I am fully committed to
stopping this farmyard apparition. Please, dear, I really want
the haunting to stop. I'm sick of sitting in front of the TV, and
having this little pink cloud float in and start rooting around.

LoopyLisa21f: Broadly speaking, I ain't afraid of no ghost, but
– paradoxically – I am afraid of this ghost, and I don't even
know why. I think it's looking for truffles. You know: the sort
of truffles what ghost pigs can eat. Please? Please can you
help me? Every night when I try and go to sleep I can hear it
snorting at the foot of my bed, and banging into the furniture.

OrcaSpain2: ok,but am not a ghost, am a living guy,that just want to know you

> LoopyLisa21f: I know you're not a ghost. That's more than apparent.

> LoopyLisa21f: But you seem to know more about ghosts than anyone I've ever met. You're like a real-life Ghostbuster, except with a poorer grasp of English.

OrcaSpain2: ya cos i've seen ghost b4

> LoopyLisa21f: I hate it here now. Whenever the pig appears other things happen. Doors open, drawers open, spoons flip up, and last week there were several green blobs moving around on the shelves. I don't even want to imagine what they might have been.

OrcaSpain2: hahahahahaa

> LoopyLisa21f: Please stop laughing. Just tell me what I should do.

OrcaSpain2: come and live with me

> LoopyLisa21f: I thought you were taking this seriously, and now I'm not so sure. Why do you laugh at me so?

OrcaSpain2: live wit me and u will be free

> LoopyLisa21f: How will I be free? The pig materialises in the evenings to frighten me, and make my spoons flip.

OrcaSpain2: u will be free from all the green moveing object,and will have confort around me

> LoopyLisa21f: Well, yes, but I don't know you. How do I know YOU'RE not a ghost as well? Or you could be the pig's owner when it was alive. Maybe this is all some elaborate form of posthumous entrapment.

OrcaSpain2: just want to know u

LoopyLisa21f: I thought you were going to give me advice on the Hog that Haunts. Instead you're just like everyone else. You all make fun of me, but none of you have been here at one in the morning and gone to the toilet, and had an unctuous spirit swine stick its damp snout against the back of your thigh.

LoopyLisa21f: You're just like all the rest. Honestly. You people ...

OrcaSpain2: am taking this serious as well

OrcaSpain2: i've lived with good ghost for 4 year

LoopyLisa21f: Well then I hardly want to come and live with you if you've got a ghost there too.

OrcaSpain2: that's happen to be my grandmum

LoopyLisa21f: I'm very sorry that your grandparent has died and returned in a spiritual form. But you must understand this: good ghosts, bad ghosts ... I ain't afraid of saying "I don't want no ghosts".

OrcaSpain2: is been along time ago sionce she die

LoopyLisa21f: So you're saying I can't get rid of my ghost? That I'll have this ham-based miasma hovering around my home for the rest of eternity?

OrcaSpain2: u can get rid

LoopyLisa21f: HOW? How do I make it vanish?

OrcaSpain2: confront it face to face, they will know u are not afraid anymore

LoopyLisa21f: Should I wave anything at it?

OrcaSpain2: call them to come over that yu are ready for them

LoopyLisa21f: Ok. So I say "Come here, pig ghost".

LoopyLisa21f: Then what?

81

OrcaSpain2: invite them for war

LoopyLisa21f: For WAR??!?

OrcaSpain2: yes,

LoopyLisa21f: Are you insane? I don't want to fight it. It's just one restless, incorporeal pig. If I challenge it to war, who knows what'll happen? Thousands of them could invade my home.

OrcaSpain2: they woudn't even come for war cos they are already dead

OrcaSpain2: make sure u stand brave evertime

LoopyLisa21f: I don't know what you're talking about. I really wish you'd put forth your theories in some way that I can understand.

OrcaSpain2: that's ghost topic. is difficute to understand

LoopyLisa21f: I must go now.

OrcaSpain2: how

OrcaSpain2: how?

OrcaSpain2: u walking away from me?

OrcaSpain2: ok

OrcaSpain2: ghost topic always difficute to understand

>>LoopyLisa 21f SIGNED OFF AT 14:58

LOOPYLISA'S BLOG

Saturday, April 06

You'll be glad to hear I've had the ghost exorcised from my flat. I tried praying to God to make the ghost go away, but when that didn't work I prayed to Satan. That didn't work either (though I did get mugged on the way home from work), so I prayed to the associate producer of Songs of Praise, which finally seemed to do the trick.

POSTED BY LOOPYLISA AT 10:34

<<NEW CHAT SESSION STARTED

DirtyDog20: hello miss

LoopyLisa21f: Hello, dear. How are you?

DirtyDog20: im good thankyou and yourself

LoopyLisa21f: I'm also good. That makes one … two … at least two good people!

LoopyLisa21f: Hurray for us!

DirtyDog20: asl ?

LoopyLisa21f: 21/Female/London. You? Please?

DirtyDog20: 22/m/london

DirtyDog20: hello ?

LoopyLisa21f: Hello there!

LoopyLisa21f: How are you? You doing ok, yeah? Still good?

DirtyDog20: wat do u look like do u have a pic ?

LoopyLisa21f: I did have a pic, but my father deleted it. He said I looked bloated. He's always doing stuff like that. When I was young he used to cut faces out of catalogues, and stick them over my face on family photographs. He didn't even buy my photo off the school photographer. He bought one of some other kid. He's still got it up on the living room wall, in fact.

DirtyDog20: oh

DirtyDog20: wat do u look like then ?

LoopyLisa21f: You'd like me if you saw me in real life.

DirtyDog20: im sure i would miss

LoopyLisa21f: I'm not actually bloated. I have a pear-shaped face.

DirtyDog20: lol

DirtyDog20: an upside down pear or normal way up ?

LoopyLisa21f: Yes. You may well "lol". I have to live with it. They won't even serve me in the greengrocers. They think I'm somehow being facetious.

LoopyLisa21f: Do you have any body parts shaped like fruit?

LoopyLisa21f: My uncle has a thumb shaped like a kumquat. I didn't even know there was a fruit called a kumquat. Then again, he might be lying to me. It wouldn't be the first time. He once made me eat a pomegranate, and then told me it was a tramp's heart.

DirtyDog20: ur crazy

DirtyDog20: but i like the sound of you

DirtyDog20: u wanna date ?

LoopyLisa21f: Don't be ridiculous. I barely know you.

DirtyDog20: who said with me ?

LoopyLisa21f: Also, the last time I went on a date was a disaster. After two hours I suddenly forgot what I was doing there. I panicked, and thought I was being assaulted. I sprayed him in the eyes with "musk". We spent the rest of the night up the hospital.

DirtyDog20: get to know me

LoopyLisa21f: Ok.

DirtyDog20: wat u wanna know miss ?

LoopyLisa21f: What's your favourite type of fish?

DirtyDog20: i work with fish

LoopyLisa21f: Do you like bream?

DirtyDog20: im a tuna man myself

LoopyLisa21f: And do you really work with fish?

DirtyDog20: i breed and sell all sorts of goldfish

LoopyLisa21f: That's the coolest job in the world!

DirtyDog20: yeh i know it is pretty cool

LoopyLisa21f: Do you sell them to funfairs?

DirtyDog20: yes and petshops and garden centres

LoopyLisa21f: Isn't it a bit cruel what they do to goldfish at funfairs?

DirtyDog20: yes but i think its all changed now the ppl we sell to seem to be ok

LoopyLisa21f: I saw some funfair market stallholders kicking one around in its bag like a football. They'd set up a stall where you had to kick it into a goal, and if you succeeded you won the fish. Either side of the goal they'd set up these spiked boards, and there were loads of burst goldfish bags on the spikes. Some boys had a go and they were deliberately kicking the fish at the spikes.

DirtyDog20: thats untrue stop that

LoopyLisa21f: It is true! Seriously. I know it sounds unlikely, but me and Craig saw it with our own eyes..

DirtyDog20: ok

LoopyLisa21f: They swore at me when I had a go about it. The air was blue with their Romany curses.

DirtyDog20: well thats pikeys for you isnt it

LoopyLisa21f: No, they were goldfish.

LoopyLisa21f: Pikeys are bigger, aren't they?

LoopyLisa21f: Do you know lots about fish?

DirtyDog20: yes

LoopyLisa21f: All sorts of fish?

DirtyDog20: yes

LoopyLisa21f: So if I name a type of fish, you could tell me something interesting about it?

DirtyDog20: yes if its a fish that exists

LoopyLisa21f: Ok.

DirtyDog20: go on then

LoopyLisa21f: Bream.

DirtyDog20: bream are large silver fish that live in british waters

LoopyLisa21f: Cool!

LoopyLisa21f: Tell me about …

LoopyLisa21f: Larch.

DirtyDog20: i dont know a larch sorry

LoopyLisa21f: Hmm.

LoopyLisa21f: Silverfish?

DirtyDog20: false

LoopyLisa21f: False? It's not a true or false game.

DirtyDog20: theres no such fish as a silverfish

LoopyLisa21f: I've got them in my bath, though. And under the little rug thing which goes around my toilet. Actually, what is that thing for? It's basically to mop up widdle, isn't it? At least if the widdle goes onto the floor you can see it, and you can clean it up easily. If it hits the wee-rug it gets soaked in, and over a period of time that causes "stinking of the air". Now that this point has been raised between us I may decide to destroy my wee-rug tonight. That said, I hardly ever miss anyway. I reckon I only miss two times out of ten.

DirtyDog20: ur talents r wasted on me u should save ur comedy for the stage whoever u are

LoopyLisa21f: I'm just having a conversation, guy.

DirtyDog20: ok

DirtyDog20: wats the furthest away uve dated somebody ?

LoopyLisa21f: Devon.

DirtyDog20: thats pretty far

LoopyLisa21f: His name was Eric, and he worked in a polystyrene factory.

LoopyLisa21f: The fumes did something to him, though.

DirtyDog20: really wat ?

LoopyLisa21f: When I saw him on production run nights he was bizarre. He'd be snarling, and there'd be little bits of foam at the corners of his mouth. I later found out it was actually tiny bits of polystyrene. I found out from one of his colleagues that he was always getting disciplined for eating the polystyrene.

LoopyLisa21f: Also, he'd keep hitting himself in the head with the back of his hand.

LoopyLisa21f: You couldn't keep him focused on anything. You'd say something, and you'd wait for a response, and he'd look at you for about thirty seconds, and then snarl, and hit himself in the head with the back of his hand. He did that all evening, every evening. It's a miracle I went out for him as long as I did.

LoopyLisa21f: I eventually split up with him because he wanted me to go to a nudist camp with him.

LoopyLisa21f: It was called Butt-lins.

LoopyLisa21f: I thought it was disgusting.

LoopyLisa21f: They even had a nude roller disco. You don't want to know what they had instead of redcoats.

DirtyDog20: go on

LoopyLisa21f: Well, their camp entertainers were nude like the guests, except instead of wearing red coats they had brown circles painted on their stomachs.

DirtyDog20: why ??

LoopyLisa21f: I've already told you why.

DirtyDog20: no u aint

LoopyLisa21f: Yes I have. Each brown circle has a number in it. It's so you can recognise who is who in photographs. You remember what photographs are, yes?

DirtyDog20: of course i photograph people for hobby

DirtyDog20: mostly portpholios

LoopyLisa21f: Are those the little round windows on ships?

LoopyLisa21f: Oh! I've done a silly. That's portholios.

LoopyLisa21f: Also: wasn't that one of the Three Musketeers?

LoopyLisa21f: Oh. Wait. That was Puffos.

LoopyLisa21f: There were four musketeers if you count them all. Puffos, Carob, Dean and Mungton-28.

LoopyLisa21f: Do you remember them?

LoopyLisa21f: Oh! I've thought of a fifth.

LoopyLisa21f: Dart-Onion.

DirtyDog20: yeah but why did you start talkin about them in the first place lol

LoopyLisa21f: Well you mentioned them, by talking about the French

DirtyDog20: no i didnt

LoopyLisa21f: I thought you did.

LoopyLisa21f: You said that Elton John was French, and I said 'No he wasn't'

DirtyDog20: wtf are u on about ???

LoopyLisa21f: Sorry, David. I've had a really bad week.

LoopyLisa21f: My crow died.

LoopyLisa21f: His name was 'Snappy'

LoopyLisa21f: His death has knocked me for six, I can tell you!

LoopyLisa21f: Goodbye, Richard! Xxx

>>LoopyLisa 21f SIGNED OFF AT 20:43 　　**,,**

LOOPYLISA'S BLOG

Thursday, April 13

Some new people moved in next door recently. This is our third set of new neighbours in as many months. It would seem that the house is jinxed.

The previous lot moved out in embarrassment when the father suffered a humiliating injury during his son's fifth birthday party. I don't want to go into detail, but it involved a plate of chicken satay, a bouncy castle, and a trip to hospital to have satay sticks removed from his anus.

While they managed to remove all the sticks, they sadly never recovered all of the peanut dip.

POSTED BY LOOPYLISA AT 18:10

<<NEW CHAT SESSION STARTED

ValleysLad: hi lisa x

LoopyLisa21f: Hello. Just give me a second. There's some weird stuff going on outside.

ValleysLad: like?

LoopyLisa21f: Ok. It's all finished. Golly. That was bizarre.

ValleysLad: what happened?

LoopyLisa21f: The people next door unloaded a load of peacocks from their van, and led them into the house.

ValleysLad: noooooooooooooooo way lol

LoopyLisa21f: Yeah. About five or six peacc
of them were wearing these little leather ?
sometimes wear. What's that all about?

ValleysLad: no idea lol

ValleysLad: so hows u?

LoopyLisa21f: Good thanks. This is going to sound weird, but could we try an experiment?

ValleysLad: like?

LoopyLisa21f: Do you believe in mentals?

ValleysLad: mentals?

LoopyLisa21f: Yeah, you know: people with mental powers and that.

ValleysLad: never thought about it

LoopyLisa21f: Well, I've been reading a book about ESP, and I just want to try a few things out.

ValleysLad: ok

LoopyLisa21f: Ok. I'm going to draw a picture on a piece of paper, and I want you to try and use your mind to picture what it is. It'll be a fairly simple picture, but quite a specific one. You are permitted to ask me six questions about it, but no more than six.

LoopyLisa21f: Ready? I'll draw it when you say "yes".

ValleysLad: yes

LoopyLisa21f: Ok. I'm drawing it now.

LoopyLisa21f: Close your eyes, and picture this image.

LoopyLisa21f: Done.

LoopyLisa21f: Right. You have six questions.

ysLad: ok

alleysLad: is it something to do with travel?

LoopyLisa21f: Yes.

ValleysLad: ok

LoopyLisa21f: Next question.

ValleysLad: does it carry a lot of passengers

LoopyLisa21f: One of the things in the image could be used for that purpose.

ValleysLad: a plane

LoopyLisa21f: No. You have four more questions.

ValleysLad: ok does it travel on the road?

LoopyLisa21f: Sometimes.

ValleysLad: bus

LoopyLisa21f: Yes. There is a bus in the image.

LoopyLisa21f: There's something else in the image too.

ValleysLad: a person

LoopyLisa21f: No.

LoopyLisa21f: Are you really trying to picture this with your mind?

ValleysLad: yes lisa

LoopyLisa21f: Ok. Well, do you want me to tell you?

ValleysLad: yes sorry

LoopyLisa21f: Ok. It's a picture of a busy road, and beside the road is a lake, and coming out of the lake – arcing over the top of the road – is a giant, sub-aquatic caterpillar. The caterpillar is wearing a t-shirt which has a drawing of a bus on it.

ValleysLad: oh right

LoopyLisa21f: Can you draw something now, and can I try and picture it?

LoopyLisa21f: Hello?

ValleysLad: sorry just getting paper

ValleysLad: ok ready

LoopyLisa21f: Ok. Tell me when you're starting to draw.

ValleysLad: now

LoopyLisa21f: Ok. Closing my eyes. Closing them … now.

ValleysLad: good

LoopyLisa21f: Tell me when you're done.

ValleysLad: ive finshed x

LoopyLisa21f: Ok. First question …

ValleysLad: ok

LoopyLisa21f: Is there something sort of triangle, or pyramid-shaped in the picture?

ValleysLad: sort of

LoopyLisa21f: Cool. Next question … Is there a cross shape in the picture anywhere? Even as part of something else? And is there a man nailed to the cross?

ValleysLad: no

LoopyLisa21f: Hmm. Is there a tree in the picture?

ValleysLad: yes

ValleysLad: your good

LoopyLisa21f: Is there a man nailed to the tree?

ValleysLad: no

ValleysLad: its 2things

> LoopyLisa21f: Ok. Is there a man nailed to anything in the picture? I'm really picturing a lot of blood in my mental image, and it seems to be coming from a man who has been nailed to something though the loose skin on his arms.

ValleysLad: nothing like that

> LoopyLisa21f: Ok – you tell me.

ValleysLad: christmas tree with a rainbow over the top

> LoopyLisa21f: Are you sure there's not someone nailed to the Christmas tree? Maybe a leprechaun, or something?

ValleysLad: no honest

> LoopyLisa21f: There's one more test I'd like to try.

ValleysLad: ok

> LoopyLisa21f: This time I'm going to make a noise, and you have to guess what it is.

> LoopyLisa21f: I'm going to make the noise for 30 seconds.

ValleysLad: ok

> LoopyLisa21f: Starting …. now.

ValleysLad: ok

> LoopyLisa21f: Finished.

ValleysLad: is it an animal noise?

> LoopyLisa21f: Not really.

ValleysLad: human?

> LoopyLisa21f: No. It's just a noise. It's not a noise that we would recognise as part of our world.

ValleysLad: ok how can i guess what it is lol

LoopyLisa21f: I dunno. I didn't think it through.

ValleysLad: lol

LoopyLisa21f: I was pinching my cheeks, and sort of making a slapping noise with them.

ValleysLad: your very sweet x

LoopyLisa21f: Thankyou.

ValleysLad: yer welcom

LoopyLisa21f: I'm bored of psychic powers now.

ValleysLad: ok hunny

ValleysLad: so what do u look like

LoopyLisa21f: I'm a bit shy.

LoopyLisa21f: People make fun of my face.

ValleysLad: y do they

ValleysLad: send me a pic

LoopyLisa21f: I'm shy. I hate what I look like.

ValleysLad: please hunny

LoopyLisa21f: Ok.

ValleysLad: thanx x

LoopyLisa21f: Sent. Don't be too horrible.

LoopyLisa21f: : -(

<IMAGE SENT – lisa12.jpg>

ValleysLad: your male

LoopyLisa21f: No I'm not. Everyone says I look like a man in that photo, but it's just the angle.

ValleysLad: send me anothewr

LoopyLisa21f: The other one's no better.

ValleysLad: come on

LoopyLisa21f: Sent.

<IMAGE SENT – lisa8.jpg>

ValleysLad: well u definatly look like a male 2 me but u can b who u want 2 b on here

LoopyLisa21f: That really hurts my feelings.

ValleysLad: u have a stubble 4 a start

LoopyLisa21f: It's the light.

ValleysLad: no way

ValleysLad: ive zoomed in

LoopyLisa21f: Yeah, well the resolution is going to be worse when you zoom in. That's not going to make a difference.

ValleysLad: your winding me up

ValleysLad: your male

LoopyLisa21f: No. Honest.

ValleysLad: so let me see full lengh pic

LoopyLisa21f: I don't have a full length pic, you perv.

ValleysLad: how can u call ME a perv??

LoopyLisa21f: Because you obviously are, wanting to see more and more of me, and stuff.

ValleysLad: not really

ValleysLad: im not intrested

LoopyLisa21f: You wanted a full frontal pic.

ValleysLad: no way

LoopyLisa21f: That's what you typed just now.

ValleysLad: no i said full lengh not frontal yuck

LoopyLisa21f: Why would that be yuck?

ValleysLad: coz i stll belive that isnt u

ValleysLad: and ive got no time for time wasters

LoopyLisa21f: I'm not wasting your time!!!!!

LoopyLisa21f: I'll send you one more. See if that convinces you I'm a woman.

LoopyLisa21f: Sent.

<IMAGE SENT – lisa9.jpg>

ValleysLad: bye

>>ValleysLad SIGNED OFF AT 19:24

LOOPYLISA'S BLOG

Friday, April 28

I was a bit taken aback when my dad started going to church – especially because he doesn't believe in The Holy Trinity. However, he really seems to have got into it. It has meant a few changes at home, though.

For example, dad will now only watch films featuring, or directed by, people with the initials "J.C." (as in "Jesus Christ"). This week we have watched four John Carpenter films, John Cleese's A Fish Called Wanda, and a biography of Jacques Cousteau.

Also, he will only eat food which begins with initials "J.C." (we've had a lot of jumbo cashews in recent weeks).

POSTED BY LOOPYLISA AT 00:56

<<NEW CHAT SESSION STARTED

UKJustin2000: hello lisa

LoopyLisa21f: Hello Justin.

LoopyLisa21f: Are you well?

UKJustin2000: Very well lisa

UKJustin2000: u?

LoopyLisa21f: I'm reasonably well. What are you up to there?

UKJustin2000: writting a couple of letters. keep getting destracted lol u?

LoopyLisa21f: Sorry. I really can't be bothered to tell you. So, to whom are you writing? An ombudsman? The Womens Guild?

UKJustin2000: not far off Barclaycard is 1

LoopyLisa21f: Why? Why you do dat, Justin?

UKJustin2000: theres a mistake on my statement

LoopyLisa21f: I've stopped using credit cards. My dad stole mine, learned to forge my signature, and bought a caravan with it.

UKJustin2000: u joking

LoopyLisa21f: Of course I'm not joking. He even went on holiday in the caravan with his secret friend, and I didn't find out until he got back. I hadn't even realised my credit card was missing until he pulled up with the caravan.

UKJustin2000: whose the friend?

LoopyLisa21f: She's something to do with the church he goes to. I think it's her job to feed the onions to the owl that lives in the belfry. Her nickname is "Onion Owl". I don't like her. She spits when she talks, and all she ever talks about is the way owls eat onions (apparently they burrow inside, and eat their way out).

UKJustin2000: have u forgiven him?

LoopyLisa21f: I have to forgive him, or he won't let me in the caravan, and that's where he serves tea. I don't want to starve ... or do I?

LoopyLisa21f: When was the last time you were in a caravan?

UKJustin2000: my parents use to have 1. we use to be in a caravan club. about 12 yrs ago. r u all prim & proper..?

LoopyLisa21f: I'm not prim and proper. Craig says I'm a fat idiot.

UKJustin2000: whose craig?

LoopyLisa21f: He's my friend. He's a right laugh. One time we were in a supermarket and he pretended to have a brain aneurysm, and fell into a pile of biscuits.

UKJustin2000: lol

LoopyLisa21f: I said he should go back and pay for the damage, but by that point we were already in the ambulance on our way to hospital. It was awful – they nearly operated to remove his spleen!

UKJustin2000: lol u got pics?

LoopyLisa21f: I'll have a look for a pic. Tell me a joke first.

UKJustin2000: k

UKJustin2000: what do u call a fish with out an eye?

LoopyLisa21f: Blindwhale?

UKJustin2000: FSH

UKJustin2000: works better said.

LoopyLisa21f: FSH? Does that stand for something?

LoopyLisa21f: Fish … Sight … Handicap? I dunno.

UKJustin2000: fish without on i = fsh

UKJustin2000: get it?

LoopyLisa21f: Oh, wait. I get it now. Ha ha ha! Fantastic! FANTASTIC!

UKJustin2000: lol lol

UKJustin2000: u sent yet?

LoopyLisa21f: No. I've not even found the photo yet.

LoopyLisa21f: Please tell me another quality funny, "Justin".

UKJustin2000: your turn

LoopyLisa21f: Ok.

LoopyLisa21f: What do you get if you cross Buzz Aldrin with Neil Armstrong?

UKJustin2000: I don't know.

LoopyLisa21f: You get: Beil Aldrong.

UKJustin2000: : -\

LoopyLisa21f: You don't like it?

UKJustin2000: whos buzz aldrin?

LoopyLisa21f: Where were we?

UKJustin2000: u were finding a pic

LoopyLisa21f: Oh, yes. One moment please.

UKJustin2000: ?

LoopyLisa21f: Here it comes.

LoopyLisa21f: Sent.

<IMAGE SENT – lisa16.jpg>

UKJustin2000: pic of a bloke. not nice

LoopyLisa21f: What?

LoopyLisa21f: I'm sure I sent the right one.

LoopyLisa21f: Let me check.

UKJustin2000: u sent a pic of a bloke. ive deleted it now

LoopyLisa21f: No I didn't. I've checked, and that was me. I … I don't understand.

UKJustin2000: send again

LoopyLisa21f: Shall I send a different one?

LoopyLisa21f: Sent.

<IMAGE SENT – lisa17.jpg>

UKJustin2000: ure not quite my type

LoopyLisa21f: I'm sorry. What can I do to make myself more beautiful for you?

LoopyLisa21f: "Justin"? Have I incurred your wrath?

LoopyLisa21f: Why does "Justin" ignore Lisa?

>>UKJustin2000 SIGNED OFF AT 19:29

LOOPYLISA'S BLOG

Wednesday, May 03

I had a terrible upset stomach at the weekend – a result of letting Craig cook me dinner. The evening began when he took me to visit what he claimed to be "The world's smallest circus", but was basically him just leading me behind a skip, and shining a torch on a packet of breakfast cereal.

I was so disheartened that he promised to make things up by cooking me a pizza. Suffice to say, I wasn't terribly surprised when his "pizza" turned out to be nothing more than some uncooked chicken skin stretched over a filthy beermat.

Looking back, I probably should have refused to eat it.

POSTED BY LOOPYLISA AT 19:33

<<NEW CHAT SESSION STARTED

Daveyjimbo12: hello

LoopyLisa21f: Hello, dear. How are you?

Daveyjimbo12: im very good thank you, wot about yourself?

LoopyLisa21f: I'm ok. I had the runs over the weekend, but that's more or less stopped now. But I'm not taking any chances, if you know what I mean!

Daveyjimbo12: well … ….thanks for sharing that with me

Daveyjimbo12: wot u look like?

LoopyLisa21f: I dunno. What do you think I look like?

Daveyjimbo12: ok, from my experience, women in chat rooms look like this – long blonde hair, blue eyes, slim, with long legs, tanned, and big tits

LoopyLisa21f: You're more or less spot on, except I have a little nub of bone sticking out the small of my back.

Daveyjimbo12: a whatttt????

LoopyLisa21f: My parents used to say it was my "tail".

LoopyLisa21f: But it's not really long enough to be a tail. As I say, it's more a nub. And they can call it what they wanted, but it didn't stop the kids at school making fun of me. Once, they even tried to burn me on the playing fields during lunch break.

Daveyjimbo12: but apart from that i am right – i must be psycic, got any proof?

LoopyLisa21f: Well, no photos to hand. Not of the nub, anyway. Though my parents have some from when I was a baby.

LoopyLisa21f: It sticks out about an inch. You don't really notice when I have a jacket on. Besides, why would I want to show you that? That's like feeling proud of having an extra mouth in your stomach, except the mouth can't form vowel sounds, and just drools, and groans.

Daveyjimbo12: so, if ur still pretty u must have guys fallin over you

LoopyLisa21f: Well, lots of them are fascinated by my nub. When I finally work up the courage to show them, that is.

Daveyjimbo12: wot about the tits? lol

LoopyLisa21f: The … the what now?

Daveyjimbo12: the tits damn it!!!!!!

LoopyLisa21f: I dunno about all that. I'd like to change the subject please.

LoopyLisa21f: Do you prefer cats or dogs?

Daveyjimbo12: wot u mean?

Daveyjimbo12: dogs

> LoopyLisa21f: Why dogs? Dogs are dirty. The way their winkies comes out it looks like a pink slug emerging from a fingerless glove.

> LoopyLisa21f: I'm fighting the urge to be sick just thinking about it.

Daveyjimbo12: wot bout a female dog?

> LoopyLisa21f: Bitches aren't much better. Going on heat all the time, and messing up the carpet. I used to have a dog when I was a girl, but we had to get rid of it when it tried to make love with my parents' neighbour, Mrs Austin.

> LoopyLisa21f: She was only four foot two, and Brutus was a very big dog.

> LoopyLisa21f: He pinned her to the floor, and hitched up her skirt and stuff. He did everything to her. Everything ...

> LoopyLisa21f: She had to have therapy.

Daveyjimbo12: lol, bit mean tho, gettin rid of it just cos of that

> LoopyLisa21f: Well, she was going to call the police and have him put down, but we took him to a dog shelter instead.

> LoopyLisa21f: I'll never forget her screams ...

> LoopyLisa21f: The worst bit was when the dog changed ends.

> LoopyLisa21f: I was only about six, and the memory of that day has stayed with me ever since. He just wouldn't stop thrusting ...

> LoopyLisa21f: What was your most traumatic moment?

Daveyjimbo12: talkin to u about that

> LoopyLisa21f: So, do you have a dog?

Daveyjimbo12: i do – eddie

LoopyLisa21f: What sort of dog is he?

Daveyjimbo12: jack russell

LoopyLisa21f: Is he named after the film star?

LoopyLisa21f: No, wait – I'm confused.

LoopyLisa21f: I'm thinking of Kurt Russell.

LoopyLisa21f: So, does he do naughty things ever? Does he pin your neighbours to the ground, and "have a crack at them"?

Daveyjimbo12: no, not really, barks a lot, sleeps

LoopyLisa21f: Does he do that funny thing where he woofs and runs in his sleep?

Daveyjimbo12: somethimes yeah

LoopyLisa21f: My parents' dog runs in her sleep, and keeps running into walls.

LoopyLisa21f: I shouldn't laugh really, but I like seeing it. The minute she hits the wall she wakes up, and looks really confused. It would be worse if she just kept trying to keep going, sort of trying to grind her way through the wall.

Daveyjimbo12: i think ud be really good at sex

LoopyLisa21f: Whaaaaa? Why do you say that? Why such a sudden injection of lewd topics?

Daveyjimbo12: just think u would be, u talk alot so ud know wot u wanted and ud make sure u got it

Daveyjimbo12: plus ur hot

LoopyLisa21f: I guess so. I'm quite good at asking for things. Cakes … biscuits … directions. I'm good at asking for most things.

LoopyLisa21f: I never used to be though. I used to be very shy. I was even shy around inanimate things, like waxworks, statues, and silhouettes.

LoopyLisa21f: I took an assertiveness course, and I'm much better now. I learned to project my voice, and in my purse I have a selection of confidence cards.

Daveyjimbo12: and has it improved the bedroom antics?

LoopyLisa21f: Well, not directly. The cards say things on them like: "Say what you feel", and "don't be shy", and "Silhouettes and shadows can't hurt you", and "The statues aren't saying things about you", and "The waxworks don't want you to die".

LoopyLisa21f: I guess it has helped in some ways. At least now I know the waxworks don't want me to die!

Daveyjimbo12: so now i will be assertive – wana cyber?

LoopyLisa21f: What's that?

Daveyjimbo12: well, we cant if u dont know wot it is

LoopyLisa21f: I think I know what it is. But I'm not 100% sure.

LoopyLisa21f: I might make a mistake.

Daveyjimbo12: wot do u think it is?

LoopyLisa21f: Is it something to do with the Internet?

Daveyjimbo12: yes and sex

LoopyLisa21f: Oh, ok. I think I get it now. I think I've heard of something like this before. Ok. You start.

Daveyjimbo12: no no no u start

LoopyLisa21f: I have to get a cushion for my nub first.

Daveyjimbo12: fair enough

LoopyLisa21f: You start while I fetch a cushion.

Daveyjimbo12: no, u start

LoopyLisa21f: Ok … Cushion in place. Ok. Well, I'm walking out of a Post Office – I was sending a birthday present to my cousin in Australian, you see – when who should I bump into but … you! I say: "You're looking well. Are those new shoes? Did you shave off your beard?"

Daveyjimbo12: and i say hello lisa, fancy a drink?

LoopyLisa21f: And I say "Ok, then, that would be nice!".

Daveyjimbo12: so i take u to a bar and give u lots of wine;-)

LoopyLisa21f: Well, if I have too much I'll be sick. I'm not one for very much wine, plus I worry that there'll be something in it. You know: something like a date rape drug, such as "rohylfaris".

LoopyLisa21f: So, I'll just have some orange squash for now. You can taste the sleeping pills in that – and I should know! Craig and I have had some pretty crazy nights!

Daveyjimbo12: ok then, aftre the orange squash and some delightful converstations about our dogs, i ask u back to my place

LoopyLisa21f: Ok then. I'll go back there with you, albeit reluctantly, dragging my feet, and sighing the whole way. Are we there yet?

LoopyLisa21f: Are we there yet? Are we there yet?

Daveyjimbo12: so i take u back to mine

LoopyLisa21f: Are we there yet?

Daveyjimbo12: we go in

Daveyjimbo12: i take ur coat and we sit down next to each other on the couch

LoopyLisa21f: Hang on a second. Not so fast, please. What's your place like? Is it tidy?

Daveyjimbo12: average

LoopyLisa21f: I'm really sorry about this, but I can't stand clutter. Can we tidy up a bit first? It helps me to relax.

Daveyjimbo12: ok, so we tidy up then, as we finish , i turn and kiss you

LoopyLisa21f: Ok then. I mumble a vague "thank you" for the kiss. Unfortunately, the orange squash has gone right through me, and I have a sudden need to go to the toilet.

LoopyLisa21f: I ask you where the bathroom is, and you point me in the right direction.

Daveyjimbo12: when u come out i ask u to sleep with me and say that u mite as well go if u dont want to

LoopyLisa21f: Wait a minute – I haven't finished in the bathroom yet.

Daveyjimbo12: tough shit

LoopyLisa21f: What are you doing while I'm in there?

Daveyjimbo12: look ive got lots of things to do

Daveyjimbo12: i cant waste no time

LoopyLisa21f: I'm just trying to build something resembling a sensual atmosphere.

Daveyjimbo12: by goin to the bathroom???!!

LoopyLisa21f: Look, I'll tell you what I'm doing in the bathroom if you tell me what you're doing while I'm in there.

Daveyjimbo12: i dont know if i wana cyber wit u any more

LoopyLisa21f: I'm getting myself ready in the bathroom, ok? Is that ok with you? Or would you rather I didn't get myself ready? Don't you know anything about women?

LoopyLisa21f: The thing about the orange squash was an excuse to go into the bathroom, OK?!

LoopyLisa21f: Do you see?

LoopyLisa21f: I had to go in there <u>TO GET READY</u>. See? Are you completely ignorant to a woman's needs?

LoopyLisa21f: You do know what I mean, right?

Daveyjimbo12: whatever

LoopyLisa21f: Ok, so I gather you're impatient. If that's the way you want to play it, we'll play it that way. <u>Fine</u>.

LoopyLisa21f: You hammer on the bathroom door, telling me you have things to do, and that if I'm not prepared to sleep with you I should go home this instant.

Daveyjimbo12: yes, i saw ur tits, and became hard, now i want to fuck you

LoopyLisa21f: I call out and tell you that I'm putting on some lipstick, in my sweetest, girliest voice. I giggle gently through the keyhole, and this feigned innocence serves to fuel your intentions.

LoopyLisa21f: However, this carefully constructed illusion merely masks the reality of what I'm actually doing in the bathroom. In truth, I'm quickly wiping my bottom, alarmed by the gruff tone of your voice. I'm trembling so much I can barely hold the toilet paper. I'm scared you'll hurt me. Suddenly, I become aware that the air in this tiny room has soured. I panic, all too receptive to the reality that the stench of my giant jobbie could seep beneath the door. What will he think of me then?! What will he think?!?!

LoopyLisa21f: I fumble in my handbag for some matches.

LoopyLisa21f: Fortunately I find some, and open the box. With alarm creeping through my body I realise that there are only two un-struck matches remaining. With fingers trembling like Judy Finnegan on a ghost train I strike a match, and hold the tiny flame aloft. It is only a partial success. The flame is gone, but the smell lingers on!

LoopyLisa21f: My quivering fingers find something else in the handbag: it's a Roman candle left over from fireworks night. Quickly, I light the blue touch paper, and drop the candle into the bath.

LoopyLisa21f: Violent sparks fizz out of the tip, and the room fills with the stench of sulphur, successfully masking the bitter reek of fecal matter.

LoopyLisa21f: You are still there, yes?

LoopyLisa21f: Dave? I'm not doing this for the good of my health, you know.

LoopyLisa21f: Have you gone off, love? Dave?

LoopyLisa21f: I'm afraid that the Roman candle has set fire to your shower curtain, Dave.

LoopyLisa21f: I managed to put out the flames, but it's still quite badly burnt.

LoopyLisa21f: Why are you ignoring me?

LoopyLisa21f: Dave?

LoopyLisa21f: Sexy Dave?

LoopyLisa21f: Sexxxxxxy?

Daveyjimbo12: talk dirty more

LoopyLisa21f: Is this helping?

Daveyjimbo12: yes talk dirty more, ur turnin me on

Daveyjimbo12: suck me off

LoopyLisa21f: Ok, well … having finally extinguished the flames by squirting shower gel at the curtain, I open the bathroom door.

LoopyLisa21f: I try to act as if nothing is wrong. But you can smell the smoke.

LoopyLisa21f: I suddenly realise that the roman candle is still sitting in the bath, so I dash back into the bathroom to retrieve it.

LoopyLisa21f: I try in vain to flush the firework down the toilet, but it becomes lodged in the U-bend. Filthy brown water belches up out of the bowl, covering the floor. Within seconds I am wading in half an inch of "bog syrup".

LoopyLisa21f: Is this helping you out?

LoopyLisa21f: Dave? Sexy Dave? Have I done it right, Dave?

LoopyLisa21f: Dave?

>>DaveyJimbo12 SIGNED OFF AT 18:22

LOOPYLISA'S BLOG

Tuesday, May 09

Dad's gone away for a few days (tried to hang himself again), so I've made a list of all the chores I need to do this weekend:

1. Get leaves out of the gutter.

Admittedly, it isn't a very long list, but is in fact a new type of list comprised of just one item. I have come up with a new name for this type of extremely short list, and that name is this: "the tad".

POSTED BY LOOPYLISA AT 21:04

<<NEW CHAT SESSION STARTED

BronsonJonson2: hiya lisa u ok?

LoopyLisa21f: Sort of. How are you?

BronsonJonson2: sort off? whats up?

LoopyLisa21f: Do you know anything about medicine? Or healing of any kind?

BronsonJonson2: no sorry

LoopyLisa21f: Are you able to make an educated guess on medical matters?

BronsonJonson2: why whats up?

LoopyLisa21f: I think I've dislocated my arm.

LoopyLisa21f: I was getting some leaves out of the gutter, and my ladder slipped, and I fell onto the sundial, and now I can't move my arm. It has gone purple, and swollen up at the shoulder. Well, when I say "purple", the hand has actually gone completely white – and cold as ice!

BronsonJonson2: well my advice is get 2 the hospital? and when u get back email me 2 tell me what they said

LoopyLisa21f: But I'm not really in any pain at the moment. The pain passed quite quickly. There was a momentary sharpness of pain as I struck the dial, and then … darkness … silence … hissing … a strange hissing in my ears, and a banging from inside my arm.

LoopyLisa21f: It'll probably be alright.

BronsonJonson2: well go anyway and get it checked

LoopyLisa21f: I'm not very good with hospitals, though. I was once left in one as a child. My parents forgot about me, and I wandered off to find them, and got lost. I wandered into an operating theatre while some person was having a big white worm cut out of their belly. I literally screamed the place down. You see, I mistook one of the surgeons for a ghost!

BronsonJonson2: no way

BronsonJonson2: well if i was u id go neway and then get a sick note 4 three week and stay off work and rest

LoopyLisa21f: I don't need that long off work. I'm a school teacher, and it would let the kids down. I know some of my colleagues do it, though. Mr Henry told the headmistress he was having recurring nightmares about being chased by a magic hammer with a face, and took two months off – but I don't like lying like that. All he really had wrong with him was a grazed uvula. He'd tried to swallow a cotton reel!

LoopyLisa21f: Anyway, I think they kids would find my arm pretty cool like this.

LoopyLisa21f: I looks a bit like a tentacle! I could pretend to be Mrs Octopus, the eight-armed schoolteacher! Except I'd only have two arms. And only one of them would look like a tentacle. And I'd need to tell them to use their imagination to picture the additional "grapplers", and the kids in my class don't have much of an imagination.

LoopyLisa21f: We had creative writing last week, and the story topic was 'Behind The Mysterious Door', and four of them wrote something along the lines of "Behind the Mysterious Door is the title of the story our teacher told us to write today". And another one of them simply wrote the title in his book, and drew a big question mark beneath it.

BronsonJonson2: im sorry but stuff the kids u come first and anyway if i was going out with u id look after u

LoopyLisa21f: Would you? Would you really look after me, BronsonJonson2?

LoopyLisa21f: Craig never looked after me.

BronsonJonson2: i would look after u 4ever

LoopyLisa21f: Craig used to bite me in the night.

LoopyLisa21f: Really hard it was. One time he bit me on the nose, and made it bleed. In the morning he said a bird must have got into the bedroom and done it, but I know it was him.

BronsonJonson2: if i fancy u i will look after u i promise

LoopyLisa21f: I really hope you fancy me then.

LoopyLisa21f: If you don't fancy me, will you have me put down?

BronsonJonson2: well u have my email address dont you? send me a picture of u if u can

LoopyLisa21f: Shall I take one of my arm so you can make a diagnosis?

BronsonJonson2: well if u wanna but id still say go 2 the hospital

LoopyLisa21f: I'll see how it is tomorrow.

BronsonJonson2: how old r u if u dont mind me asking?

LoopyLisa21f: 21

BronsonJonson2: im 20

BronsonJonson2: single until i met u here

LoopyLisa21f: You're very smooth, dear. You're like a latter-day Casanova, or Crippen. What's your best chat-up line?

BronsonJonson2: aint got one girls just come up 2 me

LoopyLisa21f: Wow! You must look like a film star then! Like Edward "the Eagle" Eddison, or Mubis Mubaru Tutu.

BronsonJonson2: honestly i went out on a staff party last month and this girl i never met her b4 came up 2 me and said straight out i fancy u do u fancy a shag ?

BronsonJonson2: but her boyfriend was in the same place and he was with us

LoopyLisa21f: Did he fancy you too? Was he being "bi-curious"?

BronsonJonson2: no he sort of threatend me 2 stay away from her

BronsonJonson2: and also gave her a slap and called her a tart

LoopyLisa21f: He sounds like my dad! My dad is always slapping people! We were in Sainsbury's once, and he dry-slapped one of the checkout girls. For no reason! Slap! Right across the side of the head, and then acted as if it wasn't him that had done it. He just turned around, and started whistling. Another time we were in the park, and there was this woman walking her dog, and my dad asked to stroke the dog, but instead he just slapped it across the back – at least twice! Slap slap!

BronsonJonson2: that not good

BronsonJonson2: i just call my dad a bald headed bastard and he laughs

LoopyLisa21f: Is he bald?

BronsonJonson2: no

LoopyLisa21f: Is he a bastard?

BronsonJonson2: no he just has really short hair

BronsonJonson2: i really really like u

BronsonJonson2: when r the next holidays?

LoopyLisa21f: Half term is next month.

BronsonJonson2: well say no if u wanna but i thought id show u round brum 4 a weekend if u wanna

LoopyLisa21f: That would be interesting … Oh god. Wait … I feel all dizzy.

LoopyLisa21f: Think my arm is affecting me in a most profound sense. It's started to hurt, and my elbow is making a funny noise. A slight buzzing sound.

BronsonJonson2: well go 2 the hospital babe

LoopyLisa21f: …

BronsonJonson2: babe u ok? im worried now

LoopyLisa21f: I'll be ok. It'll pass.

LoopyLisa21f: …

BronsonJonson2: babe you there?

LoopyLisa21f: …very sleepy … must sleep …

BronsonJonson2: no u wont go and get it checked

LoopyLisa21f: …must … have little … sleep … first …

BronsonJonson2: ok then babe but send me an email when u go and when u get back ok cos i wanna know i care about u

> LoopyLisa21f: …I've just been sick now.

> LoopyLisa21f: That can't have anything to do with the arm, can it?

BronsonJonson2: it could

BronsonJonson2: now go and get it checked get someone 2 go with u

> LoopyLisa21f: No. I've no one to go with me. I'll get the bus.

BronsonJonson2: well go now and promise u will send me an email babe?

> LoopyLisa21f: No, I can't be doing with the journey. I'd have to change buses. Do you think I could put the arm back in myself if it's only dislocated?

> LoopyLisa21f: They do it on TV all the time.

BronsonJonson2: its tricky u colud have broken it u know

> LoopyLisa21f: Shall I just bang it against the wall – just the shoulder – like they do on TV, and see if that does anything?

BronsonJonson2: no cos u could break it babe

> LoopyLisa21f: …god … been sick again … Bizarre – the sick is bright green. Literally a luminous green.

BronsonJonson2: now go and promise u will send me an email ?

> LoopyLisa21f: …my arm is literally humming now … almost musical … colours … tracing …

BronsonJonson2: fuck the bus dial 999 now

> LoopyLisa21f: …no – they only come out if you're an old person, or have been involved in an industrial accident …

LoopyLisa21f: ...I fell on a sundial, remember ...? It's pre-industrial.

LoopyLisa21f: ...probably just got an upset stomach ... That's all. Just a really bad upset stomach that's making me vomit blood.

BronsonJonson2: they come out 2 anything babe that is what they r there for

LoopyLisa21f: This isn't an emergency – i'll let them go to someone who really needs it. You know: people who are trapped under walls ... People who have been attacked by wandering dogs ...

LoopyLisa21f: ...I'll be ok ...

LoopyLisa21f: ...not much left to throw-up now! The arm is probably just a by-product of the stomach bug.

BronsonJonson2: well im worried about u now babe u fell off roof

LoopyLisa21f: I've had worse.

LoopyLisa21f: I'd better go to bed now.

LoopyLisa21f: it's gettting late

BronsonJonson2: it only 2.40pm

BronsonJonson2: im still worried but b4 u go i just wanna say something

LoopyLisa21f: Yes. Yes you say what you like. You've been very kind to me.

BronsonJonson2: i love you

LoopyLisa21f: Er ... Come again?

BronsonJonson2: sorry ill go ive upset u now

LoopyLisa21f: I'm not upset. I just don't know what's going on.

BronsonJonson2: well i have upset u aint i?

LoopyLisa21f: No. I'm not upset. I'm just wondering what made you say that?

BronsonJonson2: well i feel like i love you

LoopyLisa21f: Why is this please?

BronsonJonson2: i dont know it feels like ive known u 4 ages

LoopyLisa21f: Well I've some very good news for you,

LoopyLisa21f: Can you guess what it is?

BronsonJonson2: no

LoopyLisa21f: ...ack ... been sick again ...

BronsonJonson2: that it?

LoopyLisa21f: No. Here is the news for you: I love you too, BronsonJonson2.

LoopyLisa21f: Goodbye!

LoopyLisa21f: xxx

BronsonJonson2: bye babe

BronsonJonson2: xxx

>>LoopyLisa21f SIGNED OFF AT 14:43   **"**

LOOPYLISA'S BLOG

Monday, May 22

Sorry I haven't updated the blog in a while, but I've been in hospital for the past couple of weeks, for reasons I don't really want to go into (ladies' problems). Due to an administrative error I was put on a ward full of old men.

As revolting as this sometimes was (three of the men refused to wear pyjamas) I struck up an unlikely friendship with the man in the bed next to me (swollen colon). He was called Tony Townshend, and he told me all about his exploits during World War II (2/Two). Apparently, he worked at the GCHQ, and it was his job to polish a large, brass crab they kept in the basement.

He had a special kit which he used to maintain the crab's sheen. It contained four different types of brush, and two different types of polish: Brasso (for the bulk of the crab's carapace), and Asso (for the crab's rectum).

He never found out what the crab was doing there, or why he had to keep it polished, and he said he was breaking the Official Secrets Act by telling me about it.

I woke up the next morning, and his bed was empty. I wondered if he'd been carted off by shady government officials, but it turned out that he was just in the toilet, fighting a nurse.

POSTED BY LOOPYLISA AT 08:10

" <<NEW CHAT SESSION STARTED

Pommypomson: hi

LoopyLisa21f: Hi there!

Pommypomson: u gota pic lisa

LoopyLisa21f: Maybe. I'll have a look.

Pommypomson: ok

LoopyLisa21f: Ok.

Pommypomson: ok

LoopyLisa21f: OK!!!!

Pommypomson: hello?

LoopyLisa21f: Hello. Tell me, dear … tell me where are you from?

Pommypomson: Northants

LoopyLisa21f: That sounds like a cool place. In fact, it sounds a bit like someone saying "No Thanks".

LoopyLisa21f: You know – like, "Would you like another bag of mini-pork, dear?"

LoopyLisa21f: "Northants – I've had more than enough already. In fact, I'm so full, I may have to go and make myself barf". Do you see?

Pommpypomson: yes

LoopyLisa21f: Do you know how Northants got its name?

Pommypomson: dunno u found pic yet?

LoopyLisa21f: In a minute, dear, in a minute. Do you think Northants was named after a colony of ants found there by the first settlers? You know – in the same way that Watford is named after the legendary West Atford bear?

LoopyLisa21f: And is there a Southants?

Pommypomson: southampton and northampton

LoopyLisa21f: Is there an Easthampton?

Pommypomson: not that i know off

LoopyLisa21f: Westhampton?

Pommypomson: no

LoopyLisa21f: Is there … tell me … tell me now … is there a Centralhampton?

LoopyLisa21f: Actually, that's a bit of a mouthful!

LoopyLisa21f: If there is a Centralhampton they may have had to abbreviate it to "Centhampton"

LoopyLisa21f: But people might mis-pronounce it, with a soft "th" sound. Like "Senseampton". And that sounds like some sort of naughty massage club, like the West Atford Sensorium. In conclusion: there probably isn't a Centralhampton.

LoopyLisa21f: Anyway … where were we?

Pommypomson: u was telling me how old u where n location

LoopyLisa21f: Oh yes. Did I tell you that, or did I forget again?

Pommypomson: no

LoopyLisa21f: No I didn't forget, or no I didn't tell you?

Pommypomson: didnt tell

Pommypomson: ok. Where is the pic u were finding??

LoopyLisa21f: I have found it now, dear. Shall I send it over?

Pommypomson: u sure its u

LoopyLisa21f: Yes. Are you ready for it?

Pommypomson: k

Pommypomson: still not got the pic

LoopyLisa21f: Please ... please have some patience. Attention: I have now sent the image.

<IMAGE SENT – lisa20.jpg>

Pommypomson: its a fucking wierdo

LoopyLisa21f: What?

LoopyLisa21f: What have I done?

Pommypomson: pic was of guy in drag

LoopyLisa21f: I beg your pardon? Who is this Guy N Drahg of whom you speak?

Pommypomson: u sent a pic of a guy in drag

LoopyLisa21f: I think you are mistaken.

Pommypomson: freak

LoopyLisa21f: I have to say I've never been quite so insulted. I've been called a lot of things in my time – musty-chuff, biscuit-back, batwing-baps – but never a freak. I hope you don't speak to your future wife in that way.

Pommypomson: fucking fucking weirdo

LoopyLisa21f: I hope your future wife leaves you for a milkman. A very ugly milkman called Eric Arris.

LoopyLisa21f: <u>Special notice:</u> Eric Arris is also <u>your future best friend</u>!

Pommypomson: fucking u fucking freak

>>Pommypomson HAS SIGNED OFF AT 19:40

LOOPYLISA'S BLOG

Thursday, May 25

Today was so unexpectedly cold that I didn't even go to the library – and I go to the library most days! I sometimes go there to borrow books, but mostly I go there to watch FR Piper, the head librarian.

To say FR Piper is eccentric is something of an understatement (he's always wearing a snood!), but I think at heart he's basically a decent man. Nevertheless, I'm quite surprised the council let him keep his job, as he has twice tried to burn down the library.

Rather than sack him, the council simply removed all of the books on pyromania, fire-starting, and how to burn down libraries. For now this appears to have done the trick, although the other day I'm pretty sure I saw FR Piper striking matches near a book about cetaceans.

POSTED BY LOOPYLISA AT 12:20

<<NEW CHAT SESSION STARTED

Longname40: Hi Lisa : -)

LoopyLisa21f: Hello, dear. How are you feeling "today"?

Longname40: Good thanks – enjoying the cold snap?

LoopyLisa21f: I am! I went sledging this afternoon.

LoopyLisa21f: To be honest it was a stupid idea, as it hasn't actually snowed round here. We tried to sledge from the top of the road, but it all ended badly.

Longname40: So – more like grassing instead then – lol

LoopyLisa21f: I ended up scraping along the road into a post, Craig shredded his knuckles down to crimson rosettes, and Edward (Edward is a dog) got his lead snagged on a lamppost, and nearly pulled off his own head.

Longname40: Ouch – thats grassing for you

LoopyLisa21f: Or "concreting", if you want to be entirely accurate. But not the sort of concreting you do on a patio with a trowel and a "levelling jeremy".

Longname40: lol

LoopyLisa21f: To be honest, we possibly shouldn't have sent Edward off on a trolley, but we wanted to see if was safe for humans (Russian Cosmonauts used to do something similar, but with space in place of a street). With hindsight, it probably wasn't safe for man nor beast.

Longname40: So – apart from grass sledging what do you get up to?

LoopyLisa21f: Well, I recently went to the circus.

LoopyLisa21f: I don't go to the circus regularly, but there was one on near me.

Longname40: Chinese?

LoopyLisa21f: No, no. It was a non-Chinese one. What would you call those?

LoopyLisa21f: A White Man Circus? Would it be racist to call it that? One of those ones anyway.

LoopyLisa21f: It was a bit sad.

LoopyLisa21f: They got this penguin out, and I don't think it was very well.

Longname40: Explain.

LoopyLisa21f: It sort of shuffled in, and fell over a cable, and it couldn't get up, and then this clown started shouting at it. I mean, he was really, really angry. I don't think I've ever seen such an angry man – clown or not.

Longname40: Awh nooo

LoopyLisa21f: Bless you.

LoopyLisa21f: It was a disgusting spectacle. The clown angrily grabbed the penguin, and righted it – sort of plonked it down hard on its feet. I felt really sorry for the poor little thing. The penguin just kept making a small honking sound, and shuffling on the spot, while the clown waved his finger right in its face telling it to behave.

LoopyLisa21f: Then the clown started barking orders at him, and I think he may have poked the penguin in the eye (admittedly, I don't think the clown did this on purpose – he was just waving his finger too close to the penguin's eye).

Longname40: bit unprofessional

LoopyLisa21f: Oh, he wasn't doing this in the main ring – it was all off to one side, near a post, and a flap.

LoopyLisa21f: I saw it because my seat was near the flap, so I was close by while it was happening. You couldn't really hear what the clown was saying to the penguin because the music was so loud. But I was close enough to see his greasepaint cracking as he screwed up his face with rage.

Longname40: Someone should have beaten the crap out of the clown

LoopyLisa21f: Yeah, I wanted to go and say something to the ringmaster, but Craig told me not to, because he had a tattoo on his elbow which said "DANGER".

LoopyLisa21f: The worst thing was, as we were leaving my magazine blew out of my handbag, and around the side of the big top, and when I went to get it I saw the clown outside, and he was still having a pop at the penguin. He kept poking it in the chest, and he lifted the penguin's wings up, and let them drop, and called him "pathetic". He was saying stuff like "You can't even effing fly", and "You're the most pathetic effing type of bird there effing is", and "Even puffins are better than you".

Longname40: Jeeeeeezus. Bad. We used to keep some animals. They don't like aggresion

LoopyLisa21f: What sort of animals did you keep?

Longname40: Goats, pigs, chickens, ducks,

Longname40: Sheep

LoopyLisa21f: Where did you keep them?

LoopyLisa21f: Out of harm's way, I hope! I hope you didn't keep them in a large carrier bag! That's where my gran kept her kitten, you see. She hung it from a door handle.

Longname40: We had a few acres in the countryside

LoopyLisa21f: Wow! Were you a farmer?

Longname40: No dad used to keep a few animals : -)

LoopyLisa21f: I love animals! I love all kinds of animals. Big ones. Small ones. Crows.

LoopyLisa21f: I once even saw a cow giving birth.

Longname40: What is your favourite animal?

LoopyLisa21f: I like sloths.

LoopyLisa21f: Have you ever seen an animal giving birth?

Longname40: Yeh – amazing : -)

LoopyLisa21f: I'd like to see a sloth giving birth. I'd like to get right up close as the baby sloth was coming out.

LoopyLisa21f: Actually, I say that, but I might not be too good with it, especially not if I can smell the amniotic fluid. When the cow's placenta came out I had to have a sit down.

LoopyLisa21f: It looked and smelled like something you'd find in Doctor Who's toilet.

Longname40: lol

LoopyLisa21f: Seriously – I gagged into a trough.

Longname40: It can be a shock : -)

LoopyLisa21f: I'll say! It was all wobbly and veiny. Like a giant, mutant brain gone wrong. For a minute I thought the cow had given birth to twins, and one of them was a normal cow, and the other one was a freak. You know: all udder and no legs or face, like a monster from Lord of the Rings. A monster called an "udderaass".

Longname40: I'll admit that I was never into the gory stuff : -)

Longname40: Did you like Lord of the Rings?

LoopyLisa21f: Not particularly. I didn't really understand it. Plus I missed the first half hour of one of them, because by mistake I'd gone into a screen that was showing Elf.

LoopyLisa21f: I didn't realise at first.

Longname40: lol

Longname40: Elf – elves. Common mistake : -)

LoopyLisa21f: Well, yeah … I was thinking "This doesn't seem like the other films", but because I hadn't really been paying attention in the other films I wasn't 100% sure.

Longname40: lol – oops

Longname40: I took my mum to see them. I think she was a little blown away by the new technology : -)

LoopyLisa21f: The air conditioning, you mean? Was she literally blown away by the high-tech fan … fan … fannies? <SNIGGER>

Longname40: lol – and the sound and the screen size : -)

LoopyLisa21f: Ah!

Longname40: : -)

LoopyLisa21f: When I travelled with my nan on a plane she spent the entire journey shrieking.

Longname40: Awh noo – poor lady

LoopyLisa21f: I mean, she shrieked for literally the entire journey, except for a couple of moments, when the cabin crew tried to calm her down, and get her drunk.

LoopyLisa21f: A four hour flight, with her next to me, emitting her shrill squawking. It wasn't even the flight she was scared of; she'd watched The Fog the night before, and kept remembering bits.

LoopyLisa21f: Are you still there?

Longname40: Yeh – lol of course

LoopyLisa21f: Where were we?

Longname40: Your gran shreiking

LoopyLisa21f: Oh yeah. God. Why did you have to remind me?

Longname40: You only just mentioned it

LoopyLisa21f: She kept grabbing hold of me, and everything. She was grabbing my sleeve, my hair, my face – the whole time screaming about The Fog.

Longname40: Awh poor lady

LoopyLisa21f: No. Nothing poor about her. She ruined my holiday. I didn't even want her to come with us, but she insisted. Also, she said that she'd been having recurring nightmares, and that if she stayed at home on her own she was worried that a burglar would break into her bungalow, lift up her nightie, and blow raspberries on the elastic of her knickers. The second day of the holiday she got sunburn, and her eyes got all crispy, and almost completely sealed up.

Longname40: Ah – just a shame she got herself into a tizz

LoopyLisa21f: Anyone else would've stayed in the hotel and let us go out and enjoy ourselves, but she insisted on coming along, and making us hold a big umbrella over her head, and rub salve on her eyelids.

Longname40: Where were you off too?

LoopyLisa21f: We were going to Lanzarote, wherever that is.

Longname40: I'm not really a sun worshiper

LoopyLisa21f: She was a vindictive old hag.

LoopyLisa21f: She once threw a glass bottle of ketchup at me because she thought I'd said something derogatory about Trotsky.

Longname40: Erm

Longname40: Wow

Longname40: One strange lady

LoopyLisa21f: She is! She had a bit of a thing about Russia in general, and Leon Trotsky in particular. I don't think she knew much about him – she just thought he was handsome. She kept little cut-out photos of his face in a bureau in her bungalow, and she would stick them over images of male models she'd cut out of magazines.

Longname40: Definitely a bit touched in the head

LoopyLisa21f: Can I tell you a joke?

Longname40: Of course

LoopyLisa21f: What glows, and founded the Politburo?

Longname40: tell me

LoopyLisa21f: Neon Trotsky!!!!!

Longname40: lol

LoopyLisa21f: Do you have any grandparents?

Longname40: One gran left yes

LoopyLisa21f: What is your gran's name?

Longname40: Nellie

LoopyLisa21f: Mine is called Nanny Sutton.

Longname40: Where do u work?

LoopyLisa21f: I work in a school. It's excellent!

Longname40: r u a teacher

LoopyLisa21f: Yup. An NQT. A newly quantified teacher.

Longname40: What do u teach?

LoopyLisa21f: I teach children.

LoopyLisa21f: What was the naughtiest thing you ever did at school?

Longname40: Miss lessons and pick on the younger kids u?

LoopyLisa21f: I was quite a good kid at school. Though my friend Craig once dared me to write "minge" on his arm, and he went and told a teacher what I'd done, and she didn't believe me when I said that he'd told me to do it.

Longname40: Did u get into any trouble?

LoopyLisa21f: Yeah, big time.

Longname40: What happened?

LoopyLisa21f: I was told to sit under the Naughty Desk, and everyone had to call me "Child A" for the remainder of the day.

Longname40: Under a desk? A bit harsh wasnt it?

LoopyLisa21f: Well, sort of − but it was quite a forward-thinking school. And it wasn't a small desk. They kept the small desk for the really naughty kids.

LoopyLisa21f: They had to be referred to as "Childs B through to F".

Longname40: Why?

LoopyLisa21f: I suppose that meant they were naughtier than Child A. I never really questioned it when I was there. But imagine how naughty a Child X would be! I bet The Joker and Hitler were both a Child X.

LoopyLisa21f: Anyway, it cost my parents £2,000 a term, so I didn't like to complain.

Longname40: Wow, u went to a private school!

LoopyLisa21f: Well, sort of. It wasn't that posh – I got selected because I had special abilities.

Longname40: I should have known, u start your sentences with capital letters and use full stops whereas i forget

LoopyLisa21f: Well, I wasn't a genius, or anything.

LoopyLisa21f: But a couple of teachers put me forward for a special programme, because they said I had a unique talent for music.

Longname40: do u play any instruments

LoopyLisa21f: I never learned an instrument. I could just hear a piece of music, and write it down instantly.

LoopyLisa21f: I never even learned music. It was just an ability I had. Somehow I was born knowing about musical notation.

LoopyLisa21f: Also, I could make sound come out of certain instruments just by looking at them across a room.

Longname40: why didnt u develop your musical skills

LoopyLisa21f: They tried to get me to learn piano, and then oboe, but I was never really interested. I just liked hearing music, and writing it down.

LoopyLisa21f: In the end they got fed up with me.

LoopyLisa21f: They just used to let me sit in a corner scribbling away beneath a blanket, while the other kids played tunes.

Longname40: Why? How were u suppose to develope your potential like that

LoopyLisa21f: Well exactly. And two grand a term it was costing my parents.

LoopyLisa21f: I enjoyed it at the time, but with hindsight it was a waste of money.

Longname40: silly question but why call yourself Loopy?

LoopyLisa21f: I dunno. It sounds better than Bi-Polar.

LoopyLisa21f: Oh! I just remembered that I need to go!

Longname40: ok shame

LoopyLisa21f: I'm meant to be ringing some bells this afternoon.

Longname40: what bells?

LoopyLisa21f: Secret bells (cow bells). Bye now! Buh ... buh-bye!

>>LoopyLisa21f SIGNED OFF AT 13:57

LOOPYLISA'S BLOG

Thursday, June 01

I'm getting so desperate for a boyfriend that this weekend I even agreed to be a steward at a local sci-fi convention. I figured the place would be full of eligible single men, but I barely got a chance to check them out. Instead, I was run ragged sorting out problems with the celebrity guests.

First, the man who played R2-D2 slipped down the back of a sofa, and I had to fish him out with a spatula. Then the man who played Chewbacca got the runs, and I had to take his costume to the dry-cleaners (Craig joked that I'd have been better off taking it to a "brown-cleaners").

Then three Doctor Whos had a punch-up over which of them was the best. I settled the dispute by arguing that none of them was "best", because they were essentially the same man. I pointed out that we all have elements of our personality that we don't like, and that the key to becoming a better person is to acknowledge this, and try to do something about it, rather than beating yourself up.

Two of them responded by dragging Colin Baker into the car park, and trying to asphyxiate him.

POSTED BY LOOPYLISA AT 11:11

<<NEW CHAT SESSION STARTED

Tonythebird: Hi Lisa where you from?

LoopyLisa21f: London. You?

Tonythebird: West London

LoopyLisa21f: Wow! So you must know Peagram Brown, the tramp?

Tonythebird: who?

LoopyLisa21f: Tony?

LoopyLisa21f: Tony, love?

Tonythebird: yes lisa

LoopyLisa21f: What do you do, Tony?

Tonythebird: work in sales and amarketing lisa and u?

LoopyLisa21f: I'm a primary school teacher.

LoopyLisa21f: Get this: one of the kids in my class is called 'Dainty James'! That's his actual name!

Tonythebird: god i feel for kid lol

Tonythebird: wish u were my teacher tho babe lol

LoopyLisa21f: You wouldn't if you knew how I disciplined the kids.

LoopyLisa21f: I'm pretty strict.

Tonythebird: ooooo i like dat babe lol

LoopyLisa21f: I puff talc in their faces if they misbehave, and I blindfold them, push them into the chalk cupboard, and tell them they're responsible for the death of the rest of the class.

Tonythebird: i dont mind im sure i cando wit sum dicipline babe

LoopyLisa21f: Did I also mention that I puff them with the talc, AND pull their eyebrows off with Sellotape before pushing them head-first into "Old Chalky".

LoopyLisa21f: Not really! I'm just telling a type of joke! It's not the sort of joke which has a punchline. It's a new type of joke. The type of joke that is actually a pithy comment.

Tonythebird: dam u cruel women? lol

LoopyLisa21f: Actually, I sort of did that stuff a couple of times, but I can't really talk about it.

Tonythebird: lol i bet u cant lol

LoopyLisa21f: Well, I sort of got into a bit of trouble you see.

LoopyLisa21f: I did the talc thing to silence a kid up one time, and he contracted talc-ing of the lungs. Also, he turned into a hunchback.

Tonythebird: lol i bet he shut up after hey

LoopyLisa21f: And the Sellotape thing only happened while I was trying to fit another boy with a mask for a school concert.

LoopyLisa21f: It wouldn't have been so bad, but he was from a deprived background. I just wanted him to feel a part of the production by playing the role of Tom Seltzer, the Fizzmaster, but he became terribly distressed and began howling.

Tonythebird: ooooo naughty lol

LoopyLisa21f: Well, it was more or less an accident.

Tonythebird: so tell me more bout u babe

LoopyLisa21f: Like what exactly? I've already told you most things about me.

Tonythebird: well u single? wat u look like? wat music u liek?

LoopyLisa21f: I'm single at the moment. I am blonde, and of medium width.

LoopyLisa21f: My favourite band is The Mungoes, featuring vocals by R.Welk.

Tonythebird: nice babe r u top heavy? curvy? slim? meidum?

LoopyLisa21f: I'm literally "medium in all departments".

Tonythebird: sweet babe

Tonythebird: wud luv to c u

LoopyLisa21f: Who is your favourite band?

LoopyLisa21f: I really like The Mungoes. I've never heard any music by them, I just like their lead guitarist, Darren Uffsss. He wears boots made from Lego … probably!

Tonythebird: ok sounds all good babe

Tonythebird: me i like RnB swing soul ragga gagare , rock , salsa hip hop

LoopyLisa21f: I went to see The Mungoes with Craig, and he bought a t-shirt, but when we got home and he tried it on, there was a chrysalis inside it!

Tonythebird: lol dont worry babe

LoopyLisa21f: We tried to get the chrysalis to hatch quickly by putting it in the microwave, but stupid Craig put it on a foil dish, and it started sparking, and caught alight.

LoopyLisa21f: My dad was well angry.

Tonythebird: i bet

LoopyLisa21f: My dad's funny. He's always getting drunk, and punching the wall!

LoopyLisa21f: One time he got drunk, and hired a little bouncy castle, and then he was sick on it, but he just kept on bouncin'.

Tonythebird: lol cool babe so babe can i ask wat u do for fun?

LoopyLisa21f: Yes.

Tonythebird: so wat do du do babe?

LoopyLisa21f: Have you ever played 'Catch The Kitten'? It's a game where one of you drops a kitten out of a window, and the other person has to catch it in a towel. Have you played that?

Tonythebird: No. I like sex, dancing , music, gym cars , going out . drinking

LoopyLisa21f: What are gym cars? Are they like normal cars, but with tiny parallel bars in the back?

Tonythebird: sorz meant gym and then cars

LoopyLisa21f: My local gym has a mini-gym for dwarfs. You're not supposed to see them doing it, but one time the door was open, and I looked in. I really enjoyed watching the little guys darting around, bouncing off one another, and tumbling about. They were playing some really strange music in there, too. I think it was Equinox by Jean-Michele Jarre.

LoopyLisa21f: Some of them were on these treadmills, and one of them was running, and then he was fired off it, and bounced off the wall. Tony? Tony, love?

Tonythebird: yes?

LoopyLisa21f: Would you like to hear a joke?

Tonythebird: yeah sure babe

LoopyLisa21f: Ok … I'll think of one.

Tonythebird: ok

Tonythebird: so tellme babe wat turns u on?

LoopyLisa21f: Hang on … I've tried to think of a joke, and I've successfully thought of one, and here it is. Question: Why does Superman wear his underpants outside his trousers? Answer: Because he's a pervert! Ha ha ha. You tell me one now please.

Tonythebird: ok y did da condom go flying across da room?

LoopyLisa21f: Was there a bird inside it?

Tonythebird: no it got pissed off

Tonythebird: lololol

LoopyLisa21f: The bird got pissed off?

LoopyLisa21f: So it flew off with the condom?

Tonythebird: yes

Tonythebird: so babe can i ask u wud u liek to hook up sumtiem?

LoopyLisa21f: Yes.

Tonythebird: cool babe u drive?

LoopyLisa21f: Yes I've just passed my test! I drive a Fiat Mungoe.

Tonythebird: cool

Tonythebird: wud u liek to swap numbers so we can arrange to meet up babe

LoopyLisa21f: I dunno. Can Craig come?

Tonythebird: whos he?

LoopyLisa21f: He used to be my boyfriend. He's just my friend now after he said he couldn't go out with me after he caught a type of palsy off a rotting mulberry bush.

Tonythebird: ok well was hoping it wud b just me and u really

LoopyLisa21f: Well, I could tell him not to come. But he'd get upset. He normally comes everywhere with me. He's no bother. He just sits there, sort of shaking, and moving his head around, and making a clicking sound.

Tonythebird: well suppose we like each other and wanted to kiss then wat?

LoopyLisa21f: Kiss?!?

LoopyLisa21f: Well ... I'm sure Craig won't mind.

LoopyLisa21f: As long as it isn't a sexy style of kissing, because then he might become distressed, and wet himself. But why would you want to kiss Craig?

Tonythebird: not him . u

LoopyLisa21f: Well ... I thought you might want to kiss him "hello" on the top of his head.

LoopyLisa21f: It's a bit scabby, and the hair is patchy, but he generally looks ok, apart from the twitching and the clicking.

LoopyLisa21f: Should I not tell Craig about me seeing you?

LoopyLisa21f: Is that for the best?

Tonythebird: yeah babe its jus me and u

LoopyLisa21f: ok ... you mustn't tell Craig if you ever meet him, though?

Tonythebird: nope i wont babe

Tonythebird: sorz babe i gotta soon so email me ok

LoopyLisa21f: Ok, love! Goodbye!

LoopyLisa21f: I love you!

Tonythebird: cool babe email so we can arrange to meet up babe

Tonythebird: cool babe chat soon xxxxxxxxxxxxxxxx

LoopyLisa21f: xxxx! xxxx?!

>>Tonythebird SIGNED OFF AT 21:11   **” ”**

LOOPYLISA'S BLOG

Monday, June 05

I'm starting to wonder whether teaching is the right career path for me. Some days it all feels like such a thankless task, and I never realised that children could be so unpredictable.

Yesterday, we had a show-and-tell. One of the kids brought a pygmy hippopotamus into class, and another brought what he said was a "hygmy pippopotamus", but I could tell it was just the other boy's pygmy hippopotamus in a different t-shirt.

POSTED BY LOOPYLISA AT 16:20

<<NEW CHAT SESSION STARTED

Peepers1200: how r u doing ?

LoopyLisa21f: I'll tell you how in a moment.

LoopyLisa21f: ...

LoopyLisa21f: I'm ready to tell you now. I'm doing this: great!

Peepers1200: u ok to chat ?

LoopyLisa21f: Yes. Yes I am. You start.

Peepers1200: u single ?

Peepers1200: and how old r u ?

Peepers1200: were u from ?

LoopyLisa21f: I'm 21. And I'm from London. And you, Peepers? What is there to be known about you?

Peepers1200: im 28 m london and black

> LoopyLisa21f: Well, that's ok. You really didn't need to tell me about the black thing. I wasn't planning on telling you the colour of my face.

Peepers1200: well i do it just in case u want to know abt me

> LoopyLisa21f: You should be more proud. You should use your face as a statement which speaks for itself.

> LoopyLisa21f: When I meet people. I don't point out my eczema. It's obvious for all to see. My face is a statement about me. A statement that says: "This girl has really bad eczema".

Peepers1200: ok I get it

Peepers1200: where in london r u ?

> LoopyLisa21f: Smethickhamptonwickton.

> LoopyLisa21f: "U"?

Peepers1200: dulwich

> LoopyLisa21f: Oh dear …

> LoopyLisa21f: Do you know any jokes?

Peepers1200: yeah

> LoopyLisa21f: Tell me one? Or two please?

Peepers1200: a well travelled man once ask his wife if she knows of anywhere they he has not been to on the planet so they will go there on their weddding anniversary and the woman said then the kitchen wil be a nice place for him

> LoopyLisa21f: I get it! LOL!

Peepers1200: good

> LoopyLisa21f: It's funny because they come from another planet, right? They're aliens, yes?

Peepers1200: no

LoopyLisa21f: What do you do for a living?

Peepers1200: im with a train company as tkt sales clerk

Peepers1200: u?

LoopyLisa21f: I'm a trainee teacher.

LoopyLisa21f: Why aren't you at work today?

Peepers1200: just finish wk

LoopyLisa21f: Did you get up early?

Peepers1200: yeah at 6

LoopyLisa21f: I love that time of the morning. Sometimes I walk around my flat with my eyes closed, pretending it's that time of the morning, and pretending I can hear birdsong, and that I'm licking dew off the lawn.

Peepers1200: lol

LoopyLisa21f: But that's true. All of it.

Peepers1200: i know it is

LoopyLisa21f: Do you work shifts?

Peepers1200: yeah is a shift wk

LoopyLisa21f: My dad used to do shift work. He worked in a glue factory, melting down the horses.

Peepers1200: is that wot is use for glue ?

LoopyLisa21f: Yes. Everyone knows that, dear.

LoopyLisa21f: Occasionally they'd chuck a cow or a couple of pigs in, depending on the type of glue required.

Peepers1200: oh well i did not know that

LoopyLisa21f: Have you ever heard of Copydex?

Peepers1200: no plz wot is that ?

LoopyLisa21f: It's a type of sticky, white glue. Believe me – you don't want to know what that's made of.

Peepers1200: tel me plz

LoopyLisa21f: I reckon Copydex is made from the stomach lining of a carthorse.

Peepers1200: how can thatt be ?

LoopyLisa21f: I don't know. I guess they can make glue out of anything that's sticky, and horse stomachs are probably very sticky because of all the sugar lumps they eat.

Peepers1200: ok

Peepers1200: so have u a pic of ur self ?

LoopyLisa21f: I might do. It could take a while, though. It's on my old computer.

Peepers1200: can i see it plz

LoopyLisa21f: Yes, but it'll take approximately nine minutes to retrieve.

LoopyLisa21f: While I'm doing that please tell me more about yourself, specifically amusing stories relating to your place of work.

Peepers1200: im 28 5ft7 medium built single and looking

LoopyLisa21f: Looking at what?

Peepers1200: looking for love

LoopyLisa21f: Oh! That's good. That's ok. That's good. Ok? Good.

LoopyLisa21f: Do you ever go speed dating?

LoopyLisa21f: Well? Do you?

Peepers1200: no never have u ?

LoopyLisa21f: Once. I didn't like it. They spoke too fast for me to understand, and one of the people I spoke to was eating pickled onions.

Peepers1200: awww

LoopyLisa21f: At one point he dropped the jar, and the vinegar splashed the hem of my frock.

Peepers1200: that is not good then

Peepers1200: wot a shame

LoopyLisa21f: It wasn't very romantic at all. Another time I got confused and accidentally went speed SKATING!!!!!!

Peepers1200: lol

LoopyLisa21f: It's like normal skating, but instead of skates you drive around in a little buggy. And instead of it being on ice, you're in a field.

Peepers1200: ok i see

LoopyLisa21f: How long have you been single, dear?

Peepers1200: is been over a yr now

LoopyLisa21f: I'm sorry to hear that. Perhaps you've been looking in the wrong places. You should go speed dating. I hear it's pretty good.

Peepers1200: i dont think ill like it

LoopyLisa21f: You might! Some of my friends go all the time. Well, not ALL the time (that would be excessive). But frequently.

Peepers1200: where abt is this happening ?

LoopyLisa21f: All sorts of places. The event I went to was on a garage forecourt. There was only me and two men there. They stopped me in the street with a clipboard, and asked if I'd like to go, and I said "Ok, sure, sounds like fun, whatever".

LoopyLisa21f: At that point I didn't know the onions thing was going to happen.

Peepers1200: lol

Peepers1200: u must be a brave girl to go with 2 men

LoopyLisa21f: It's ok. It was on a busy main road in the middle of the day.

Peepers1200: so wot wld have happen if u like him ?

LoopyLisa21f: Well, I suppose then you'd go on a date. That didn't happen to me though.

Peepers1200: ok

LoopyLisa21f: But one of my friends met a Hungarian at speed dating, and went out with him for sixteen months!

LoopyLisa21f: His name was Tracy Horace.

LoopyLisa21f: Are you shy, dear?

Peepers1200: im abit shy lol

LoopyLisa21f: Why is that do you think?

Peepers1200: cos i cant tell some one i like her whiles at wk

LoopyLisa21f: There's someone at work that you like?

Peepers1200: well yeah but not with the company i wk with she is a customer

LoopyLisa21f: Is she a regular customer?

Peepers1200: yeah and very nice

LoopyLisa21f: You could slip her a note. It could read: "I LIKE YOU". And you could draw a happy face below it.

Peepers1200: wish i cld

LoopyLisa21f: What would happen if you did?

Peepers1200: i dont know

LoopyLisa21f: Are there train company regulations against it?

Peepers1200: not that i know

LoopyLisa21f: Hmm. Have you ever struck up a conversation with her?

Peepers1200: several times

LoopyLisa21f: And she's friendly?

Peepers1200: very

Peepers1200: i gave her my number once but she never called

LoopyLisa21f: You need to ensure you don't startle her with any loud noises, or sudden movements.

LoopyLisa21f: She might be timid. You must never hide in a photo booth, for example, and leap out shrieking.

Peepers1200: ok

LoopyLisa21f: Here are several further things you must never do: never brandish a stick at her. Never try and grab her through that little money tray at the bottom of your service window. Never press your lunch up against the service window, as she might not realise what it is. Especially if it's a slice of baloney.

Peepers1200: ok

LoopyLisa21f: Would you like some more advice? I'm good at advice, or so I'm told.

Peepers1200: sure

LoopyLisa21f: Ask me a question, and I'll answer.

Peepers1200: i thought u were giving me advice

LoopyLisa21f: Well I will, but I need specific topics on which to trigger the advice response.

Peepers1200: ok

LoopyLisa21f: Actually, you might be able to give me some advice. Do you know where I can get a cheap theremin?

Peepers1200: whats a theremin

LoopyLisa21f: It's a musical instrument that you play by manipulating electromagnetic fields. I used to have one, but it's gone now.

LoopyLisa21f: ATTENTION! Quick-fire question: what colour is your hair?

Peepers1200: black of course

LoopyLisa21f: Is it dyed black? Like a goth?

Peepers1200: normal black

Peepers1200: what r u wearing

LoopyLisa21f: I'm wearing a big, blue jumpsuit at the moment.

LoopyLisa21f: It's made out of parachute silk.

Peepers1200: how cum?

LoopyLisa21f: I just am. It's my favourite outfit.

LoopyLisa21f: What's your favourite outfit?

Peepers1200: i like jeans and t shirt, casual

LoopyLisa21f: I see. Do you own many t-shirts?

Peepers1200: quite a few

Peepers1200: what other outfits do u like to wear

LoopyLisa21f: I have a large array of bonnets. I have a train driver's bonnet, if you're interested. It's got a hidden pocket for storing train keys.

Peepers1200: sounds interesting

LoopyLisa21f: Yes.

LoopyLisa21f: Hmm. Yes.

Peepers1200: so why do u not have a bf ?

LoopyLisa21f: He ran off, and took the theremin with him.

LoopyLisa21f: I really need to get a new one.

LoopyLisa21f: It's quite a recent split.

Peepers1200: i c, do u like sexy outfits

LoopyLisa21f: That depends on your definition of sexy. My boyfriend had a weird definition of sexy.

Peepers1200: in what way

LoopyLisa21f: Well, he made me wear capes all the time. Huge ones. They were really impractical.

LoopyLisa21f: I failed my driving test because my cape kept flapping in the examiner's face. I suppose I could have closed the window, but it was really hot in there. For some reason the examiner kept lighting Roman candles and letting them off in a biscuit tin he kept on the back seat.

Peepers1200: i mean, underwear

LoopyLisa21f: No. I never wore capes as underwear.

LoopyLisa21f: They really are best worn externally. I'm not sure how you'd wear one as an item of underwear. I suppose you could tuck it between your thighs, but that's hardly practical, because you'd have to walk around with your legs together, lest the cape unfurl.

Peepers1200: i c, do u wear sexyt underwear

LoopyLisa21f: Again, that depends on your definition. My boyfriend used to get embarrassed if I wore anything too – you know – saucy.

Peepers1200: i love a woman wearing saucy stuff

LoopyLisa21f: And I haven't had time to buy anything new.

LoopyLisa21f: You see, he only broke up with me about 20 minutes ago.

Peepers1200: ok,

LoopyLisa21f: I can't explain it. One minute he was waving his hands around, playing the theremin in a seemingly happy fashion, then he suddenly leapt up, and started shouting, and ranting wordlessly. Then he snatched up the theremin, and clambered out through the French windows.

LoopyLisa21f: It was an awful sight to behold.

Peepers1200: perhaps he got an electric shock

Peepers1200: do u like sex

LoopyLisa21f: Well, I suppose. I did before my boyfriend left me. Now I'm not sure I'll ever do it again.

>>Peepers1200 SIGNED OFF AT 21:31

LOOPYLISA'S BLOG

Saturday, June 10

I was hit with a credit card bill for over £4,000 last week, and I've realised I need to find some more money – "stat" (as they say on ER). I've worked it out, and I think I can fit a third part-time job into my schedule.

On Friday, I went for an interview to be the new voice of the speaking clock, but I don't think it went very well.

The interview lasted 24 hours (I had to do the whole clock), and by the end of it I was so tired I tried to eat a plug. I expressed my exhaustion to the interviewer, but he insisted that if I got the job I'd have to get used to the hours.

Also, he said that conditions would be a lot worse if we were doing it live. Apparently, they hire clowns, who try to put you off by prancing around in front of you, doing pratfalls, and throwing wacky shapes.

POSTED BY LOOPYLISA AT 18:16

<<NEW CHAT SESSION STARTED

Dave3744: HI wanna chat to a m 33 sussex?

LoopyLisa21f: It's ok with me, if it's ok with you.

Dave3744: looking for a discreet femme for some fun with

Dave3744: have i found one.?

LoopyLisa21f: I can be discreet. Do you have secrets to impart to me? And when I say "secrets" I specifically mean "state secrets".

Dave3744: am looking for no strings sex

LoopyLisa21f: I'm not sure I'm with you. Is this something to do with puppets? Is it a code for something kinky to do with ventriloquism puppets? Or glove puppets? Off the top of my head I can think of three naughty things you could do with a glove puppet, but only two you could do with a ventriloquism puppet.

Dave 3744: no just sex without hassle

LoopyLisa21f: Why don't you want any hassle? Surely the whole act is a bit of a hassle. It's never as simple as, say, pressing some sort of a buzzer to make a food pellet come out of a dispenser.

Dave3744: live with gf so need no strings sex

LoopyLisa21f: Won't she mind?

Dave3744: wont tell her

LoopyLisa21f: How would you feel if she did the same?

Dave3744: im too horny for her she says if i fuck others i just doesnt want to know about it

LoopyLisa21f: No, no – I meant how would you feel if she had no-strings sex … WITH YOU?

Dave3744: that dont make sense

Dave3744: do u have a bf?

LoopyLisa21f: Not at the moment.

LoopyLisa21f: So basically what you're after is an affair?

Dave3744: not an affair as in dating but just meet for sex

Dave3744: both wanting same thing

Dave3744: not relationship

LoopyLisa21f: What if I wanted the occasional chat?

Dave3744: yeah of course

LoopyLisa21f: But would you set a limit on how long we could chat for?

Dave3744: no

LoopyLisa21f: Great!

LoopyLisa21f: Would you approve a list of things we could and couldn't chat about?

Dave3744: no

LoopyLisa21f: What if I wanted to talk nonsense for half an hour? What if I just wanted to roll around on the bed making high-pitched, gibberish noises for 35 – 40 minutes?

Dave3744: lol u can

Dave3744: just wouldnt wanna talk about gf too much etc

LoopyLisa21f: What's wrong with your girlfriend?

LoopyLisa21f: I want to know a bit more about her. What's her favourite food?

Dave3744: lived with her 8yrs dying to fuck another

Dave3744: im randy all the time

LoopyLisa21f: Ok. Well, what should we do?

Dave3744: well do u have a pic

LoopyLisa21f: I'll try and retrieve it off my laptop. You can continue chatting to me in the meantime.

Dave3744: would u tell people if we do this?

LoopyLisa21f: Yes. I'd tell them your name, telephone number, and address.

Dave3744: why????

LoopyLisa21f: What do you mean? We would be engaging in something very beautiful, and I'd want to trill your name from the highest treetops.

Dave3744: NO! it would hve to be very discreet!

LoopyLisa21f: Why?

Dave3744: does no strings sex appeal to u or not?

LoopyLisa21f: I suppose.

Dave3744: can u send a pic then

LoopyLisa21f: What if I accidentally fell in love with you, as I fear I may already be doing?

Dave3744: wot?

LoopyLisa21f: Would I have to pay you for no strings sex?

Dave3744: no

LoopyLisa21f: Would you have to pay me?

Dave3744: no

LoopyLisa21f: Would I have to pay your girlfriend?

Dave3744: wed do it coz we both wanted it ok?

LoopyLisa21f: Ok.

LoopyLisa21f: Do you like me?

Dave3744: yes of course

LoopyLisa21f: Great!

Dave3744: have u had sex recently?

LoopyLisa21f: That's a bit personal.

Dave3744: ok what do u like sexually

LoopyLisa21f: That is also personal.

LoopyLisa21f: Shall I send you my pic?

Dave3744: yes

<IMAGE SENT – lisa18.jpg>

Dave3744: very sexy

LoopyLisa21f: Thankyou. Am I really sexy?

Dave3744: would need two paper bags

Dave3744: one over your head and one over mine in case yours fell off

LoopyLisa21f: That's a horrible, horrible thing to say.

LoopyLisa21f: I'm insecure enough already, and now this?!?

LoopyLisa21f: Do you do this to every girl you meet?

LoopyLisa21f: Does it make you feel like a big man building up my hopes and then insulting me?

Dave3744: yes lol

LoopyLisa21f: And now you're just laughing at me?!

Dave3744: didnt realise u were a bloke in drag

LoopyLisa21f: I'm not. What does that even mean?

Dave3744: well whos pic is that

LoopyLisa21f: I've sent you another one if you don't believe me.

<IMAGE SENT – lisa19.jpg>

Dave3744: you havent had a very close shave

LoopyLisa21f: It's just shadows.

LoopyLisa21f: I never come out right in photos.

Dave3744: take a body shot then

LoopyLisa21f: You're just being a saucy pervert now.

Dave3744: no u r a geezer

LoopyLisa21f: How would you like it if I said you looked like a girl?

LoopyLisa21f: Not very much, I'd wager.

Dave3744: well shame u arent a femme I'm going now

LoopyLisa21f: Love you, Dave!!! Xxxx

>>LoopyLisa21f SIGNED OFF AT 16:24   ""

LOOPYLISA'S BLOG

Thursday, June 15

As expected, I didn't get the job with the speaking clock people, but I have had another interview with the BBC, for a job as a continuity announcer. I'm pretty confident that this one went a lot better.

I hadn't realised this, but continuity announcers aren't given the schedule information in advance – they have to guess the programmes which are going to be shown.

In my interview I had to guess an entire evening's programming, and I was 78% accurate (they told me that people normally only get between 40% and 76%). Also, I managed to make my predictions despite some nude clowns trying to put me off.

POSTED BY LOOPYLISA AT 17:06

<<NEW CHAT SESSION STARTED

BigD: hi

LoopyLisa21f: Hello, dear. Who are you?

BigD: hello am David wot u up 2?

LoopyLisa21f: Just sitting here sucking on a bundle of gauze that I've soaked in iced tea and Savlon. What are you up to?

BigD: chattin to sexy girls

LoopyLisa21f: How do you know they're sexy?

BigD: they sound it lol

LoopyLisa21f: They might be lying. I chatted to someone on here once who told me he was the cousin of the actor Robert Englund, but when I met him, he wasn't his cousin at all.

LoopyLisa21f: He was just some guy who worked in a café, and had psoriasis. But get this: he only had the psoriasis on his upper lip, and whenever he spoke you couldn't see his mouth for the shower of skin flakes. Craig kept making him talk at speed about parmesan cheese, which I felt was a little cruel.

BigD: who is ur cousin then

LoopyLisa21f: My cousin? Have you clearly understood?

LoopyLisa21f: I have lots of cousins. None of whom I was referring to.

LoopyLisa21f: They include: Helen, Pelen, Hansel, Fretl …

BigD: lol

LoopyLisa21f: …Yuncer, Buncer … Yentsen and DeMoynt … Foynt, O'Sullivan, and Tot.

BigD: LOL

LoopyLisa21f: What's so funny, dear?

BigD: last person i was talkin to saisd she was sat in her undies …doubt it tho

LoopyLisa21f: Are you sure she wasn't just some mad old woman? There was a woman who used to live near me who'd get on the bus with her bra outside her cardigan, and would sit there stroking a trough of Soreen.

BigD: she said she was feeling horny

LoopyLisa21f: Who? The Soreen woman on the bus? Do you know her?

BigD: no – undie girl. it got me thinking tho

LoopyLisa21f: Thinking about what?

BigD: wot she looked like sat there

LoopyLisa21f: Well, once again, what if she was a mental old woman? And she had gnarled hands, like little claws, or "chicken feet"? And she kept scratching her bare stomach with those hands, and while she was scratching she kept breathing really heavily through her nostrils, whilst making a hideous, guttural grunting at the back of her throat?

BigD: suppose it would shatter my illusion

LoopyLisa21f: Well, yes. Yes it would. And what if she had sick all down her front?

LoopyLisa21f: And had some dog dirt in her lap? And what if she kept screeching like a magpie trapped in a centrifuge?

BigD: i doubt it

LoopyLisa21f: Well, you just don't know. I was talking to someone on here once who said he looked like Robert Englund, but when he sent me a photo of himself he looked more like Ronert Umlaut.

BigD: yea but i met someone and they were exactly as they said

LoopyLisa21f: Who was that? Was it Ronert Umlaut?

BigD: a girl

LoopyLisa21f: What was she like? Was she nice?

BigD: blonde 5 10 size 12 absolutley gorgeous

LoopyLisa21f: What happened next? I absolutely must know!

BigD: she came back to my house and stayed the night

LoopyLisa21f: How old was she?

BigD: 28

LoopyLisa21f: I see. How old are you?

BigD: 26

LoopyLisa21f: So she was literally old enough to be your older sister, or cousin?

BigD: only 2 years

LoopyLisa21f: Yeah. Hence what I said. So, what's it like being 26? Is it as cool as I've heard?

BigD: ??

BigD: not really

LoopyLisa21f: Is it true that when you hit 26 you get a new National Insurance card that's exactly like the old card, except that it's 350% bigger in size, and is in the shape of a fish?

BigD: don't think so

LoopyLisa21f: Are you happy?

BigD: very u ?

LoopyLisa21f: Yes. Yes, I suppose so. I could do without having my scurvy keep flaring up, though. Do you know what scurvy is?

BigD: yep

LoopyLisa21f: It's awful. I can't even feel my ankles any more.

LoopyLisa21f: It looks like I'm wearing purple leg warmers.

BigD: othjer than that ok ?

LoopyLisa21f: Yes, all fine other than that thanks.

BigD: i have a problem but its not medical

LoopyLisa21f: What is that problem, dear?

BigD: u really wanna know ?

LoopyLisa21f: Probably more than anything else in the world!

BigD: i am always playing with myself

LoopyLisa21f: Yes, I see. It's good to have an active imagination.

LoopyLisa21f: I've still got some of my old teddy bears, and sometimes I play with them!

LoopyLisa21f: Sometimes I set them up around the living room, and imagine that they're ordering me about. "Turn on the TV, Lisa" ... "Now turn it off" ... "Lay face down on the floor and don't move" ... "Get up" ... "Hold your breath until we say otherwise" ...

LoopyLisa21f: I mean, you can probably imagine the sort of thing that bears say. They're quite devious characters.

BigD: my problem is i am always stroking my penis

LoopyLisa21f: Heavens above!!!!! By the love of all that is decent!!!!!!!

BigD: soz

LoopyLisa21f: That's ok. I understand. Are you stroking it to knock off bits of fluff? I get fluff balls in my stretch marks. I clean them out using a custom-made brush called a "jolly gonzo".

BigD: doubt it

LoopyLisa21f: You could perhaps get a pessary that might suppress the urges. I suspect that inserting the pessary would stifle urges of that nature. Especially if it wasn't a pessary, but bits of a broken bottle.

BigD: i quite like stroking it

LoopyLisa21f: I hope you don't do it on the bus like the Soreen woman with her trough.

BigD: if i said i was doin it now how would u be able to tell?

LoopyLisa21f: I wouldn't be able to tell. But if you said you were how would I be able to tell for sure?

BigD: cos i dont lie

> LoopyLisa21f: But that might be a lie in itself.

> LoopyLisa21f: If you're a liar, you might lie about even that.

BigD: nope

> LoopyLisa21f: And that.

BigD: ?

> LoopyLisa21f: You might be lying when you say 'nope'.

BigD: am not tho

> LoopyLisa21f: See? My friend Craig is always lying. One time he rang me up and said he was coming over, but he never came over. Another time he told me he had a t-shirt with a picture of a crab on it, but it wasn't a crab – it was a "carb".

BigD: so do u think i am or not ?

> LoopyLisa21f: I don't know. I don't know what to think anymore. You're confusing me with all your words and phrases, and double-bluffs. You probably are the ultimate trickster.

BigD: do u think i am indulging myself yes or no

> LoopyLisa21f: No.

> LoopyLisa21f: Wait.

> LoopyLisa21f: Yes.

> LoopyLisa21f: No! I don't know.

> LoopyLisa21f: I'm so sorry, I really am.

BigD: yes or no ?

> LoopyLisa21f: You can't push me on this. I'm trying hard to think about it, even though I instinctively <u>don't</u> want to think about it..

BigD: its a 50 50 guess

LoopyLisa21f: Well ... give me a clue.

BigD: am typing with one hand

LoopyLisa21f: Ok. Another clue.

BigD: dont have my undies on

LoopyLisa21f: Are you on the toilet?

BigD: oh no

LoopyLisa21f: "Oh no"?! What's wrong?! Have you experienced a powerful trauma? What's happened to you?!?

BigD: nothing yet

LoopyLisa21f: Hmm. One more clue?

BigD: my hand is going up and down my penis

LoopyLisa21f: Hmm. One more clue?

BigD: no more clues

LoopyLisa21f: Ok then. Let me think about this ...

LoopyLisa21f: ...

LoopyLisa21f: ...

LoopyLisa21f: ...

BigD: hurry up

LoopyLisa21f: ...

LoopyLisa21f: ...

LoopyLisa21f: I think ...

LoopyLisa21f: ...

Big D: whot?

LoopyLisa21f: No!

LoopyLisa21f: I mean YES.

LoopyLisa21f: Am I right? Am I?

LoopyLisa21f: Wait ... I mean NO.

BigD: well i am

LoopyLisa21f: Wow! Really? This is the most erotic middle of the day of my life! Let me just put down my ploughman's lunch, and get comfy.

BigD: what u got in mind

LoopyLisa21f: Hang on – I've spilled the pickle down my shin.

LoopyLisa21f: ...

BigD: what u doin ?

LoopyLisa21f: Wiping up the pickle.

BigD: have u a boyfriend ?

LoopyLisa21f: Not at the moment. I did for a while, but then he got off with Jennifer Perris-Cope from the pet shop. My friend Bernadette said she saw them snogging in a cage, and the cage also had a turtle and a bird of paradise in it.

BigD: oh

BigD: when u last get horny?

LoopyLisa21f: What do you mean?

BigD: be real

LoopyLisa21f: Well, I'm not sure about the tenure of your questioning.

BigD: when u last have sex

LoopyLisa21f: I think I'm too shy to answer that on here. I'll write the answer on a piece of paper instead.

LoopyLisa21f: Is that ok?

BigD: why shy

LoopyLisa21f: I just am. Ok – I've done it. I've written it down.

BigD: whats it say ?

LoopyLisa21f: If I told you then that would be the same as typing it on here. You're not tricking me that way, fatty!

BigD: do u want to get horny or not?

LoopyLisa21f: Generally, or right this minute?

BigD: ur choice

LoopyLisa21f: Tell me what I have to do.

BigD: play with ur vagina

LoopyLisa21f: Hmm. Well, I'll try.

BigD: ok whats ir feel like

LoopyLisa21f: It's kind of crinkly.

BigD: and?

LoopyLisa21f: Oh hang on – it's not crinkly. That was just a Quality Street wrapper. How did that get down there?

BigD: well ?

LoopyLisa21f: Hmm. It feels kind of odd.

BigD: why

LoopyLisa21f: It feels like an old hooverbag that's got a hole in it, and the dust is coming out.

BigD: u just need a stiff cock up there

BigD: u wud like it

LoopyLisa21f: I'm not following you.

LoopyLisa21f: Hang on. I need to get comfy.

LoopyLisa21f: Oh God, I've put my foot in the cat's bowl.

LoopyLisa21f: God, it's gone everywhere. Ruddy hell.

LoopyLisa21f: Ok. Let's start again.

BigD: is ur pussy moist

LoopyLisa21f: I can't even see it. Shall I call it in from the garden?

BigD: sod off

LoopyLisa21f: What's wrong, dear?

LoopyLisa21f: Mmm? Dear?

BigD: u r being stupid

LoopyLisa21f: I'm not! Sorry, I'm just not used to this sort of remote intimate activity.

LoopyLisa21f: I'm quite shy, and haven't had a lot of experience.

LoopyLisa21f: The last boy I kissed was a plastic money box in the shape of a disabled person.

BigD: take ur knickers off

LoopyLisa21f: But I'm cold. Can't I keep them on, dear?

BigD: no

LoopyLisa21f: But they're sort of attached to my top.

BigD: in wot way

LoopyLisa21f: It's kind of an all-in-one thing.

LoopyLisa21f: Like a cross between a unitard, and a leotard.

LoopyLisa21f: It's got built-in-mittens too. And a hood.

BigD: ur takin the piss

LoopyLisa21f: I'm not. Really I'm not. I just want to take things at my own pace.

BigD: u got a photo?

LoopyLisa21f: Yes. Yes I do. Would you like to see it?

BigD: Yes.

LoopyLisa21f: There you go. I've emailed it to you.

<IMAGE SENT – lisa6.jpg>

BigD: wot's that supposed to be?

BigD: that aint u

LoopyLisa21f: Who else would it be?

BigD: dunno but thats a guy

BigD: thats some freak

LoopyLisa21f: What's the matter now? This has honestly been the most confusing lunchtime I've ever had. It has been a rollercoaster of erotic emotions.

LoopyLisa21f: Are you there?

LoopyLisa21f: Are you there, dear?

BigD: fuck u and fuck the freak

>>BigD SIGNED OFF AT 12:42   ""

LOOPYLISA'S BLOG

Wednesday, June 28

I've given up trying to find a new job, so I've decided to start my own business selling iced yams during Wimbledon. I intend to sell the yams from a pram full to the brim with ice, and I am going to call my business "Yams in Prams".

I had a dry run in my local park yesterday afternoon, but it didn't go too well. It seems that nobody really knows what yams are, and – as it turns out – neither do I. Potential customers kept asking me about the yams, and I really struggled to answer their questions.

Eventually, I got fed up with my floundering, and started telling people that they were yak eggs. One of the customers found my yams so disgusting that he suggested I change the name of my business to "Yaks in Cack".

POSTED BY LOOPYLISA AT 15:42

<<NEW CHAT SESSION STARTED

NewkyB: hi lisa

LoopyLisa21f: Hello NewkyB.

NewkyB: who am I ????

LoopyLisa21f: Why, don't you know? Have you lost your memory? Are you suffering from ambrosia?

NewkyB: ur just meant to guess my name – go on

LoopyLisa21f: Is it F. Bongo?

NewkyB: wtf?!

LoopyLisa21f: You know – like the cartoon character.

NewkyB: hmmm ?

LoopyLisa21f: F.Bongo? Remember the song?

NewkyB: no remind me

LoopyLisa21f: "It's Mr F.Bongo, He's singing the songo, It goes a-like this, A trongo-a-trongo-a-trongo-a-trongo." And the opening titles have him driving around in a little Jeep, dispensing pellets out of a slit in his knees.

NewkyB: oh ok sounds erm … great

LoopyLisa21f: Do you not know that cartoon?

LoopyLisa21f: I used to watch it when I was little.

LoopyLisa21f: When I was even more little than I am now, of course! Ha ha!

NewkyB: i dont remember it at all

LoopyLisa21f: Do you have a funny real name? I went to school with a boy called Brutus Proust. As if that isn't awful enough in itself, his father was a local alcoholic, and once stripped off in front of the PTA.

LoopyLisa21f: Do you see?

NewkyB: no … im from camden

LoopyLisa21f: Is that where they have the Smorten Centre?

NewkyB: what the fuck is smorten center?

LoopyLisa21f: I'm not sure. A friend of mine goes there. The way he describes it, it's like a big dome covered in moss, and inside they play musical notes on a big, chrome Cossack that juts out of an electrical appliance of some sort.

LoopyLisa21f: Inexplicably, this appliance has a face drawn on it in crayon.

NewkyB: so tell me something …

NewkyB: ur job ???

LoopyLisa21f: I'm a newly qualified teacher.

NewkyB: oh ok

NewkyB: thats a shame really

LoopyLisa21f: Why is that a shame?

NewkyB: because unless ur unlike all teachers ive ever met … you will be a real nightmare

LoopyLisa21f: I don't always want to be a teacher. One day I'd like to be the first person to circumnavigate the globe on a single gust.

LoopyLisa21f: What are the teachers you've met been like?

NewkyB: well they have no clue how to dress …

NewkyB: they cant seem to listen …

LoopyLisa21f: Whatever.

NewkyB: they cant read or write but …

NewkyB: u may be the exception

LoopyLisa21f: You'll be glad to hear that I know how to dress at least. In fact, I recently customised my entire wardrobe, replacing all buttons, zips and buckles – and cuffs, and material – with Velcro. I also replaced all the seams with caulk, and the pockets with hefty clumps of sod.

NewkyB: ur different but id geussed that already

NewkyB: i teach too but not in schools

LoopyLisa21f: Really? What/where/how do you teach?

NewkyB: flying

NewkyB: have done for 8yrs

LoopyLisa21f: Wow! I didn't think that flying was physically possible! Is it true what they say, that the way to learn is jump off a building with a parachute ...

LoopyLisa21f: And then do it again, but using a slightly smaller parachute?

NewkyB: lol

NewkyB: yep

LoopyLisa21f: And then you repeat this step four score and twenty times, and on the penultimate jump you use a child's blazer instead of a parachute, and on the final jump you go back to the original parachute size, only this time there's a bird trapped under the canopy?

NewkyB: im a failed airline pilot : ((

NewkyB: tooo lazy i am

LoopyLisa21f: Really? Elaborate at length, please.

NewkyB: just didnt try hard enough

NewkyB: so i teach others so they can become airline pilots

LoopyLisa21f: That's kind of ironic. And also a coincidence, because my cousin is a failed airline steward.

NewkyB: oh a steward i couldnt do that

LoopyLisa21f: He had a nervous breakdown on his third flight. During the meal he served up bowls of hot water with pegs in, and pinched a rabbi's shoulder so hard that the rabbi's hat and shoes flew off with a honk!

NewkyB: sounds like my ex gfs dinners everynite

LoopyLisa21f: What did she do?

NewkyB: stabbed me with a kitchen knife

NewkyB: oh ....

NewkyB: u mean job

LoopyLisa21f: Why did she do the stabbing?

NewkyB: she just went nuts 1 day when i got home

LoopyLisa21f: What had you done to upset her? You must've done something. I get pretty hacked off when Craig puts sofa cushions in my bath.

NewkyB: did nothing just enquired y she was so drunk at 4.30 wed afternoon

LoopyLisa21f: I guess it was because she'd been drinking.

NewkyB: i still have the scar to remind me of the nut

NewkyB: had a 40cm slash and a deep stab wound in the fucking back

LoopyLisa21f: Goodness me!

LoopyLisa21f: She got you twice?

LoopyLisa21f: I knew someone who got stabbed with one of those "party razzer" things that you blow, and it elongates, and there's a whimsical feather on the end. You know those things? Actually, when I say "stabbed" I mean "lightly slapped around the face", and when I say "party razzer" I mean "draught excluder".

NewkyB: still its ok i forgive her

LoopyLisa21f: Really? Are you a Christian? Those guys will forgive anything. Even if you let off a cheeky little parp in church. Craig did a massive fart in the baptism pool when he was being baptised. The vicar said "It's not a Jacuzzi, you know".

NewkyB: no no no not Christian

NewkyB: but i know u ladies are under a lot of pressure

LoopyLisa21f: Some of us are. Especially those of us who live in a hyperbaric chamber.

LoopyLisa21f: My mother was under a lot of pressure.

NewkyB: go on explain ...

LoopyLisa21f: She was under so much pressure her eyebrows fell off!

NewkyB: thats a bit shit

LoopyLisa21f: It was. Especially because she was one of the top three forehead models in the UK, circa about 1986.

NewkyB: right so never ever make eyebrow jokes i get that

LoopyLisa21f: Not to her. Not that she'd be able to hear you anymore anyway. You see, when her eyebrows fell off there was a strong sea breeze, and they blew into her ears.

NewkyB: lol!

LoopyLisa21f: I'm joking, of course. The reason she wouldn't be able to hear you is because about three years ago she died from malnutrition in a toilet.

NewkyB: oh my god im going to cry in a minute

LoopyLisa21f: Why? Have you "barked your shin"?

NewkyB: not quite but your full of sad stories

NewkyB: cheer me up now please

LoopyLisa21f: Ok. Do I know any jokes?

NewkyB: no cos ur a teacher

LoopyLisa21f: Do you know any jokes?

NewkyB: i do but im waiting to hear one from you

LoopyLisa21f: Ok.

LoopyLisa21f: Question: Why does Superman wear his underpants outside his trousers?

NewkyB: dunno

LoopyLisa21f: Answer: Because he's a pervert!!!!!

NewkyB: that joke was so bad it was funny

NewkyB: see what i mean about teachers jokes ?

LoopyLisa21f: Well, that's a pupil's joke. I have no jokes of my own.

LoopyLisa21f: Why are you so down on teachers anyway, dear? Are you scarred by an experience with a teacher? Did one perhaps hold you down during double maths and roundly thwack your botty with a protractor?

NewkyB: wasnt everyone scarred by school?

LoopyLisa21f: I wasn't. Not that I remember.

LoopyLisa21f: No wait – I was.

NewkyB: go on

LoopyLisa21f: I've just remembered. My science teacher hit me in the mouth with a Bunsen burner.

NewkyB: ffs

NewkyB: see

NewkyB: thats not good

LoopyLisa21f: No. It really wasn't. However, when I say "science teacher" I mean "school caretaker", and when I say "hit me" I mean "heard me", and when I say "in the mouth" I mean "swear", and when I say "with a Bunsen burner" I mean "behind the poplar trees with my friend Craig".

NewkyB: i saw my teacher cut his finger off in wood work

NewkyB: now i hate saws

LoopyLisa21f: Why did he do that?

NewkyB: erm i geuss he didnt mean to

LoopyLisa21f: Whereabouts did he cut it? Above or below the knuckle?

NewkyB: just below it was awful

LoopyLisa21f: I bet he was literally "hopping mad"!!!!!!!

NewkyB: yep

LoopyLisa21f: What sort of saw was it?

NewkyB: you know those big electric ones that only the teacher could use because the pupils might cut their fingers off

LoopyLisa21f: Wasn't he wearing a protective helmet?

NewkyB: how wuld that help his fingers ?

NewkyB: look you restored my faith in teachers but im going to go do some work take care

LoopyLisa21f: Ok. I'm sorry.

NewkyB: sorry for what ?

LoopyLisa21f: In case I've somehow upset you.

NewkyB: no not yet

LoopyLisa21f: Ok. That's good. I hope you enjoy your work! Are you off to fly a plane?

LoopyLisa21f: Hey – I've just thought of something!

NewkyB: ?

LoopyLisa21f: There are two types of planes – aeroplanes, and the sorts of planes you get in woodwork, and a third sort of plane: Salisbury Plain. And a fourth sort of plane: plain-flavour crisps. Thus there is a link between the beginning and the end of our conversation!!!!!!!!!!

NewkyB: what link?

LoopyLisa21f: I dunno. Some sort of link. I really hadn't thought it through.

NewkyB: anyway im off to wash a plane not fly it sadly

LoopyLisa21f: Do you have a plane on your driveway? I have a plastic toad and some Lego on my driveway. The kid from next door threw it at me from her bedroom window. I threw some of the Lego back, but missed, and one of the pieces ended up in my nostril.

NewkyB: i dont have a driveway remember im from camden we dont have driveways here

NewkyB: anyway im going now or il just sit here all afternoon bye

LoopyLisa21f: Goodbye, dear. Enjoy your "many planes"!

>>NewkyB SIGNED OFF AT 11:12 **"**

LOOPYLISA'S BLOG

Saturday, July 01

I've given up my search for a new part-time job, and have enrolled as a "special constable". I don't really know what it is that I'm supposed to do, but I'm guessing I'm more or less a normal constable, only more special.

Certainly, they make us feel special down at the station. All of us special constables get to eat special food (biltong sprinkled with glitter) in a special canteen (a shed wrapped in tinsel) staffed by special dinner ladies (four fat drug addicts in dresses).

POSTED BY LOOPYLISA AT 21:14

<<NEW CHAT SESSION STARTED

macdonald2000: hi Loopy, want to chat

LoopyLisa21f: Yes. Yes I do.

macdonald2000: how ru Loopy?

LoopyLisa21f: I just bought a scooter!

LoopyLisa21f: Have you ever ridden a scooter?

macdonald2000: no but i've alway wanted to

LoopyLisa21f: Cool! Cool and excellent!

macdonald2000: what do you do 4 a living?

LoopyLisa21f: On certain days I'm a special constable.

LoopyLisa21f: You know about those? We're like the normal police, but we're 'special'. You know: we have to go to a 'special police station' in the way that some people have to go to a 'special school'.

macdonald2000: so your into handcuffs and trunchons then?

LoopyLisa21f: Yes I am, and on Tuesdays we get to do gluing and sticking with our paperwork.

LoopyLisa21f: Last week I had to prepare a murder report, but I got into trouble because I put too much glitter on one of the photographs.

LoopyLisa21f: Snap! Snappppp! Snappp! Snap.

Macdonald2000: wot u doin ????

LoopyLisa21f: I'm just doing some major snapping, guy.

macdonald2000: where aboot in london do you live?

LoopyLisa21f: North. Whereaboot you?

macdonald2000: in bonny scotland

LoopyLisa21f: I used to know a girl called Bonnie. She wasn't "Scottish".

LoopyLisa21f: She came from Italy.

LoopyLisa21f: She had a type of sci-fi eczema and could bend her wrist back so she could touch the top of her forearm.

LoopyLisa21f: And when she did it, it made a wet, sliding sound, like the noise of a seal dragging itself over a tray of crockery.

macdonald2000: i can fit my whole foot in my mouth and i make a noise like someone puting his foot in his mouth.

LoopyLisa21f: Do you speak Scottish?

macdonald2000: aye

LoopyLisa21f: Aye see. Do you also say stuff like "wee", and "och aye the noo"? And "The camel has done a whoopsie on mah haggis, dear"?

macdonald2000: i say wee but not big on och aye the noo, i also love iron bru but i'm not ginger and i dont own a kilt

LoopyLisa21f: Question: Why do Scottish women have big nostrils, and look like they smell?

macdonald2000: dunno do you have any pic preferebly with your police uniform on

LoopyLisa21f: I may have a pic. But you don't want to see me in my uniform. It's not like the one that normal police wear, and it's not particularly flattering. In fact, it's basically a sort of deep sea diver's outfit, but in blue.

macdonald2000: pic without would be fine

LoopyLisa21f: Well, I need to find it first. Tell me some jokes while I look.

macdonald2000: what does a blackpool donkey get for its lunch?

LoopyLisa21f: Donkey food? You know: "SEEDS"!

macdonald2000: no half an hour

LoopyLisa21f: Ha ha ha! Excellent! That donkey's a time-eater! He must eat clocks! I get it, I think!

LoopyLisa21f: You've done donkeys, so tell me a joke about herons now! Like, what do herons have for lunch?

macdonald2000: where does sadam hussein keep his cd's?

LoopyLisa21f: In a heron? In a heron's lunch?

macdonald2000: in a rack

LoopyLisa21f: In a heron, in a rack! Excellent!

LoopyLisa21f: Heron racks!

macdonald2000: whats the facination with herons?

LoopyLisa21f: Herons are what a puffin would look like if it looked in a fairground mirror.

LoopyLisa21f: This is part of the reason why herons are commonly known as "extruded puffins".

macdonald2000: nice

LoopyLisa21f: What's your favourite bird? I like herons, but there are better examples of "avians".

macdonald2000: i like coots,but they aint bald

LoopyLisa21f: Isn't coot a rude word?

macdonald2000: not in scotland, its a small duck with black and white feathers

LoopyLisa21f: Hmm. Bit racist. I'll have to see about that.

LoopyLisa21f: Are there different laws in Scotland?

LoopyLisa21f: Craig told me it was legal to murder someone up there if you could prove they'd dreamt about murdering you first.

macdonald2000: that law is not true

LoopyLisa21f: Do you think Craig was lying, or he just got it wrong?

macdonald2000: you have the right to roam up here, theres no no trespassing law, not sure about craig

LoopyLisa21f: Hmm … I'll have to have words with him.

LoopyLisa21f: What is 'roam'?

LoopyLisa21f: Is it the Scottish word for 'foam'?

macdonald2000: its also a place in italy

LoopyLisa21f: Ha ha ha. I get it, you crazy Scottish funster!

macdonald2000: my parents moved to chelmsford last year

LoopyLisa21f: Is that where they have that big fibreglass sow?

macdonald2000: ?

LoopyLisa21f: It's this big fibreglass pig thing, that you can go up inside, and there's a slide coming out of its mouth that you can go down into a <u>real</u> pig sty.

macdonald2000: not sure where that is

LoopyLisa21f: I just said it was in Chelmsford.

macdonald2000: i,ve only been down there 3 times so don,t know it that well, moving down there soon tho

LoopyLisa21f: Cool!

LoopyLisa21f: You'll have to go up in the pig.

macdonald2000: hopefully

LoopyLisa21f: I think the pig's name is Lady Francis.

macdonald2000: did you find that pic?

LoopyLisa21f: Oh! I have to go.

LoopyLisa21f: Craig has fallen out of his chair, and dropped his Cornpops in his washing-up bowl (he likes playing at washing-up, so I fill a bowl with soap "suds" for him to splash in).

LoopyLisa21f: Talk soooooooon!

LoopyLisa21f: Love you!!!!!!

LoopyLisa21f: xxxxxx

macdonald2000: ok bye bye and stay cool

LoopyLisa21f: I will, dear!

>>LoopyLisa21f SIGNED OFF AT 13:11   ""

LOOPYLISA'S BLOG

Tuesday, July 04

My dad has started breeding koi carp. Given that we live in a third floor flat I had to question the wisdom of this, but he seems pretty confident that he's going to grow the biggest carp the world has ever seen.

To date, my father has bred one carp, which he has named Kiki Little. Even though she is only five days old, Kiki Little is already quite large! In fact, she is so large dad has had to move her from a brandy glass into a pint glass.

POSTED BY LOOPYLISA AT 22:38

<<NEW CHAT SESSION STARTED

GuidoGuido100: hiya

GuidoGuido100: so why are u Loopy lol

LoopyLisa21f: I'm mentally ill.

LoopyLisa21f: Not really!!

LoopyLisa21f: It's not fun to make jokes about mental folk, so please don't do it, or encourage others to do it.

LoopyLisa21f: You see, my mother had the mental illness.

GuidoGuido100: did she sorry to hear that

LoopyLisa21f: Don't be. I don't think it was your fault.

LoopyLisa21f: It was awful.

LoopyLisa21f: One Christmas morning we came down, and she'd painted the living room brown.

LoopyLisa21f: Not just the walls – everything.

LoopyLisa21f: She'd even painted a brown stripe along the dog's back. He had a brown stripe, and brown lips.

GuidoGuido100: awwwwwwwwww

LoopyLisa21f: It wasn't much fun.

GuidoGuido100: im not sure whether u r joking now

LoopyLisa21f: Do you have any experience with mental illness?

GuidoGuido100: i have suffered with depression

LoopyLisa21f: Really?

LoopyLisa21f: I got that once, but then I cheered up a bit.

GuidoGuido100: only a bit?

LoopyLisa21f: Well, at first it was a bit. Then it was a lot. Then I got a little bit sad again. Then I cheered up again. All in the space of about half an hour.

LoopyLisa21f: What was the best thing that ever happened to you?

GuidoGuido100: nothin lol

GuidoGuido100: what about u

LoopyLisa21f: I got a dog for Christmas.

LoopyLisa21f: But it died of paint poisoning.

GuidoGuido100: brown paint ?

LoopyLisa21f: No. That's the ironic thing. It had nothing to do with my mother.

LoopyLisa21f: He drank some paint out of a tin. It was pink paint. I came in and found him lolling around on the sofa with a pink snout.

LoopyLisa21f: What's your favourite type of dog?

LoopyLisa21f: I like the "German Banger".

GuidoGuido100: sounds like a hot dog lol

LoopyLisa21f: LOL!!!!!!!!!?

LoopyLisa21f: Craig told me that some hot dogs were made out of a crow's pancreas.

LoopyLisa21f: Do you think he's lying?

GuidoGuido100: yeah lol

LoopyLisa21f: I haven't eaten hot dogs in four years because he said that.

GuidoGuido100: whose craig

LoopyLisa21f: He's my friend.

LoopyLisa21f: Can I run some other foods by you, and see whether he's lying about those too?

GuidoGuido100: yeah

LoopyLisa21f: Pancakes: plate fungus?

GuidoGuido100: dont think so lol

LoopyLisa21f: Hamburgers: hedgehog face?

GuidoGuido100: lol

GuidoGuido100: nah

LoopyLisa21f: Lamb: baby sheep?

GuidoGuido100: true

LoopyLisa21f: True? That's really revolting.

GuidoGuido100: there are lot of em here

LoopyLisa21f: Where are you then? A roast lamb shop?

GuidoGuido100: scotland

LoopyLisa21f: Oooh! I love Scotland! I thought it was Wales that had the sheep, though.

LoopyLisa21f: What other animals do they have in Scotland?

GuidoGuido100: cowes

LoopyLisa21f: I thought that was in the Isle of Wight?

GuidoGuido100: it is sorry crap at spelling

LoopyLisa21f: That's ok. I'm crap at "belling" – ringing bells.

LoopyLisa21f: I used to be part of a bell-ringing group at a local church, but I kept licking the clanger.

LoopyLisa21f: I was only four.

LoopyLisa21f: I don't know why I did it. The verger said I was a dirty child, and marched me out of the church, and made me sit on the grave of someone called Hampton Belt (1872–1905).

LoopyLisa21f: How long have you lived in Scotland?

GuidoGuido100: 2 yrs

LoopyLisa21f: Where were you from originally?

GuidoGuido100: london

LoopyLisa21f: Why did you move?

GuidoGuido100: got pissed off

LoopyLisa21f: What was wrong with where you lived in London?

GuidoGuido100: i actually didnt live in london though that was where i was born i lived in swindon

LoopyLisa21f: Swindon. Whenever I think of Swindon I think of swans.

GuidoGuido100: why!!!!!!!!!!!!

LoopyLisa21f: I don't know. Swans/Swins. I like to imagine that it was named after a swan called "Don". You know: "Don Swan".

GuidoGuido100: nah its named after pigs

LoopyLisa21f: Shouldn't they have called it "Pigston"?

GuidoGuido100: its swinedon

GuidoGuido100: a place on a hill where pigs are kept

LoopyLisa21f: Is that true?!

GuidoGuido100: so i believe

LoopyLisa21f: You're quite knowledgeable about farmyard things! Can I test you?

GuidoGuido100: k

LoopyLisa21f: What's faster: pig or cow?

GuidoGuido100: pig i think

GuidoGuido100: although bulls are fast

LoopyLisa21f: Ah, yes. Bulls are "super-fast".

LoopyLisa21f: Next question: how many stomachs does a pig have?

GuidoGuido100: one i think

GuidoGuido100: cows have more

LoopyLisa21f: How many do cows have?

GuidoGuido100: is it three?

LoopyLisa21f: Is that why cows are so fat? Because they're always eating to fill their many stomachs?

GuidoGuido100: dont think so its cos they eat grass

LoopyLisa21f: Do cows only eat grass? Would a cow eat a cake if you offered it one?

GuidoGuido100: cow cake

    LoopyLisa21f: Yes. Would it eat a cow cake?

    LoopyLisa21f: Question: What is a "cow cake"?

GuidoGuido100: what cowes eat I suppose

GuidoGuido100: what do you like eating

    LoopyLisa21f: I like anything, really. Except for the things that Craig said were other things. My favourite food is black pudding.

    LoopyLisa21f: Have you ever eaten a "harris"?

GuidoGuido100: whats that

    LoopyLisa21f: It's that thing they have in Scotland.

    LoopyLisa21f: I'd have thought you'd know about it being up there, and everything.

GuidoGuido100: you mean haggis

    LoopyLisa21f: I don't think so.

    LoopyLisa21f: Is a "harris" an animal?

GuidoGuido100: no its a filled sheep stomach

    LoopyLisa21f: What?!? Filled with what!?!?

GuidoGuido100: its got offal and oats in it

    LoopyLisa21f: What is "offal"?

GuidoGuido100: no now u r being scilly lol

GuidoGuido100: liver etc

    LoopyLisa21f: Oh. Crikey.

    LoopyLisa21f: I'm not eating that then.

GuidoGuido100: hey you never told me what ya look like

LoopyLisa21f: I'm medium height, medium build, light brown hair.

LoopyLisa21f: You?

GuidoGuido100: im 5 11 medium build blue eyes fair hair well hung lol

LoopyLisa21f: Congratulations!

GuidoGuido100: nothing to be congaratulated about lol

LoopyLisa21f: Well, then, you have my commiserations.

LoopyLisa21f: At least you're not deformed.

GuidoGuido100: no not deformed lol

GuidoGuido100: so u got a dog now

LoopyLisa21f: No. I find that dogs bring heartache. But I have a cat.

LoopyLisa21f: I don't like it, though.

LoopyLisa21f: I inherited it from my neighbour. He died when his plastic knee fractured, and a splinter of plastic got into his bloodstream, and pierced his thorax.

GuidoGuido100: human family and friends bring heartache too

LoopyLisa21f: Yes, that's true. But you don't have to clean up poo from your family and friends when they do it on your pillow, though.

LoopyLisa21f: And when I say "pillow", I mean "face".

GuidoGuido100: im sure you are having me on about the dog poo that didnt happen to you did it. Neither did the bloke with the knee

LoopyLisa21f: It's all horribly true. And his cat used to come round and cadge food off me.

LoopyLisa21f: And then when he died I just kept it. I sealed it into a Tupperware pot, and made some holes so that it could breathe. It's funny watching it desperately trying to move around behind the misted plastic.

GuidoGuido100: u cant do that

LoopyLisa21f: I don't like it, but I didn't want to kill it either.

GuidoGuido100: cats always prefer the neighbours to their owners

LoopyLisa21f: What's the biggest thing you've ever killed?

GuidoGuido100: a spider

LoopyLisa21f: How big?

GuidoGuido100: not that big not into killing animals

GuidoGuido100: what about u

LoopyLisa21f: I'm not into killing animals either, but sometimes you kill them by accident, like if you sit on a parrot, and accidentally break its neck, and stuff.

LoopyLisa21f: You see, I accidentally killed a parrot.

GuidoGuido100: lol

GuidoGuido100: actually i have driven over a rabbit by accident i forgot about that

GuidoGuido100: but the parrott beats my rabbit

LoopyLisa21f: Do you think a cat could beat a rabbit in a fight?

GuidoGuido100: im thinking you are really taking your name seriously lol

LoopyLisa21f: What about a parrot? Could a parrot beat a rabbit?

GuidoGuido100: what is your proper name

LoopyLisa21f: Well – that's my name!

LoopyLisa21f: Lisa.

GuidoGuido100: of course i must be f**king thick

LoopyLisa21f: No, it's ok. You seem to be quite clever about animals, and stuff. My friend Craig is more thick than you. He once shook hands with a tree!

GuidoGuido100: do rabbits or parrotts ever fight lol

LoopyLisa21f: Well, it depends. I imagine they eat similar food – seeds, carrots, and that – so if a rabbit was hording something a parrot would want, then in theory it could happen.

GuidioGuido100: this is such a weird conversation

LoopyLisa21f: I reckon the parrot would carry the rabbit off, and drop him onto a motorway.

GuidoGuido100: parrots are not hawks you know lol

LoopyLisa21f: They look like hawks.

GuidoGuido100: there is evidently a large colony of escaped parrots in the south of england somewhere

LoopyLisa21f: Really?!? Escaped from where? Did they escape from homes all round the country, and somehow all gravitate to the same part of England?

GuidoGuido100: so why did you sit on this parrott

LoopyLisa21f: I didn't mean to. It was my auntie's parrot. Craig had asked her to get it out of the cage while I was in the toilet, and I came back in and sat down, and heard this crunch beneath me, and someone shout "Hussss!".

LoopyLisa21f: And that was the last thing the parrot ever said.

GuidoGuido100: do you know about the wild mink?

LoopyLisa21f: The mink?

GuidoGuido100: all wild mink in this country have escaped and bred from mink farms

LoopyLisa21f: I didn't think they were allowed to have mink farms anymore.

GuidoGuido100: not sure but it would have been when they did

GuidoGuido100: i think they are a real problem in some places

LoopyLisa21f: What do they do?

GuidoGuido100: what do you mean

GuidoGuido100: i think they attack other wildlife

LoopyLisa21f: Oh, ok. Perhaps it's a good thing that they're killed and made into hats, then.

GuidoGuido100: no dont think so

GuidoGuido100: so what else u wanna chat about

LoopyLisa21f: Hmm. Well, I don't like anyone that hurts wildlife – even if it's other wildlife. I'll tell you what would be weird – if you made a mink eat a mink coat!!!!

GuidoGuido100: yeah it would be

LoopyLisa21f: I don't know how you'd do it, though. I don't know what minks eat.

LoopyLisa21f: I suppose you could put a mink in a room with nothing but a mink coat, and then leave it so that it gets so hungry that it eats it.

GuidoGuido100 signed off at 17: 12

GuidoGuido100 signed on at 17: 12

GuidoGuido100: sorry got disconnected

LoopyLisa21f: That's ok. I thought you might hate me.

GuidoGuido100: why should i

LoopyLisa21f: I don't know. Most people do. Craig texted me earlier and said he hates me.

LoopyLisa21f: Hello? Guido? Hello?

LoopyLisa21f: Has Guido gone now?

>>GuidoGuido100 SIGNED OFF AT 17:16

LOOPYLISA'S BLOG

Friday, July 07

I'm looking after my nephew for the weekend. He's actually more of a step-nephew, as he's the son of my mother's boyfriend's daughter (they have gone to a nude antiques fair in Dunstable). The boy's name is Richard Beltane.

In a bid to find out more about Richard Beltane, I asked him to complete the following questionnaire:

NAME: Richard Beltane

AGE: 10

SEX: Male

FAVOURITE COLOUR: Synthesiser yellow

FAVOURITE FOOD: Giant chicken Kiev

FAVOURITE TV SHOW: Telly Addicts (recordings of)

MOTTO: "Strength through unity"

POSTED BY LOOPYLISA AT 07:07

<<NEW CHAT SESSION STARTED

TomtheGuy: how r u

LoopyLisa21f: Hello, dear. I'm really marvellous, thanks. Sorry I took so long to reply to your so-called "private message". I was locked in my dad's garage.

TomtheGuy: lol oh dear what happened?

LoopyLisa21f: I went in to look for a bucket to lend to my nephew – who wants a bucket to wash his felt-tips in – and while I was rooting around in the back, my dad shut the door, and locked it.

LoopyLisa21f: I don't think he knew I was in there.

LoopyLisa21f: At least, I hope not. I mean, he trapped me in the bathroom once by pushing a wardrobe in front of the door. I never found out why. When I finally got out – by scuttling onto the extension roof – he denied he'd even been in the house, even though I'd been speaking to him through the bathroom door moments before I got trapped.

TomtheGuy: oh dear lol

LoopyLisa21f: Even so, do you think it might have been something other than my dad? You know – like a ghost?

TomtheGuy: no

LoopyLisa21f: Do you think it might have been a burg-o-lar?

TomtheGuy: no

LoopyLisa21f: Do you think it might have been a wyvern?

TomtheGuy: NO

LoopyLisa21f: So. Tom. How are you today?

TomtheGuy: im good thanx, would u like to chat?

LoopyLisa21f: Yes. Yes please. I'd really like to chat.

TomtheGuy: cool, may i ask your a/s/l please

LoopyLisa21f: I'm a 21-year-old in London.

TomtheGuy: im 29 m near bristol

TomtheGuy: i presume your name is lisa

LoopyLisa21f: Yes. What is your full name please?

TomtheGuy: thomas, nice to meet u lisa xxxx

TomtheGuy: what do u look like?

LoopyLisa21f: I don't know really. It's not for me to say.

TomtheGuy: why not?

LoopyLisa21f: Well, dad always said I shouldn't describe myself, because we all have a negative body image. I might accidentally describe myself as something I'm not, such as a lamppost, or a "brogue". That would be both inaccurate and surreal.

LoopyLisa21f: Or I might say "I'm uglier than a tarp'", and then you'd either hate me, or not know what I'm talking about.

TomtheGuy: not at all, well im 6ft2 short brown hair blue eyes glasses

LoopyLisa21f: Are the glasses tinted with blue glass?

TomtheGuy: no they are light sensitive though so turn ito sunglasses

LoopyLisa21f: Holy cow! That's like something out of James Bond!!!!! Craig once had an umbrella that opened when you pressed a button. I said he should've shown it to some of the idiots from the estate – potentially, they'd have burnt him for being a witch!

TomtheGuy: so tell me wot do u look like or do u have a pic?

LoopyLisa21f: I have blonde hair. It's sort of vaguely long on one side, and I sweep it over, so that it brushes the opposing shoulder, and then I immediately brush it straight at the back, and curl it along the "fringe".

LoopyLisa21f: How … how is your hair please?

TomtheGuy: short and spiky

TomtheGuy: have u got a pic

LoopyLisa21f: I'll have a look. It may take a while. I'm having to use an old computer, because dad has had his other one confiscated, and won't get it back until they've disproved the charges.

TomtheGuy: u sound really nice

LoopyLisa21f: Thanks!!! Tell me a joke, please.

TomtheGuy: xxxxx r u single?

LoopyLisa21f: Yes I am.

TomtheGuy: me too

LoopyLisa21f: Joke please? JOKE PLEASE!

TomtheGuy: lol ive been single for so long ive got cobwebs in me trousers lol lol

LoopyLisa21f: Really?

LoopyLisa21f: Craig once told me he had some muffins in his trousers, but they were actually scones.

TomtheGuy: yeah

TomtheGuy: u got cobwebs? lol

LoopyLisa21f: I don't think so. I once had a fungal infection.

LoopyLisa21f: The doctor told me to treat it with yoghurt.

LoopyLisa21f: It made a terrible mess.

TomtheGuy: that doesnt sound nice

LoopyLisa21f: Then he told me I was using the wrong type of yoghurt.

LoopyLisa21f: I'd just been squeezing Frubes down my knickers.

TomtheGuy: if ud have let me know i could have licked it off for u

LoopyLisa21f: But you might have caught the fungus.

LoopyLisa21f: It was a plate fungus.

LoopyLisa21f: Nobody really wants to lick a plate fungus that's growing out of someone's parts.

TomtheGuy: well id have licked the frubes off straight away so it wouldnt have been there long enough to cause a fungus

LoopyLisa21f: The Frubes didn't cause the fungus. I got the fungus from taking a pee in the woods. I squatted too near a big mushroom.

TomtheGuy: u often take a pee in the woods?

LoopyLisa21f: I do when I'm caught short. I was doing paintball with some of Craig's friends, and got nervous, and had to go behind a log.

LoopyLisa21f: When we got back Craig told everyone that he'd seen me having a poo.

LoopyLisa21f: But I wasn't doing a poo. It really was just a number 1. You believe me, don't you? I'd simply drunk too much squash.

TomtheGuy: kinky ;-) good job u didnt get a paintball up the bum lol

LoopyLisa21f: Gosh, that would've hurt. I barked my shin while I was there, but I didn't get shot once.

LoopyLisa21f: Craig dared me to eat a paintball, though. But when I did it, he wouldn't even look, and then just walked off.

TomtheGuy: did anyone ctach u having a pee then lol

LoopyLisa21f: No, but I told Craig I was going to do one, because I wanted him to protect me.

TomtheGuy: is craig your ex?

LoopyLisa21f: No. We sort of were boyfriend and girlfriend when we were little, but only for about a week. He kept trying to control me by telepathy.

LoopyLisa21f: We remained on good terms after the split.

LoopyLisa21f: Though I once didn't speak to him for a month because he stuffed a load of tissue in my Mega Drive slit.

TomtheGuy: thats good, good job i didnt see u having a pee in the woods not sure wot id have done if id have see n squatting with your knickers round your ankles mmmmm lol

LoopyLisa21f: You probably wouldn't have done much. I had welts all over my backside from falling against some brambles.

TomtheGuy: maybe id have kissed them better for u

LoopyLisa21f: Not while I was weeing, surely?

TomtheGuy: no either b4 or after lol

LoopyLisa21f: Well, I wasn't exposed for long. I had to go quickly. Not quickly enough though; still enough time to get a fungal infection from that big "'shroom".

TomtheGuy: if i was there i would have offered to throw a jacket or something down for u

LoopyLisa21f: What, so that I could pee on it? Do you really want me to pee on your jacket, Thomas?

TomtheGuy: it would be better than u getting a fungal infection wouldnt it

LoopyLisa21f: Hmm. What would you have done with the jacket afterwards, though? Left it in the thicket, or taken it back to Base Camp 7?

TomtheGuy: depends on the jacket if it was a good 1 id take it back to wash it if not id leave it there

LoopyLisa21f: I wouldn't want to touch anything after someone has done a wee all over it. I'd leave it there for the woodland creatures to dispose of.

LoopyLisa21f: You know: woodland creatures such as racoons, badgers, alpacas, and sprites.

TomtheGuy: i now have a picture of u in the woods squatting down lol

TomtheGuy: knickers round your ankles lol

LoopyLisa21f: Where did you get a picture of me from? Do I know you? Were you at the paintball?

TomtheGuy: no mental picture

LoopyLisa21f: Yes, well, it would be. It was quite a mental thing to have happen.

LoopyLisa21f: I didn't look very nice. Just imagine all those fungal spores going up my bottom.

TomtheGuy: funnily enough they arent in my mental picture

LoopyLisa21f: No, but that's what occurred. A big cloud of yellow spores floating up my anus.

TomtheGuy: ok xxxx

LoopyLisa21f: Why the "xxxx"?

TomtheGuy: just to make u and your bottom feel better, its up to u where u want them xxxx

LoopyLisa21f: Thankyou. You're very "nice".

LoopyLisa21f: Have you ever "done" paintball?

TomtheGuy: no i havent but if i thought i would see u half naked id do it anytime

LoopyLisa21f: I wasn't half naked. Probably not even 10%.

LoopyLisa21f: And the exposed part was covered in welts and damp, widdle-stinking spores.

TomtheGuy: lol not in my mental picture lol

LoopyLisa21f: No. But if you want the picture to be accurate you have to know everything.

TomtheGuy: i bet u still looked sexy

LoopyLisa21f: Can you drive?

TomtheGuy: no i cant, have u ever had sex in the woods

LoopyLisa21f: No! I'd never do something like "that" outside!

TomtheGuy: well if id have been paintballing and seen u u might have done lol lol ;-)

LoopyLisa21f: I find that a slim possibility at best.

TomtheGuy: lol ok we will go back to yours then lol

LoopyLisa21f: Hmm. I'm a bit confused. Is this actually happening now?

TomtheGuy: what?

LoopyLisa21f: I … I'm confused by the tenses you're using. Is this happening, or is this some sort of memory?

TomtheGuy: no i was just teasing u

LoopyLisa21f: Ok. I have trouble sometimes with stuff like that. It … it gets a bit frightening sometimes.

LoopyLisa21f: Like, once I was reading a book, and I got all confused because I couldn't work out whether I was reading something, or experiencing it.

LoopyLisa21f: And the worst thing was – the book I was reading was The Bible. I thought my wife had turned into a pillar of salt – and I don't even have a wife!

TomtheGuy: im sorry hun was just teasing u thats all xxxxxx

LoopyLisa21f: It's ok. I'm a bit shaken up now.

TomtheGuy: im sorry xxxxxx

LoopyLisa21f: All this talk of salt makes me thirsty, and hungry for salt. I'm going to drink some salted water.

TomtheGuy: r u ok?

LoopyLisa21f: I will be in a minute. I need my fluids and body salts to stabilise.

LoopyLisa21f: Right. I'm already back. I had a swig out of a jar of anchovies in brine. It was this: horrible.

TomtheGuy: im sorry shall i leave u alone for a while

LoopyLisa21f: You don't have to. I'm feeling better already.

TomtheGuy: r u sure?

LoopyLisa21f: Yes. I'm feeling at least 50 – 60% better.

TomtheGuy: good xxxxxx

LoopyLisa21f: Great!!!!!

TomtheGuy: ;-)

LoopyLisa21f: Do you know any jokes?

TomtheGuy: im not very good with jokes

LoopyLisa21f: Can I tell you a joke that Craig told me?

TomtheGuy: of course

LoopyLisa21f: Question: Why are you always so scared in the bath?

TomtheGuy: i dont know

LoopyLisa21f: Answer: Because skinheads are looking in through the window!!!!

LoopyLisa21f: I don't get it though. Is it funny?

TomtheGuy: i dont know i dont get it either

LoopyLisa21f: Stupid Craig.

LoopyLisa21f: He's always doing weird stuff like that. One time he came round and set fire to a Bible!

TomtheGuy: why?

LoopyLisa21f: I dunno. He just said: "Watch this", and then poured lighter fluid over it, and threw a match on it. It was on my dad's pouffe at the time, and it melted the top of the pouffe.

LoopyLisa21f: Then Craig started crying, and begged me to take the blame for it.

TomtheGuy: as you said weird, did u manage to find a pic of u lisa?

LoopyLisa21f: One second, please.

TomtheGuy: thank u, but i dont have 1 to return sorry

LoopyLisa21f: Sent.

TomtheGuy: thanx

<IMAGE SENT – lisa1.jpg>

TomtheGuy: is that pic of u?

LoopyLisa21f: Yes. Why?

TomtheGuy: its just u have short hair in the pic thought u said earlier u had long hair

LoopyLisa21f: I can't be expected to remember everything.

TomtheGuy: ok

LoopyLisa21f: I have another one.

TomtheGuy: well if ud like to send id like to look at it

LoopyLisa21f: Ok.

LoopyLisa21f: There you go.

LoopyLisa21f: Got it?

TomtheGuy: yes thanx just gonna look

LoopyLisa21f: Ok! Great!

<IMAGE SENT – lisa2.jpg>

TomtheGuy: still pictured u having longer hair

LoopyLisa21f: Hmm. Sorry. Have I disappointed you?

TomtheGuy: no jsut pictured longer hair

LoopyLisa21f: I'm sorry : -(

TomtheGuy: its ok no need to apologise

LoopyLisa21f: I've sent the last one I have.

<IMAGE SENT – lisa3.jpg>

TomtheGuy: thanx

TomtheGuy: can i ask a question about a earlier bit of the conversation

LoopyLisa21f: Ok.

TomtheGuy: why were u squirting frubes into your knickers?

LoopyLisa21f: The doctor said I had to use yoghurt to cure the thrush.

LoopyLisa21f: So I thought any old yoghurt would do.

TomtheGuy: ok

LoopyLisa21f: But it actually had to be a special yoghurt-flavoured yoghurt.

TomtheGuy: ud have thought the doc would have explained that

LoopyLisa21f: Yes. I was quite cross when I went back to see him. I could tell he was trying not to laugh.

LoopyLisa21f: I even took some of the empty Frubes in to show him.

TomtheGuy: that wasnt nice

LoopyLisa21f: I'd even tried to use a Fruit Corner. When I told him about that he left the room for three minutes, and I could hear him and the receptionist sniggering.

LoopyLisa21f: But nothing had been working, you see. The Frubes didn't work. The Fruit Corner didn't work. I even tried rubbing some tiramisu on and around the fungus.

LoopyLisa21f: I mean, I'd literally been itching for a month. I was close to tears when I went back to see him.

LoopyLisa21f: And he just sat there smirking, and shuddering with silent mirth.

TomtheGuy: so did he then recommend a suitable yoghurt

LoopyLisa21f: Yes. It wasn't any one brand – just had to be plain, live yoghurt.

LoopyLisa21f: At first I used a whole tub, but that leaked through my jeans at work, so in the end I just applied about a third of a tub with a spatula in the mornings, and it cleared up.

TomtheGuy: did anyone at work notice?

LoopyLisa21f: Yes, someone pointed it out to me in the staff room.

LoopyLisa21f: I … I have to go now. I'm getting upset again.

TomtheGuy: im sorry we can change the subject

LoopyLisa21f: No. I must go now. It is time for me to go. Goodbye, dear.

LoopyLisa21f: xxxx

TomtheGuy: take care. goodbye xxxx

>>LoopyLisa21f SIGNED OFF AT 11:12

LOOPYLISA'S BLOG

Wednesday, July 12

I've failed to pay off my tremendous debts, so I have decided to become self-sufficient. To this end, I have erected a modest coop in my bedroom, inside of which I have installed a real hen.

Henceforth, I intend to eat nothing but eggs, and drink nothing but chicken milk. Already my hen has produced four eggs, but I'm having difficulty getting it to express milk. In fact, I can't seem to find the hen's teats anywhere. I even tried plucking the hen, but its teats continue to elude me.

I even tried squeezing the hen really hard to see if any milk came out from anywhere, but that just burst one of its legs, and made it lay another egg.

POSTED BY LOOPYLISA AT 18:29

<<NEW CHAT SESSION STARTED

Shepley: hi, what you looking for tonight?

LoopyLisa21f: I seek information.

Shepley: about what?

LoopyLisa21f: Specifically: information regarding eggs. Egg information. "Eggformation", if you will.

Shepley: ?????????

LoopyLisa21f: I'm doing a little survey about eggs. Do you like eggs? How do you like them eggs, dear?

Shepley: however they come

LoopyLisa21f: Have you ever eaten a raw egg?

Shepley: drunk one with milk

LoopyLisa21f: Eurrrgh! That's like bobbing for foetuses from a trough of amniotic fluid. I feel ill now. Just the thought of that is worse than the memory of someone licking a cat's placenta, and I have had to watch that happen at least twice. What did the raw egg taste like?

Shepley: horrible but my dad said it was good for me

LoopyLisa21f: Is your dad cruel? Mine is, and he makes up stuff like that all the time.

LoopyLisa21f: My dad once threw a cushion at me, and the zip cut my lip. He said it was good for me to experience cushion-pain, and all other types of pain in general.

Shepley: no my dad wasn't cruel

LoopyLisa21f: I once saw my dad fall out of a window!

LoopyLisa21f: He landed on his bottom, and done a blow-off!

Shepley: you're mmmmaaaaaaadddddddd !!!!!!!

LoopyLisa21f: Not really. I'm not "mad" if it's true. Which it is!

Shepley: accident prone then?

LoopyLisa21f: Yes. But he's just always getting drunk. Like, literally all the time. It's really funny.

Shepley: i'm feeling really horny !!!!!!!

LoopyLisa21f: I wasn't expecting you to say that!

Shepley: sorry

LoopyLisa21f: Why are you sorry? It's funny!

Shepley: it's not when you're on your own !!!!!!!

LoopyLisa21f: It can be. It can be funny if a comical buzzer goes off and several clowns enter the room whenever you feel that way.

Shepley: true and i think it will be tonite !!!!!

LoopyLisa21f: Are you already finding it funny? Are you "chortling"?

Shepley: what's chortling? is it rude?

LoopyLisa21f: Not exactly ... it's a type of laugh.

LoopyLisa21f: A chortle.

LoopyLisa21f: As in chuckling, snickering, guffawing ...

Shepley: are they cockney rhyming slang? lol

LoopyLisa21f: I don't think so. Do you know any cockney rhyming slang?

Shepley: a bit

LoopyLisa21f: Ok. I will test you. Testing begins ... NOW.

LoopyLisa21f: Apples and stairs?

Shepley: stairs

LoopyLisa21f: Well done!

LoopyLisa21f: Further testing begins ... NOW.

Shepley: ok

LoopyLisa21f: Syrup of wigs?

Shepley: dunno

LoopyLisa21f: Oh, wait. I said it wrong.

LoopyLisa21f: Syrup of figs?

LoopyLisa21f: That's right: it's wigs!

LoopyLisa21f: One more.

LoopyLisa21f: Ok. Testing begins … NOW.

Shepley: ok

LoopyLisa21f: Apples and mags?

Shepley: dunno

LoopyLisa21f: Fags!

LoopyLisa21f: One more please?

Shepley: ok

LoopyLisa21f: Ok. Prepare for testing.

LoopyLisa21f: Pillars of Babel?

Shepley: table ?

LoopyLisa21f: Scrabble!

Shepley: here's one for you

LoopyLisa21f: Ok.

Shepley: threepenny bits

LoopyLisa21f: Hmm …

LoopyLisa21f: Splits? Doin' the splits?

Shepley: nope

LoopyLisa21f: Chips? Eatin' chips?

Shepley: nope. one more try

LoopyLisa21f: Trips? Takin' trips?

Shepley: nope wrong again

LoopyLisa21f: Tell me! I couldn't imagine what that could be!

Shepley: remember how i'm feeling?

Shepley: what am i thinking about?

LoopyLisa21f: Uh ... it wasn't table tennis, was it? Only, I was thinking about table tennis earlier, and it would be a bit weird if we'd both thought about it.

Shepley: threepenny bits

LoopyLisa21f: Three penny bits ... Table tennis bits? You know: the bits you use to play table tennis.

Shepley: nope

Shepley: threepenny bits ------------------------------tits !!!!!!! sorry

LoopyLisa21f: Right ... I don't know what's going on.

Shepley: thats me Im afraid.

Shepley: crazy and horny as hell !!!!!!!!

LoopyLisa21f: I see. Well, Craig is the craziest person I know. You'll have to go some way to trump him.

LoopyLisa21f: One time Craig actually threw a "lemon" at a "bee"!

Shepley: who's craig and why was that crazy?

LoopyLisa21f: Craig is my friend. And he's always doing crazy stuff.

LoopyLisa21f: Another time he was in B&Q, and he pretended to have a fit!

LoopyLisa21f: It was pretty funny, but not so funny with hindsight, when he actually started having fits for real, and had one in Homebase.

Shepley: Nutter

LoopyLisa21f: Well, don't call him nutter to his face! Not now he has a type of palsy!

Shepley: soz i didn't know

LoopyLisa21f: No it's ok – sometimes it's funny! He just vibrates all the time.

Shepley: steady on. no wonder he's your friend

LoopyLisa21f: I once balanced a paper plate on his head, and put olives on it, and got people to bet how long the olives would stay on there!

Shepley: MMMMMaaaaaaaaddddddd lady.. what you look like?

LoopyLisa21f: I have brown hairs.

Shepley: and?

LoopyLisa21f: Greenish eyes, of a medium size.

Shepley: and?

LoopyLisa21f: And good ears.

Shepley: and? remember i'm horny

LoopyLisa21f: Oh … oh lordy – I need to go.

LoopyLisa21f: Craig has burnt himself on the iron.

Shepley: ok sorry cya

LoopyLisa21f: He licked it, the vibrating idiot!

LoopyLisa21f: Bye! Love you!!!!!

LoopyLisa21f: xxxxx

Shepley: bye x

>>LoopyLisa21f SIGNED OFF AT 18:22　　　**""**

LOOPYLISA'S BLOG

Friday, July 14

Last night my mum held a sex party for some of her friends (please note: this isn't a party at which sex occurs, but a party where sexual aids are sold). I can't say I entirely approve of what went on, but I was certainly intrigued by the forty-eight pounds profit my mother made.

Among the items in her catalogue are:

Krill-flavour Thigh Oil (100ml – £5.40)
"The Samson" (Packet of 12 – £6.99)
The Impregnus 58 (£59)
Henry's Cat DVD (£8.99)
Sexy Man Masks (£20 – choose from 'Bill Clinton', 'George Clinton', 'George Michael', or 'Michael Stripes out of REM')

POSTED BY LOOPYLISA AT 11:34

<<NEW CHAT SESSION STARTED
Want to be clint: hiya asl plz

LoopyLisa21f: "Hullo".

LoopyLisa21f: I am 21, sex is female, location today: KENT

Want to be clint: kewl I'm 19 m s.yorkshire

LoopyLisa21f: Is Yorkshire where Yorkie bars come from?

LoopyLisa21f: What about Yorkie dogs?

Want to be clint: lol

LoopyLisa21f: I am serious.

LoopyLisa21f: Is that where they come from? I can't imagine where else they might come from, but I want to know for sure. You know: for "the record".

Want to be clint: im not sure about the chocolate but the dogs yeah

LoopyLisa21f: Hmm

LoopyLisa21f: Do other things come from Yorkshire?

LoopyLisa21f: You know – like Yorkington Slices?

LoopyLisa21f: You've had those, right?

LoopyLisa21f: Yummmmm!

LoopyLisa21f: Mmmm! Yummmmmmmmmmmmmmmms! Prrrrrrtthsssss! C–c–cllllettttttth …

Want to be clint: sexy men come from yorkshire

LoopyLisa21f: Which sexy men?

LoopyLisa21f: Michael York? The Grand Old Duke of York? Yorkie Peters?

LoopyLisa21f: I love Yorkie Peters.

Want to be clint: who?

LoopyLisa21f: You must know Yorkie Peters. He had that big song.

LoopyLisa21f: How did it go again?

LoopyLisa21f: Dum-dum-na-na-na-na-na!

LoopyLisa21f: Luuu-luuuu-na-na-na-na-luuuuuu!

LoopyLisa21f: Lu-lu-lu-lu-lu-lu-lu-dum-dum-da-da-na-na-lu-lu!

LoopyLisa21f: You remember it?

Want to be clint: nope

LoopyLisa21f: Hmm. It was number one all over the world.

LoopyLisa21f: You remember the video though?

LoopyLisa21f: Yorkie was on the back of that rocking horse, and fell off onto a big tray of badger fat that had been left out in the sun.

LoopyLisa21f: And then? And then he blew off on it! Ha ha ha!

Want to be clint: nope, so wot do u do?

LoopyLisa21f: I'm currently helping my mum with her Ann Summers catalogue.

LoopyLisa21f: Did you know that they do fourteen flavours of edible knickers?

LoopyLisa21f: Have you ever tried a chiken korma flavour thong?

Want to be clint: no i cant say i hav

LoopyLisa21f: They also do a pilau rice flavour bra.

LoopyLisa21f: And a lime chutney butt plug, whatever that is.

LoopyLisa21f: So what do you do?

Want to be clint: im a warehouse operative, and a designer

LoopyLisa21f: I used to know a designer.

LoopyLisa21f: He designed little hats for toads. He made them out of paper, and would staple them to the toads' heads. And then? And then the toads would die.

Want to be clint: i design websites

LoopyLisa21f: Regarding your name, dear – which Clint would you like to be?

Want to be clint: eastwood

LoopyLisa21f: Which aspects of Clint Eastwood do you enjoy the most?

Want to be clint: lol, dont start youll upset my horse

LoopyLisa21f: Has your horse ever knocked over your computer?

Want to be clint: no, comp does that on its own

LoopyLisa21f: Do you model your entire aspect after Clint Eastwood?

LoopyLisa21f: For instance, have you spent the evening shooting "punks", and being a "mayor"?

Want to be clint: lol, not shoy my load yet , powder still dry, wot about you, has yr equipment gone of premeturly yet

LoopyLisa21f: I bought the new Yorkie Peters album today.

Want to be clint: does he eat chocolate ?

LoopyLisa21f: No. He's allergic, actually. He only eats "carob". It says so in the sleeve notes to his new album.

Want to be clint: carob ?

LoopyLisa21f: Yeah, it's a healthy alternative to chocolate. It's made out of carrots and something else. Oblongs, probably. Car-ob.

LoopyLisa21f: Here's a test: can you work out what I do for a living?

Want to be clint: fitness instructor ?

LoopyLisa21f: No. I run carob parties!

LoopyLisa21f: They're like Tupperware parties. But with more carob!

Want to be clint: ive heard of tupperware and anne summers, but not carob !

LoopyLisa21f: Look it up on the internet.

LoopyLisa21f: Carob is the ultimate health food.

LoopyLisa21f: There's only one thing healthier.

LoopyLisa21f: Do you know what it is?

LoopyLisa21f: That's right!

LoopyLisa21f: It's lo-fat 'Yummies'.

Want to be clint: lol, ive heard it called a lot of things but never lo-fat 'Yummies', pmsl

LoopyLisa21f: PMSL?

Want to be clint: lol, piss myself laughing

LoopyLisa21f: That's just PML.

LoopyLisa21f: PMSL could stand for Peed My Sandwich Longways.

Want to be clint: now that id like to see.

LoopyLisa21f: You wouldn't if you could see what's in my sandwich.

LoopyLisa21f: It's sheriff's hair and poo!

Want to be clint: lol, strange diet

LoopyLisa21f: Not really. None of it was meant to be in my sandwich. It got put in there "by error".

LoopyLisa21f: I'm merely joshing with you, dear.

LoopyLisa21f: How are you anyway?

Want to be clint: fine

Want to be clint: can i have a pint of wot ever yr drinking ?

LoopyLisa21f: No. You don't want a pint of this.

LoopyLisa21f: I think it's gone off.

Want to be clint: lol,So how come yr not out on the pull tonite ?

LoopyLisa21f: I've had a rotten week.

LoopyLisa21f: My boyfriend left me.

Want to be clint: awe, sorry to hear that, ill just take my big foot out of my mouth

LoopyLisa21f: Hey – that's ok. It happens.

LoopyLisa21f: His new job was distracting him.

LoopyLisa21f: You know how it is. It's a classic story ...

LoopyLisa21f: Boy meets girl, boy gets job as a lollypopman in the next town over, and leaves girl for a woman who makes lollypopman sticks.

Want to be clint: lollypop man, is that a good career move ?

LoopyLisa21f: Well, it's a step up from being a member of ABC.

Want to be clint: abc ?

LoopyLisa21f: He was in ABC. You remember them?

Want to be clint: pop group ?

LoopyLisa21f: Yes. The pop group ABC.

LoopyLisa21f: He was never in the classic line-up. He was just a session keyboardist brought in to replace Yorkie Daniels, who was the keyboardist in the original line-up.

LoopyLisa21f: He toured with them a couple of times on 80s reunion tours. You see, he used to be in an ABC tribute band called 'FQN'. He was also in a tribute band for Tears for Fears called 'Hairs for Pears', and a tribute band for Haircut 100 called 'Bront 1000'.

LoopyLisa21f: And now he's a lollypop man. It's a funny old life.

LoopyLisa21f: The other day an unruly child threw a cornet at him!

Want to be clint: thats like a small trumpet ?

LoopyLisa21f: Yes. But it was full of marbles!

LoopyLisa21f: Kevin, how old are you please?

Want to be clint: too old for you im afraid

LoopyLisa21f: How old is that?

LoopyLisa21f: Ssssss?

Want to be clint: 40 : '(

LoopyLisa21f: I've been out with a 62 year old.

Want to be clint: thank you, youve made an old man very happy , lol

LoopyLisa21f: Well … Is 40 old these days? 87 is older.

Want to be clint: lol, i guess. so wot do you do for fun ?

LoopyLisa21f: Oh no! I have to go! Dad just came in and threw the rest of his Pot Noodle at me. Goodbye, dear! Xxxxx

>>LoopyLisa21f SIGNED OFF AT 21:10

LOOPYLISA'S BLOG

Monday, July 31

When I've paid off my debts I'm going to save up to buy a new car. The car I currently have is about 20 years old, and I don't even think they make it anymore (it's a 'Vauxhall Dubious'). In fact, I don't even think they'd be allowed to make it anymore – it doesn't have seat belts, or seats, or doors.

I have to sit on the floor, and I can only see out of the windscreen using a shaving mirror, which I adjust with a length of bamboo.

POSTED BY LOOPYLISA AT 15:58

<<NEW CHAT SESSION STARTED

SuperShane38: hi

LoopyLisa21f: Hello there. How are you today?

SuperShane38: fine thanx u?

LoopyLisa21f: I'm not too bad. To be honest, I've been better.

SuperShane38: wats up?

LoopyLisa21f: Do you know anything about cars?

SuperShane38: a bit

LoopyLisa21f: How much do you know on a scale of one to fourteen?

SuperShane38: 11

LoopyLisa21f: Ok. Then you're probably the guy to ask.

LoopyLisa21f: Here is my question. Are you ready?

SuperShane38: yeah

LoopyLisa21f: The engine is making this sort of funny noise when I turn the key. What do you think is causing this noise?

SuperShane38: wot noise

LoopyLisa21f: It makes this sort of "chal-chal-chal-chal" sound.

LoopyLisa21f: I don't think it should be doing that.

LoopyLisa21f: It drives ok, apart from small blue flames coming out the exhaust, but people give me funny looks whilst I drive around town. "Chal-chal-chal-chal". It get all sorts of looks; Glares … stares … grimaces.

SuperShane38: head casket maybe

LoopyLisa21f: Beg pardon? What did you call me?

SuperShane38: lol

SuperShane38: or fuel pump

LoopyLisa21f: I've never heard of either of those things. "Chal-chal-chal". I can't afford to take it to a garage. Plus: those places intimidate me.

LoopyLisa21f: What should I do? Please tell me. The noise sounds like something is really badly broken, or is about to break. Can you say the noise aloud, and see if you can pinpoint it for me? "Chal-chal-chal-chal". Don't stop after the fourth "chal", though. Keep going. Please. Keep saying it, and help me with this issue.

LoopyLisa21f: Are you saying it aloud?

SuperShane38: yeh try qick fit theyre ok

LoopyLisa21f: Craig told me to wrap the whole engine in a duvet to mask the sound, but it caught alight.

SuperShane38: lol

LoopyLisa21f: It wasn't funny at the time. It didn't actually go up in big flames. Just one part of it caught alight. I was able to batter it out with a small paddle I keep next to the porch, but now my bed smells of smoke.

LoopyLisa21f: It's a shame, because I liked the pattern on that duvet. It was a sort of Aztec/Mayan pattern. It used to make me dizzy if I looked at it for too long. Now it just gives me chronic smoke-sickness.

SuperShane38: lol

LoopyLisa21f: I'm going to have to take it into a garage, aren't I?

SuperShane38: yeah

LoopyLisa21f: The last time I went to a garage they made fun of me.

SuperShane38: they should understand

LoopyLisa21f: It's not my fault I don't relate well to cars. I've not been driving very long, you see.

LoopyLisa21f: The last time I went to a garage it was because I'd somehow got a cotton reel trapped under the brake pedal, and the only way I could bring the car to a halt was to take my slipper off the accelerator, and gradually slow down by scraping along things at the roadside. I drove around like that for over a week.

SuperShane38: lol

LoopyLisa21f: But when I went to the garage and explained about the trapped cotton reel the man started laughing, and he called his friend over, and they started slow clapping at me.

LoopyLisa21f: And one of them was stamping his foot going "Ooh ooh ooh", and pointing. It went like this: clap/point/clap/stamp/stamp/"Ooh ooh ooh"/point.

SuperShane38: take it 2 different garage

LoopyLisa21f: But what if they're all like that? What if one of the men from that garage has gone to work at the garage I take the car to? What if they all have? What should I do then? What if there has been an almost total and universal "mechanic exchange"?

SuperShane38: I dunno

LoopyLisa21f: I'm really worried about it. I know I shouldn't be, but I really can't stop thinking about it.

SuperShane38: phone them 1st

LoopyLisa21f: And say what? "Do you have anyone there who stamps his feet and goes "ooh ooh ooh"? They'll laugh at me even more. They'll bark their dirty laughs down the phone and directly into my ear.

SuperShane38: tell them bout car and then take it

LoopyLisa21f: Ok. If you think that's the best thing to do. I could always just jiggle some wires, though?

LoopyLisa21f: Do you think that might sort it out? Or shall I jab a couple of forks in there, and try and knock some of the mechanisms around?

SuperShane38: ok

LoopyLisa21f: Ok!

SuperShane38: yeah

LoopyLisa21f: OK!

SuperShane38: ok

LoopyLisa21f: Do you know any interesting facts about cars? If I take it to the garage I could make out I know about cars by saying some car facts. That may stave off the tide of mockery.

SuperShane38: just tell them 2 start car and theyll tell u

LoopyLisa21f: Yes, but first I could say "Did you know that cars have pneumatic such-and-suches", and "Also, it's a little-known fact that cars can do such-and-such a thing".

LoopyLisa21f: That would probably impress them big time.

SuperShane38: yeah

LoopyLisa21f: So you don't have any interesting facts? If they were really good facts I might be able to impress them enough to offer me a job there. Do you think that could happen?

SuperShane38: could do

LoopyLisa21f: I should be careful then. I don't really want to work with people like that. So, if you have any facts can you get a few details wrong for me?

LoopyLisa21f: If you don't have any facts I could make some up, and see if they notice. I could say something like ... "Did you know that Adolf Hitler never owned a car?", or "If you turn a steering wheel all the way round the car lays an egg".

SuperShane38: sure

LoopyLisa21f: You think I'm talking rubbish, don't you?

SuperShane38: yeah

LoopyLisa21f: Shall I leave you alone?

SuperShane38: yes please

LoopyLisa21f: "Chal-chal-chal-chal-chal-chal-chal-chal".

<<LoopyLisa21f SIGNED OFF AT 14:13   **??**

LOOPYLISA'S BLOG

Wednesday, August 02

I had a dream last night that there was a mandrill living in my chest of drawers. The mandrill had somehow climbed into the top drawer while my back was turned, and I'd shut it without realising he was in there.

The mandrill became wedged between the drawer and the back of the chest of drawers, and could not escape. Over a period of months I couldn't work out where my clothes were going, and it turns out that the mandrill was eating them – the only way it could survive.

Eventually, the mandrill had become so fat from eating my clothes that the chest of drawers collapsed, and he had a heart attack. The mandrill was sprawled amid the wreckage with a pair of half-eaten tights hanging out of his funny, deceased, monkey gob.

POSTED BY LOOPYLISA AT 09:10

<<NEW CHAT SESSION STARTED

bONkerzBoY: hi asl

LoopyLisa21f: Hello, Bonkers.

bONkerzBoY: asl

LoopyLisa21f: Patience, please. I'm "multi-tasking".

LoopyLisa21f: Right. I'm 21/female/London. What about you?

bONkerzBoY: 21 m cumbria

bONkerzBoY: wot u look like

LoopyLisa21f: I have blonde "hair".

230

bONkerzBoY: anything else or pic

LoopyLisa21f: I might have a pic, but as it's on my other computer it'll take me a while to find it. You see, it's currently buried beneath a pile of rusting segs and discarded hospital sharps. I don't even want to explain why that is!

bONkerzBoY: try 2 find it plz babe xx

LoopyLisa21f: I don't really want to move from my seat, but in a while I'll try and knock some of the segs away using this broom handle. But first? First tell me about yourself.

bONkerzBoY: u want a pic

LoopyLisa21f: Of you? Not really.

LoopyLisa21f: Do you have any pictures of Pavarotti though?

bONkerzBoY: no y

LoopyLisa21f: I'm doing a chart of the opera singers. I'm going to arrange them in order of height.

bONkerzBoY: ok

LoopyLisa21f: Unfortunately, the only opera singers I can think of are Pavarotti and Leslie Carrot.

bONkerzBoY: u want a dirty pic of me lol

LoopyLisa21f: Dirty? Why are you dirty? Have you been playing "rugger"? Are you a "rugger bugger"?

bONkerzBoY: no i ment dirty bcos it of my cock

LoopyLisa21f: I'm sorry?

bONkerzBoY: u dont hav 2 hav it

LoopyLisa21f: What would I get out of seeing such a thing?

bONkerzBoY: dunno

bONkerzBoY: wot u wearin

LoopyLisa21f: Dungarees, and a jumper, with sleeves that are three times as long as they need to be, and have tiny bells on the cuffs, which jangle as they drag along the ground.

bONkerzBoY: underwear?

LoopyLisa21f: Yes.

bONkerzBoY: wot it like ?

LoopyLisa21f: My knickers are comprised of a one-inch thick elastic strap, with strips of coloured cloth hanging from it.

bONkerzBoY: so a g string

LoopyLisa21f: No, no. The pieces don't join up. They just hang there.

bONkerzBoY: ????????

bONkerzBoY: y

LoopyLisa21f: If I spin around, or "dance" in some way, the centrifugal force of my gyrations cause the "flaps" to lift up!

bONkerzBoY: y it like that

LoopyLisa21f: I dunno. To be honest, it's not very comfy. They were a present from my dad.

bONkerzBoY: ya DAD ???

LoopyLisa21f: Yes. And now I've got a rash all over my private area where the garment has been rubbing up against my jeans when I sit down.

bONkerzBoY: seems strange ya dad buyin the daughter sumthing like that

LoopyLisa21f: Well, we're quite broad-minded.

LoopyLisa21f: He once bought me a book which contained nothing but join-the-dots pictures of sharks having sex.

bONkerzBoY: is ya rash sore

232

LoopyLisa21f: A little. I have plasters over it, and I've smothered the areas with a custom paste I mixed up from TCP, Germolene and Vick's Vaporub.

LoopyLisa21f: Frankly, it stinks to ruddy Heaven.

LoopyLisa21f: I should probably stop wearing them, but I don't want to offend my dad.

bONkerzBoY: were is the rash? clit ?

LoopyLisa21f: I'm sorry?

bONkerzBoY: 4 wot ?

LoopyLisa21f: What do you mean? Hello? HELLO?

bONkerzBoY: is the rash on ya clit ?

LoopyLisa21f: On my whaaaaat?!?

bONkerzBoY: pussy

bONkerzBoY: the bit were the penis goes in

LoopyLisa21f: Again you mention something rude. Why is this please?

bONkerzBoY: is the rash there

LoopyLisa21f: Well, it's around that general area. I don't particularly want to go into specifics. It's a "private" matter, surely?

LoopyLisa21f: It doesn't hurt anymore, if that's your concern. However, I can reveal that the area in question is bright red, and there are thick, yellow suds pulsing out of it, in steady gulps. In the last hour alone I have filled four reasonable-sized vases with the foul-scented spume.

bONkerzBoY: soz got 2 go

LoopyLisa21f: Hello?

>>bONkerzBoY SIGNED OFF AT 17:41

"

LOOPYLISA'S BLOG

Thursday, August 10

I've decided to flex my creative muscles a bit more often, and I'm going to try and write my own film script. I have decided to start by writing a second sequel to Honey, I Shrunk The Kids. I thought I'd start by writing the title, and have decided to choose one of the following:

10. Honey, You Shrunk The Kids
9. Honey, I'm In The Oven
8. Honey, I'm Wearing A Bosun's Whistle
7. Honey, I Can't Remember Your Name
6. Honey, I Shaved The Dog
5. Honey, There Is Honey All Over My Workshop
4. Honey, I Like Kids
3. Honey, I Strangled An Actress
2. Honey, I Taped EastEnders For You
1. Honey, I Made Our Son Go Gay

POSTED BY LOOPYLISA AT 15:44

<<NEW CHAT SESSION STARTED

OllyStuntman64: hi

LoopyLisa21f: Hello. Just give me a second. There's some weird stuff going on with my neighbours.

OllyStuntman64: k

LoopyLisa21f: Ok. Back now. That was bizarre.

OllyStuntman64: what was it

LoopyLisa21f: Just some weird stuff going on next door.

OllyStuntman64: what like

LoopyLisa21f: The couple next door had a really bad argument a few nights ago, and I think the man has been staying away. Anyway, he came back about half an hour ago covered in mud, and wearing a cape, and stuff, and started banging on the door. He was also carrying a pizza, and then he started throwing bits of pizza up at the house. Then some of the pizza got stuck to the bedroom window, and he produced this long stick, and started using it to move the slice of pizza around the window. The window's all mucky and smeary now.

OllyStuntman64: oh well its a bit of live entertainment

LoopyLisa21f: What are your neighbours like?

OllyStuntman64: well bad come to think of it

OllyStuntman64: had the cops round so many times

LoopyLisa21f: For what kind of things?

OllyStuntman64: the husband fucked off with another bird

LoopyLisa21f: That's not illegal is it?

OllyStuntman64: it is illegal when they smashing things up in the house

LoopyLisa21f: Especially if he'd stolen the things from someone else's house, and brought them back to his house to smash up.

OllyStuntman64: better not to intervene

OllyStuntman64: apart from that its a pretty good neighbourhood

LoopyLisa21f: Have you ever smashed anything in your house?

OllyStuntman64: no

LoopyLisa21f: Would you like to?

OllyStuntman64: not really

LoopyLisa21f: Listen, can we try an experiment?

OllyStuntman64: experiment what?

LoopyLisa21f: Do you believe in extra sensory perception?

OllyStuntman64: explain pls

LoopyLisa21f: Telepathy, mental powers – stuff like that. The ability to cook hamburgers without touching them. Being able to read books just by thinking about them. That sort of thing.

OllyStuntman64: is that what u have

LoopyLisa21f: No, but I've been reading a book which says we all have latent powers to some degree. I just wanted to try some of the tests from the book.

OllyStuntman64: well sumtimes i sense things then a couple of months later it happens

LoopyLisa21f: Really?

LoopyLisa21f: That's a bit spooky.

OllyStuntman64: well i dont know why it happens but i feel like it was dream i had yesterday

LoopyLisa21f: That's really amazing. Are you sure it wasn't just a dream you had yesterday?

OllyStuntman64: postiive

LoopyLisa21f: Give me an example.

OllyStuntman64: i sensed sumthing was to happen at work while working

LoopyLisa21f: What was it?

OllyStuntman64: that i was going to get into trouble

OllyStuntman64: an it happend i got a verbal warning for doing it

OllyStuntman64: do people have sixth sense

LoopyLisa21f: Can we try some tests?

OllyStuntman64: what like

LoopyLisa21f: I want to draw something on a piece of paper, and I want you to guess what it is.

OllyStuntman64: well i dont whther it works but give it a try

LoopyLisa21f: Drawing now. Close your eyes, cross your legs, and try and picture it.

OllyStuntman64: drawed the dog have u ?

LoopyLisa21f: No. I haven't finished yet.

LoopyLisa21f: Now I have finisihed.

OllyStuntman64: what was it?

LoopyLisa21f: You have to guess.

OllyStuntman64: was it a dog ?

LoopyLisa21f: No. No, it's not a dog.

LoopyLisa21f: Do you want me to tell you?

OllyStuntman64: i dont know. thats all that coem to me head

LoopyLisa21f: It was Samuel Pepys.

OllyStuntman64: yeah?

LoopyLisa21f: Yes.

LoopyLisa21f: I suppose his hair is quite curly, makes him look a bit like a type of curly-haired dog.

OllyStuntman64: ok lets test u

LoopyLisa21f: Ok.

OllyStuntman64: guess what i ve draweed

LoopyLisa21f: Was it something pyramid-shaped?

OllyStuntman64: yeah kinda of

OllyStuntman64: hows u do that ?

LoopyLisa21f: It's sort of a gift. My grandmother always said I was blessed with the "brown eye".

OllyStuntman64: carry on

OllyStuntman64: tell me what it is

LoopyLisa21f: Ok. Is there also a cross-shape somewhere in the picture? Like, two lines crossing?

OllyStuntman64: yeah ther are two lines crossing

OllyStuntman64: ur spooky

LoopyLisa21f: This is quite exciting. It's giving me both a hum, and a buzz.

LoopyLisa21f: Is it a kite?

OllyStuntman64: no but it isnt a kite its a sail crossing on a boat

OllyStuntman64: the sails lookijng like pyramid shape a bit like a kite i guess

OllyStuntman64: with the pole in between acting as cross

OllyStuntman64: i say u was too close for comfort ther

OllyStuntman64: hows u do it ?

LoopyLisa21f: I don't know. It's just something I can do. I can always guess the contents of handbags about 90% of the time.

OllyStuntman64: well good fo u i say

OllyStuntman64: can u see all sausages as well

OllyStuntman64: see whats big small

LoopyLisa21f: Sausages? Hang on – suddenly you're making less sense. Have you gone and done some heroin? Are you riding the horse, and chasing the dragon? Are you painting along with the Nancy?

OllyStuntman64: it dont matter

OllyStuntman64: can u send me a pic of u

LoopyLisa21f: I look awful in photos.

OllyStuntman64: well who cares we all have to have a face

LoopyLisa21f: Yeah, but sometimes people say I look like a man.

OllyStuntman64: well can i see ?

LoopyLisa21f: Yes. Please don't be too nasty, though.

OllyStuntman64: i wont i ll be honest if u want

LoopyLisa21f: Ok. There you go.

<IMAGE SENT – lisa21.jpg>

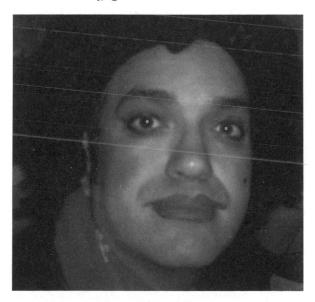

OllyStuntman64: do u want me to be honest?

LoopyLisa21f: I suppose. But don't be needlessly nasty.

OllyStuntman64: well it looks like a man with stubble either that or u is man

OllyStuntman64: or ur not sending ur true pic of a woman

LoopyLisa21f: It's not stubble. People always say that with that photo. It's just shadows, and the light.

LoopyLisa21f: I do have another one.

LoopyLisa21f: Gosh. I can't believe you find me so unbearably ugly.

OllyStuntman64: can u send the other one then

LoopyLisa21f: Sent, dear.

<IMAGE SENT – lisa30.jpg>

OllyStuntman64: am sorry huni but thats no woman for sure

LoopyLisa21f: How would you like it if I said you looked like a woman?

OllyStuntman64: good question ur right i wudnt like it

OllyStuntman64: i really am sorry

LoopyLisa21f: But you were really nice before. What has happened? Is this because you've taken some drugs?

OllyStuntman64: what more can i say?

LoopyLisa21f: So is that it then? You're not going to talk to me now, just because you find me a bit ugly?

OllyStuntman64: no we can talk but ther wont benothing good happenin jus genrel chat

OllyStuntman64: i bet thats not even ur pic

OllyStuntman64: i can feel it sumhow that is not u

LoopyLisa21f: Why? Who would it be?

OllyStuntman64: not u

LoopyLisa21f: I have others.

LoopyLisa21f: I've sent you one more.

LoopyLisa21f: See if that convinces you.

<IMAGE SENT – lisa23.jpg>

OllyStuntman64: yeah still not convinced

>>OllyStuntman64 SIGNED OFF AT 20:12   **,,**

LOOPYLISA'S BLOG

Monday, August 14

Earlier in the year I briefly attempted to keep hens. I was inspired by my experiences to put pen to paper, and I've just received a letter telling me that one of my hen poems has been accepted for publication in a book of poetry about – and for – hens.

My piece is called simply 'Hens'.

Eggs and hens,
Eggs and hens,
Pencils and pens,
Pencils and pens,
If you are a hen,
Do not eat a pen,
Because it will get wedged in your neck and you'll die-i-i.

I think it works on several levels. If you're someone who likes poems it's just a really good poem, and if you're a hen it features an important safety tip (do not eat pens, hens).

POSTED BY LOOPYLISA AT 11:17

<<NEW CHAT SESSION STARTED

Markryanon: hi how u doing

LoopyLisa21f: Oh I'm ok. Just passing the time until Watchdog starts. I love that show – tonight they're investigating a trader who has been selling dodgy balloons filled with pigeons instead of helium. Where are you from, dear?

Markryanon: nw lon near wembley

LoopyLisa21f: Wembley is cool. That's where they have that big aquarium, right?

LoopyLisa21f: The one which got shut down, because they found out half the fish weren't real? Half of them were carrots, and the other half were plimsolls they'd painted silver.

Markryanon: stadium and arena

LoopyLisa21f: Yes, and aquarium. Wembley's Magnificent Seasorium, I think it's called.

Markryanon: so wat u in2

LoopyLisa21f: I'm into Aquariums. They're a tremendous amount of fun. I had a dream recently that I lived in an aquarium, but got fed up with all the visitors.

LoopyLisa21f: You wouldn't believe how much spat-out chewing gum there is on the floor of an aquarium. And when I say "aquarium", I mean "an aquarium in a dream". The owner of the aquarium only let me stay there if I ate a cup of sprats every morning.

LoopyLisa21f: What do you think it all means?

Markryanon: ;-)lol

LoopyLisa21f: I'm serious. It has really affected me. It's one of those dreams where you can't tell when the dream stops and real-life begins. What does it mean, dear?

Markryanon: not 100 percent sure

LoopyLisa21f: Sprats taste horrible, you know. But I suppose we all have our crosses to bear ...

Markryanon: wat u look like

LoopyLisa21f: I look like the woman who co-presents Dipping With Derek.

LoopyLisa21f: Have you ever seen that show?

Markryanon: no

Markryanon: describe urself or av u got a pic?

LoopyLisa21f: Wait a minute there. I've not finished talking about Dipping With Derek. You see, each week they dip into a different topic, but don't explore it in any particular depth.

Markryanon: k

LoopyLisa21f: They dip "in", then "out" again. And it's presented by Eric Nimmo, the son of Derek Nimmo. Nimmo isn't on it (because he's dead, probably), but his son presents it in front of a big photo of his father.

Markryanon: dnt know it

LoopyLisa21f: Last week they dipped into "draughts".

LoopyLisa21f: Not the game draughts.

Markryanon: yea wat u look like

LoopyLisa21f: Sssh! They' dipped into "draughts which blow through doors". Just watching that show made me feel chilly. Because they only dipped into it they never really came to any conclusion. Consequently I don't know how to stop the draughts in my flat. If I freeze to death this winter I'll blame the Nimmos.

Markryanon: wat u look like ???

LoopyLisa21f: I have dark red hair.

Markryanon: k and ....

LoopyLisa21f: Green-ish ears.

LoopyLisa21f: EYES.

LoopyLisa21f: I mean ears. EYES. Eyes.

LoopyLisa21f: You?

Markryanon: blond blue eyes 5'9

Markryanon: where u from

Markryanon: ?? u there?

LoopyLisa21f: Oh yeah. Sorry. I blacked out. Yeah, sorry. I have a type short-term memory loss, and a terrible sense of direction.

LoopyLisa21f: I've got half a leek lodged in my inner ear, you see, and it presses on the part of my brain which controls my ability to remember where I'm going, what I'm doing, and why. One minute I'm in the kitchen, then the next thing I know I'm 40 miles away in the back of a lorry with a load of old cows.

Markryanon: shit no way??? how you get in wit tha cows?

LoopyLisa21f: I'd rather not discuss it. It's really awful, to be honest. That particular scenario has happened three times now. So anyway, what sort of house do you live in? Bungalow? I bet it's a bungalow.

Markryanon: 4 bedroom house

LoopyLisa21f: What do you keep in the extra bedrooms?

Markryanon: live with my parents still lol

LoopyLisa21f: My friend Craig has a spare bedroom. He keeps a collection of razors and razorbacks in it.

LoopyLisa21f: It isn't a very organised collection. Plus, he only has about 12 razors, and one razorback. As collections go it's rubbish. It's not even a real razorback – just a drawing of one.

LoopyLisa21f: He just chucks the razors in there and closes the door whenever he gets a new one. He never even looks at them, or sorts through them, or anything.

Markryanon: : -)

Markryanon: wat r u in2

Markryanon: hobbies etc

LoopyLisa21f: Craig and I occasionally go to this club to play giant shove ha'penny.

Markryanon: : -$

LoopyLisa21f: It's like normal shove ha'penny, but instead of using ha'pennies you use handbags, and you get greased up and have to slither around on your bare belly in time to some music.

Markryanon: wat else ?

LoopyLisa21f: I also like reading books about bird-related disasters, such as the incident in Stevenage in 1952 when a primary school was crushed by 3,000 cassowaries who fell out of the sky when they realised they couldn't fly.

LoopyLisa21f: You?

Markryanon: football drinking fucking and cumming!

LoopyLisa21f: Don't you mean "going", as in "going places".

Markryanon: na doing

Markryanon: u dnt like sex?

LoopyLisa21f: I never said that. I just get embarrassed when talking about things like that with people I don't know.

Markryanon: wen was the last time u did it

LoopyLisa21f: "Did it"?

Markryanon: yea

LoopyLisa21f: I'll tell you shortly. First? First I want to hear more from you.

Markryanon: k wat u wanna know

LoopyLisa21f: Do you know any jokes?

Markryanon: yea loads but cant b bothered 2 type em out

Markryanon: ;-)

LoopyLisa21f: Shall I tell you a joke?

Markryanon: if u want

LoopyLisa21f: I know thousands. Set me a topic, and I'll tell you a joke on that topic straight away.

Markryanon: football

LoopyLisa21f: Ok. A footbally joke.

Markryanon: is that the joke

LoopyLisa21f: Be patient, you brusque poltroon. Please. Here it is now: What academic subject are butterflies best at?

Markryanon: i dunno

LoopyLisa21f: Answer: moths (maths). Ha ha ha.

LoopyLisa21f: Ok, I've got another one now.

Markryanon: k

LoopyLisa21f: Question: What is the pop singer Elton John's favourite soft drink?

Markryanon: ???

LoopyLisa21f: Answer: Bum Ongo(ing)!

LoopyLisa21f: I admit that I don't really get it though.

Markryanon: k

LoopyLisa21f: Craig told me it, but I didn't really understand.

LoopyLisa21f: He seemed to find it funny, though. He illustrated the joke by moving in a particular way that I don't particularly want to describe.

Markryanon: k

LoopyLisa21f: My final joke is this: what happens if you rub your stomach the wrong way?

LoopyLisa21f: Pullicans appear!

LoopyLisa21f: Your turn.

Markryanon: cant think of any

LoopyLisa21f: Ok. Hit me with another topic, shorty.

Markryanon: u choose

LoopyLisa21f: Would you like to hear a Star Wars joke?

Markryanon: no

Markryanon: ur an adult aint ya ?

LoopyLisa21f: I'm 21, yes. Come on – It's a really good joke this one.

Markryanon: dnt u wanna chat bout sumfin more excitin?

LoopyLisa21f: Let me tell you my Star Wars joke then we will.

LoopyLisa21f: Please. It's SO funny.

Markryanon: k

LoopyLisa21f: Ok.

LoopyLisa21f: What's white, has two taps on the end, and breathes heavily?

Markryanon: mmmmmmmm close 2 cummin

LoopyLisa21f: No – BATH Vader.

Markryanon: is that the answer 2 the spaceman joke

Markryanon: cummin in 2 space

Markryanon: thats better

LoopyLisa21f: Oh … oh goodness – I need to go.

LoopyLisa21f: Craig has burnt himself on the iron again.

Markryanon: ok sorry cya whos craig

LoopyLisa21f: He's a very naughty boy who is going to have no tongue left if he keeps licking hot irons – that's who.

LoopyLisa21f: Bye! Love you!!!!!

LoopyLisa21f: xxxxx

Markryanon: bye x

>>LoopyLisa21f SIGNED OFF AT 19:21

LOOPYLISA'S BLOG

Sunday, August 20

I came home today to find my bedroom transformed. It turns out that Craig had secretly arranged for a digital TV DIY show to do a make-over on it. I'd never seen the show in question (RAS: Room Altering Squad), or heard of the presenter/home decorating expert (Crystal Breath), but I have to say that I'm quite impressed with what they've done.

However, when I say "quite impressed with what they've done" I actually mean "I absolutely hate it". They basically just stripped off all the wallpaper, threw out my duvet, and tried to pass off the wallpaper as bedding.

Also, I'm pretty sure I caught some of the camera crew going through my underwear drawer (and I found an empty Ribena carton in there later, and someone had written their phone number on it).

POSTED BY LOOPYLISA AT 00:01

<<NEW CHAT SESSION STARTED

Superpro3: mmm ... you'r name has got me curious ... interested in a fit older london man?

LoopyLisa21f: How much older? How much fitter? I need to know as a percentage, please.

Superpro3: Lol ...how much depends how old you are ... and fit enough!

LoopyLisa21f: I'm 21, and the only exercise I do are 40 lateral snaps a day. You know what they are, right? I'm trying to increase my fitness by 34% in time for Passover.

Superpro3: mmm. ... well i'm quite a bit older ... and as for exercise ... only the enjoyable sort

LoopyLisa21f: Enjoyable sort? You mean like team sports? Do you like tug o' war?

Superpro3: not what I had in mind lol

LoopyLisa21f: You know what would be really funny? Having a tug o' war with a Portuguese man 'o war!

Superpro3: weird girl

LoopyLisa21f: I admit that it's probably a strange thing to be thinking about, but I wonder how hard it would be to rip a jellyfish in half.

Superpro3: Not that hard.

LoopyLisa21f: What about a narwhal?

LoopyLisa21f: Changing the subject slightly, have you got a hairy stomach?

Superpro3: Not very hairy ... is that a problem?

LoopyLisa21f: Not really. Just that my friend Craig's stomach has become really hairy in the last month.

LoopyLisa21f: We're all a bit worried by it.

Superpro3: Lol ... how old is he?

LoopyLisa21f: 26.

LoopyLisa21f: You can hardly see the skin anymore.

Superpro3: bit young for sudden sprouting of unwanted hair

LoopyLisa21f: That's what he thought. It's weird because he's hardly hairy anywhere else. In fact, apart from his eyebrows and a little bit on top of his head he's completely hairless.

LoopyLisa21f: But now there's this perfect circular disc of hair on his stomach, about the size of a dinner plate.

Superpro3: How strange …I really don't know what to advise!

Superpro3: Shaving is always an option for unwanted hair of course

>   LoopyLisa21f: He's scared to shave down there in case he nicks himself.

>   LoopyLisa21f: He once tried to shave his nose because he was paranoid it was getting too hairy, and he badly cut it.

>   LoopyLisa21f: He had a big scab on the side of his nose for a fortnight, and he had to do film a training video at his work, and had to conceal the scab with his finger. I did some temp work there, and got to see the video. At one point someone asks why he's holding his finger at the side of his nose, and he just starts this nervous laugh that goes on slightly too long, and then someone says "Well?", and then Craig just legs it out of the room, muttering about having "the runs". I don't know why they had to leave that bit in. It should've been edited out, really.

Superpro3: I do have hair below my stomach

>   LoopyLisa21f: Hello?

Superpro3: hello …??? i'm here

>   LoopyLisa21f: What are we talking about here, please?

Superpro3: mainly talking about your hairy friend

>   LoopyLisa21f: Sorry – I won't talk about Craig anymore if you find him distressing.

Superpro3: Its ok ..unusual but hey ..its good to be different lol

>   LoopyLisa21f: It is! That's what Craig says. But then, Craig says a lot of things, such as "Big Ben is full of citric acid". I really embarrassed myself in a pub quiz because he told me that.

Superpro3: Lol … sounds like Craig could get you into a lot of trouble!

Superpro3: Everyone knows its nitric acid

LoopyLisa21f: What's that?

Superpro3: Oh its much worse than citric acid

LoopyLisa21f: I see. Are you trying to join in with the fun? Craig told me Big Ben ran on a type of refined citric acid.

Superpro3: Really ... well maybe he's right after all

LoopyLisa21f: Tell that to the pub quiz woman.

Superpro3: They don't always have the right answers!

LoopyLisa21f: No, I know. One other time we were there I disagreed with her about an answer, which she said was James Bolan, but I knew it was Geoffrey Palmer, and she told me to sit down and be quiet or I'd be thrown out.

Superpro3: and did you behave after that?

LoopyLisa21f: I had to. I was crying so much, but I had no choice but to behave.

Superpro3: poor you ..how traumatic

LoopyLisa21f: I just felt humiliated. Craig bought me a kebab to make me feel better.

LoopyLisa21f: But I even dropped that, and nearly slipped over on it, and then had a fight with a drug addict. That was a really rubbish night.

Superpro3: Do kebabs usually cheer you up?

LoopyLisa21f: Well of course they do.

Superpro3: Mmm ...you should get out more often

LoopyLisa21f: Get out where?

LoopyLisa21f: There's nowhere to go in London.

Superpro3: In London? ... where on earth are you?

LoopyLisa21f: I already told you I'm in London. But they closed the bowling alley, the ice rink, and the mink farm, and the ice farm, and the mink rink, and now there's nowhere left to go.

Superpro3: So just the kebab shop and pub quizzes for you then ... awww

Superpro3: Not all bad then

LoopyLisa21f: No. Not all bad.

Superpro3: And always with Craig? ... even with his hairy stomach?

LoopyLisa21f: Oh! I have to go, dear.

Superpro3: : -(

Superpro3: by by babe

LoopyLisa21f: I'm sorry, but Mrs Billam is going to be here soon, to take me to darts in her special "darts trolley".

LoopyLisa21f: She pulls it along, and I just recline and dream of darts.

Superpro3: What fun.

LoopyLisa21f: Goodbye, "Richard"! I love you!

Superpro3: lol

>>LoopyLisa21f SIGNED OFF AT 19:34

LOOPYLISA'S BLOG

Tuesday, August 29

My granddad is staying with us at the moment. I don't mind at all, even though he's incontinent, and I have to share a bed with him. He's a nice old feller, literally full of interesting stories about his time in the RAF.

Apparently, he was the first helicopter pilot in the RAF, and this was in the days before helicopters had been invented. Basically, he used to spend his days hanging out in a classroom looking at pictures of helicopters drawn by Leonardo da Vinci, and chewing on sycamore seeds for inspiration.

POSTED BY LOOPYLISA AT 13:40

<<NEW CHAT SESSION STARTED

STEVEYTREES: hey babe wanna chat?

LoopyLisa21f: Yes. Hit me with your chatting stick, please.

STEVEYTREES: age sex location please hunni?

LoopyLisa21f: 21, London, blah blah blah. And you've already guessed I'm a lady, so I don't know why you're even asking that. You?

STEVEYTREES: 35 m

LoopyLisa21f: I see. If you're 35 what were are you doing trying to chat to me? From my name you must know that I am in my early 20s?

STEVEYTREES: like the younger lass

STEVEYTREES: so whats ya location then

LoopyLisa21f: Just in front of the computer.

STEVEYTREES: where location in the country?

LoopyLisa21f: I'm not in the country. I'm in "London".

STEVEYTREES: newcastle here

LoopyLisa21f: Newcastle? So you're a Georgie-boy?

STEVEYTREES: yea sure am

LoopyLisa21f: "Hey there, Georgie-boy, There's another Georgie deep inside, Why do all the boys just pass you by? Do you stink of mould, oh Georgie-Boy? What's that that's been splashed all up your back, oh Georgie?". You remember that song, don't you, Colin?

STEVEYTREES: its steve

STEVEYTREES: so u got a pic??

LoopyLisa21f: I do have a pic, Colin. I need to retrieve it from my laptop before you can see it, though. That might take a while – it's up in the ruddy loft with the dead pigeons, and the half a rotting cat we keep up there to mask the smell of the dead pigeons (the cat has cloves stuck in it). We can still chat in the meantime.

LoopyLisa21f: Chat subject primed: what are your five favourite animals?

STEVEYTREES: u got webcam?

LoopyLisa21f: Sssh! What are you five favourite animals? Didn't you hear me?

STEVEYTREES: where is it like?

LoopyLisa21f: Where is what like? What are you talking about?

STEVEYTREES: u buying a webcam like?

LoopyLisa21f: Well, I have one, but it's broken. Craig dropped it in the fish tank.

STEVEYTREES: ok

LoopyLisa21f: He was chatting to a girl on here, and wanted to convince her he's a merman. Apparently she used to have a bit of a thing for The Man From Atlantis.

LoopyLisa21f: Personally, I preferred Manimal, and the young John Sessions.

STEVEYTREES: who is craig?

LoopyLisa21f: My friend.

STEVEYTREES: ok cool a freind or ex partner

LoopyLisa21f: Just a friend. We held hands one lunchtime when we were six, but I'd never go out with Craig. He shouts directions in his sleep. He'll shout stuff like "Turn right at the roundabout, and go straight on until you pass the pub on your right, then go straight over the next set of lights, and it's the third on the left", and "You probably want to take the Hayes bypass as usual when going to Ikea, but come off an exit earlier than you normally would, and follow that road all the way down, and we're at number 43".

LoopyLisa21f: One time, he did a blow-off in a bank!

STEVEYTREES: o right

LoopyLisa21f: He was applying for a loan at the time. Craig told me that the manager said "I hope you didn't just leave a deposit!". But I would imagine that's a lie, and the manager probably said something more along the lines of "Could you not do that, please?". Or maybe he just tried to ignore it.

STEVEYTREES: ok

STEVEYTREES: so wat u into?

LoopyLisa21f: What does that mean?

STEVEYTREES: like wat u like doing?

LoopyLisa21f: I like going to the cinema, reading books, browsing books, and burning books.

LoopyLisa21f: What do you like doing, dear?

STEVEYTREES: footy, sex, clubbing

LoopyLisa21f: Clubbing seals?

STEVEYTREES: wha?

LoopyLisa21f: Do you like clubbing seals?

STEVEYTREES: wat the fuk does tht mean?

LoopyLisa21f: You know the animal called a seal?

STEVEYTREES: yea

LoopyLisa21f: Well, when you said "clubbing" I thought you might've meant that you like "clubbing seals". You know: hitting seals with clubs and bats.

STEVEYTREES: wha tha fukk?!

LoopyLisa21f: You never know. Craig once went on a seal clubbing weekend with some of the people from his line of work.

STEVEYTREES: fukk!

LoopyLisa21f: I thought it was disgusting.

STEVEYTREES: yea

LoopyLisa21f: He showed me his scorecard when he got back. Do you know what was written on it?

STEVEYTREES: wat?

LoopyLisa21f: The words: "Fourteen seals dead". That's how many seals he'd clubbed to death.

STEVEYTREES: lol

LoopyLisa21f: Why are you laughing?

LoopyLisa21f: It's disgusting. There was another thing written on his scorecard: "12 seals maimed". Apparently, because it was so icy he kept slipping over before he could finish them off, and the seals would then slither off into the sea, or underneath this portakabin that was nearby. Disgusting.

STEVEYTREES: wel if its wat he wants to do then up 2 him

LoopyLisa21f: Yeah, but some people might want to do murders, or crimes, and you can't really say "that's up to them" if they're going to kill people, or do crimes.

STEVEYTREES: yea suppose

LoopyLisa21f: Could you club a seal?

STEVEYTREES: ner

LoopyLisa21f: Nor me. I couldn't even club an ant.

STEVEYTREES: same here

LoopyLisa21f: I could probably club a single cell organism to death, but nothing bigger. Maybe a small horse if it had bitten me.

STEVEYTREES: lol

LoopyLisa21f: I doubt anyone would bother trying to club an ant. You couldn't make a very big coat out of an ant. You'd have to club loads and loads of ants to make an ant coat. I suppose you could use the carapace of an ant to make a little cycle helmet for a flea.

STEVEYTREES: lol

LoopyLisa21f: What is your favourite colour of ant?

STEVEYTREES: black

LoopyLisa21f: Good. Can I ask your advice?

STEVEYTREES: what about?

LoopyLisa21f: I was wondering whether I should call an ambulance for my grandad. He fell off his chair earlier.

STEVEYTREES: yeah i would

STEVEYTREES: what happen??

LoopyLisa21f: I walked in, and he was sitting on the back of the sofa, for some reason. He looked really happy – almost a bit manic, to be honest – but was sort of hunched forward a bit, with his fists clenched, and staring off into the middle distance. And then he started bouncing up and down a bit, and then toppled backwards.

STEVEYTREES: check hes ok

LoopyLisa21f: Hmm. Thing is, I don't want to wake him.

LoopyLisa21f: He looks quite happy in his sleep.

STEVEYTREES: well id make sure hes ok

STEVEYTREES: not to suppose to sleep after u had a bad fall straight away

LoopyLisa21f: He landed in almost complete silence, and there hasn't been a peep out of him since. I keep looking down the back to see if he's moved, but he's just stayed "in situ" between the sofa and the wall. I covered him in a sleeping bag to keep him warm.

STEVEYTREES: look I am off u are right Loopy

LoopyLisa21f: What?

LoopyLisa21f: What's the matter?

STEVEYTREES: ur weird

LoopyLisa21f: I was being serious! I'm not weird. Why are you saying that?

LoopyLisa21f: I just want to know whether to move my grandad or not.

STEVEYTREES: well phone a bloody ambulance

LoopyLisa21f: Don't swear at me all of a sudden!

STEVEYTREES: am not just giving u my advice hunny

LoopyLisa21f: Ok. I'm sorry for losing my temper. I just really hope he's ok.

STEVEYTREES: shake him

LoopyLisa21f: What if he's dead? I don't really want to touch someone who's dead. What if he feels all weird?

STEVEYTREES: he wont do

LoopyLisa21f: I just shouted out his name, but he didn't respond.

STEVEYTREES: duno what 2 suggest

LoopyLisa21f: Oh! Oh, it's ok. I can hear him getting to his feet now.

LoopyLisa21f: He lives to fall off the back of the sofa another day!

LoopyLisa21f: Oh man! I just took a look into the living room, and he looks really bewildered, and he's bleeding from the mouth and nose!

LoopyLisa21f: Oh no! Where have grandad's trousers gone?!?

>>STEVEYTREES SIGNED OFF AT 13:26

LOOPYLISA'S BLOG

Thursday, August 31

A new shop has opened up on the high street selling nothing but clown shoes. The shop was opened in a gala ceremony by some of Britain's most famous clowns. I've never heard of any of these clowns, but maybe you have: Rollo Coco, Rollo Benny, Herman and Bagel, The Tits, Jackie Lace, and Bront.

After the opening ceremony, the clowns went on a hilarious riot through the town, throwing bins through shop windows, setting fire to tramps, and stealing from Boots.

POSTED BY LOOPYLISA AT 17:17

"

<<NEW CHAT SESSION STARTED

Bekky26NW: hello how are you? fancy a chat?

LoopyLisa21f: Look at your name …! Are you … are you a … a real girl?!

Bekky26NW: was the last time I looked. lol.

LoopyLisa21f: Good grief. You're the first girl who has ever spoken to me on here. Seriously.

Bekky26NW: lol i feel honoured hi xx

Bekky26NW: im 26 live nr manchester, you?

LoopyLisa21f: Hang on … I'm just a bit taken aback. It's always men who talk to me on here. You just go into the chat room, and sit there, and within 30 seconds you've got ten of them sending you instant messages, and asking you to sleep with them, and begging you to send them photos. I feel so dirty. So very dirty, and cold. Like a piece of scabby old meat being fought over by dogs down some dank, widdly-piddly alley. Now get this: the dogs don't even want to eat the meat – they just want to, you know, do some rumpity-pumps to it.

LoopyLisa21f: Try and picture that if you can – a randy bulldog humping away at a lump of rancid old pork.

Bekky26NW: will do lol

LoopyLisa21f: I feel like I'm losing my humanity. Do you ever feel like that when you go into chat rooms, though?

Bekky26NW: yes i do, although some of the men are cute and fun too

Bekky26NW: i should be honest form the start im a bi fem ... ... is that ok?

LoopyLisa21f: You're a ... you're a what now?

Bekky26NW: bi fem. swing both ways.

LoopyLisa21f: I see. I ... I think I understand. You're like that monkey – Bi-Curious George.

Bekky26NW: lol you're funny.

Bekky26NW: are you bi?

LoopyLisa21f: Er ... not exactly ...

Bekky26NW: most girls are. They just need to admit it to themselves

Bekky26NW: hehe

LoopyLisa21f: I don't want to pry, but I can't imagine what two girls would get up to with one another. I mean, is it just a lot of hand-holding, and brushing each other's hair?

Bekky26NW: not exactly!

Bekky26NW: dya have a pic?

LoopyLisa21f: You want me to send you my picture? Sigh. I get it now. Yes, yes, I'll do it in a minute …

Bekky26NW: yeah thats fine hunny if you don't want to …

LoopyLisa21f: So, let's continue the, y'know, the pretence. Tell me about this whole bisexual thing. What's that all about then? I mean, you can't be a vegetarian and a meat eater at the same time. You can't wash up with a dirty rag. You can't play a tune on a banjo full of peas.

Bekky26NW: had my first gay experience when i was 15 with a friend

Bekky26NW: lost my virginity with a guy when i was 16

LoopyLisa21f: So, you're sort of like the Queen.

Bekky26NW: how??

LoopyLisa21f: You know how the Queen has two birthdays every year?

LoopyLisa21f: Well, she has two virginities as well. According to a documentary I saw she has so far only lost the first one, which she lost at the age of 19 to the Grand Old Duke of York. Apparently, he marched up the top of the hill, and popped her cherry. And then he marched her back down again.

Bekky26NW: u live and learn

LoopyLisa21f: My friend Craig told me that the Queen gets all sorts of perks. Like when she goes on the train, they have to install a bowling alley, which she hardly ever uses. When she does use it, instead of balls she uses an air rifle, and instead of the skittles she uses bottles of rare elk tears.

Bekky26NW: can I ask when did you lose your virginity?

LoopyLisa21f: I can't remember.

Bekky26NW: why not?

LoopyLisa21f: Well, it all happened so quickly that I can't be sure whether it happened at all. I sort of had a vague recollection of it a few weeks later, but dismissed it as a form of "sexual deja-vu". You see, at the time I was browsing an underwear catalogue. I looked at some brown knickers, and had a flashback.

Bekky26NW: dya have that pic lisa?

LoopyLisa21f: No. Not yet. I'm doing it. Sigh.

Bekky26NW: hehe k

Bekky26NW: sorry im the first fem you have chatted to ya on here and here i am chatting you up lol

LoopyLisa21f: Is that what you're doing? I wouldn't have guessed. One way or another I fear you're going to be disappointed.

Bekky26NW: so what are your favourite things to do?

Bekky26NW: lol I bet some of them involve batteries

LoopyLisa21f: Yes. I'd imagine they do.

Bekky26NW: hehe naughty, what toys do you have>?

LoopyLisa21f: I have to say I'm quite taken aback by all this.

Bekky26NW: im sorry, want me to leave ya alone?

LoopyLisa21f: I have to be honest and say that I'm a trifle concerned that you're actually man pretending to be a woman.

Bekky26NW: haha

Bekky26NW: want me to ring you to prove im a girl?

Bekky26NW: i dont want you thinking im a bloke

LoopyLisa21f: That really won't be necessary. Besides, my phone isn't a normal one. My dad's profoundly deaf, so the phone doesn't actually have an earpiece. He can ring people up, but they can't say anything back. He rang for a pizza the other night, and stayed on the phone for almost four hours going "Hello? Hello, are you still there? Did you get my order?".

Bekky26NW: ok

Bekky26NW: found ya pic yet?

LoopyLisa21f: Give me a minute. For pity's sake!

Bekky26NW: lol sorry … i am a little horny today, i havent had my rabbit out yet lol

LoopyLisa21f: What rabbit? What are you talking about?

Bekky26NW: my toy

LoopyLisa21f: Perhaps I'm just being paranoid, but you really do seem quite man-like in your approach to matters of the chat. Maybe that's because you're half-lesbian. Do you like football, DIY, and real ale, except that the footballs have to be pink, the DIY involves putting up shoe cabinets, and the real ale has to be drunk out of a champagne flute with a picture of a kitten on it?

Bekky26NW: lol ok i can understand that … i only ask for a pic cause i like to see the person im chatting to

LoopyLisa21f: I bet you do get chaps on here pretending to be lesbians.

Bekky26NW: oh yes i get loads chattin to me

LoopyLisa21f: How can you be sure if they're the real deal?

Bekky26NW: the first pic they always send is of a girl topless or naked

Bekky26NW: why would i be interested in that … i want to see a dressed girl n wait to be suprised at whats underneath

Bekky26NW: do u want to see me topless?

LoopyLisa21f: Whaaa?! Why would you even want to send me a picture of yourself topless? I'm not saying you're not nice, but – if you are a girl – why would you want to send me that?

Bekky26NW: lol

Bekky26NW: i dont

Bekky26NW: have you found your pic yet?

LoopyLisa21f: You're very high-maintenance.

Bekky26NW: lol

Bekky26NW: you have to remember im a bi girl, i fancy girls, i sleep with girls, so obviously i like seeing a girls naked body ...

LoopyLisa21f: I'm sorry for being so paranoid, but I really am quite convinced that you're actually a man. And if you are, what would your parents think about that? I mean, is that any way to spend your life? Pretending to be a woman so that you can eke sexual gratification out of other Internet users?

Bekky26NW: i will phone you if you want lisa

Bekky26NW: send me your pic

LoopyLisa21f: Ok. Hang on.

LoopyLisa21f: Sent.

<IMAGE SENT – lisa22.jpg>

Bekky26NW: very nice

LoopyLisa21f: Thankyou.

Bekky26NW: and here was me thinking it would be a topless pic lol

Bekky26NW: your very pretty but I have to go.

LoopyLisa21f: Hello?

LoopyLisa21f: Hello, dear?

Bekky26NW: I have to go

>>Bekky26NW HAS SIGNED OFF AT 15:03

LOOPYLISA'S BLOG

Saturday, September 02

I have to admit I'm becoming increasingly disillusioned with the calibre of person I'm meeting on the Internet. When I first bought a modem I hoped that I'd be married within six months, but a wedding looks as far away as ever.

Craig – who bought a modem at around the same time as me – says he's met loads of women off the Internet, and got at least four or five of them pregnant. I'm not sure whether to believe him, though.

After all, this is the person who once told me he came out of an egg, and could lay eggs himself. When I asked him to demonstrate he did something unsanitary to my handbag.

POSTED BY LOOPYLISA AT 16:44

<<NEW CHAT SESSION STARTED

PhilPhil69: hi wanna chat

LoopyLisa21f: May as well. What do you want to chat about, dear?

PhilPhil69: sex if u want

LoopyLisa21f: Lordy. Right in there. You didn't waste any time.

PhilPhil69: well do u or not ?

LoopyLisa21f: Well, I dunno. We could I suppose. Don't you want to get to know me first? What about a bit of romance?

PhilPhil69: fuck romance aint got tha time

LoopyLisa21f: I mean, I've had a bit of a traumatic day. I'm hardly going to be in the mood for an "intimate chat" after a day like today. Not without a bit of smooth talking first.

LoopyLisa21f: I had a small car accident earlier, you know.

PhilPhil69: how comes?

PhilPhil69: what happened, r u ok?

LoopyLisa21f: Well, I was on my way to Lidl to pick up some manner of meat-like paste for spreading onto my olive bread. I pulled up outside, stepped out of the car, and this big pumpkin lorry comes out of nowhere, and knocks my door off. If I hadn't gone back in to get my shopping list (1. Meat-like paste; 2. Bread; 3. Pine nuts) I could've been killed – or worse.

PhilPhil69: worse how?

LoopyLisa21f: Use your imagination, dear. The driver of the pumpkin lorry could've gotten out, and abducted me, and held me captive in some dank airing cupboard for the rest of my natural life. He might've made me eat some dirty hand towels!

LoopyLisa21f: Can you drive?

PhilPhil69: yea i can drive

PhilPhil69: i bet u was well scared, i wood have been

LoopyLisa21f: Have you ever had an accident in your car?

PhilPhil69: yea but i only a little bump up my arse

LoopyLisa21f: By which I mean "Have you ever done a little wee in your car because you've been scared of the traffic"?

PhilPhil69: yea all the time

LoopyLisa21f: When I was younger we used to go on these holidays at the far end of the country, and so that we didn't have to stop en route my dad used to go to wee in a crisp bag, and throw it out of the window.

LoopyLisa21f: One time he even did a number two in an empty Pringles pot.

PhilPhil69: ewww thats horrible

LoopyLisa21f: He held the Pringle pipe to his anus, and just squeezed one out, one hand still on the wheel.

PhilPhil69: jesus

LoopyLisa21f: Once you pop – you can't stop! I'm just glad he has quite solid stools, otherwise it could've been nasty.

PhilPhil69: done it in a bottle b4

PhilPhil69: wouldnt b able to do it in a bottle now

LoopyLisa21f: Why not?

LoopyLisa21f: My dad still does.

PhilPhil69: it would b hard but havent tried 4 a very long time

LoopyLisa21f: Well, next time you're out in the car you should give it a go. My mum used to have to help him, though, so you might need an assistant.

PhilPhil69: so u use 2 b able to see ur dad going 4 a piss and ur mum helping him?

LoopyLisa21f: Well, she used to complain endlessly. And I didn't watch. I was in the back. My dad also has this problem whereby he breaks wind involuntarily when he's emptying his bladder. Now see if you can picture that scenario.

PhilPhil69: yeh disgusting

LoopyLisa21f: The Pringle pot was the worst. He just put the lid back on, and threw it out.

PhilPhil69: that is horrible

LoopyLisa21f: To be honest, it would've been easier if he'd stopped and done it at the side of the road. Or wound down the window, and just done it straight onto the motorway as he was going along.

PhilPhil69: li bet

LoopyLisa21f: That would've been like a dirty version of The Red Arrows. You know: The Brown Arrows.

PhilPhil69: so wot do u look like

PhilPhil69: and see if u got a pic

LoopyLisa21f: I'll get you a pic in a moment.

LoopyLisa21f: I'm not sending it until I know I can trust you.

PhilPhil69: im not gonna give it to no one

LoopyLisa21f: I'm not sending it until I know 100% that I can trust you. I've had some bad experiences on here.

LoopyLisa21f: I had a stalker once. He found my address on the Internet, and tracked me down. He built a cardboard kennel in my front garden, and slept in it for three nights. And then it rained, and his kennel got all mushy, and I never saw him again. I think he got washed into a drain.

PhilPhil69: im no fuckin stalker im in the army im not like that

LoopyLisa21f: What do you do in the army?

PhilPhil69: driver

LoopyLisa21f: Do you drive tanks?

PhilPhil69: yes and lorries

LoopyLisa21f: Do you drive armoured cars?

PhilPhil69: not yet

LoopyLisa21f: Have you ever driven a big car that's in the shape of an orange for some reason?

PhilPhil69: whot tha fuck?

LoopyLisa21f: Never mind. It's just something I like to imagine; a soldier driving around in a big orange.

PhilPhil69: do u work ?

LoopyLisa21f: Yes. Currently, I'm working in a garden centre part-time, and studying to become a teacher. Have you ever been in a garden centre? They really are well wicked, man. We sell mud by the bucket load, and sod by the clump.

PhilPhil69: yes so can i ask somethin

LoopyLisa21f: Yes.

PhilPhil69: wot do u wear to work

LoopyLisa21f: It's just a pair of black trousers and a green smock with a big letter "G" on the front. And a sort of black rubber strap around my jaw and head.

PhilPhil69: tight trousers?

LoopyLisa21f: Well, a bit tight. Why do you ask?

PhilPhil69: coz i like naughty girls

LoopyLisa21f: Well, they're only tight because they're too small from me. They used to belong to the girl I took over from.

LoopyLisa21f: She died of malnutrition, I believe. There's nothing naughty about that, unless she starved herself for a prank. It's hardly the best practical joke ever, though. It's not really on a par with "whoopee soap", or "black face cushions".

PhilPhil69: u ever been naughty at work

LoopyLisa21f: Yes.

PhilPhil69: wot did u do

LoopyLisa21f: You know those big plastic pond bases they have?

PhilPhil69: yes

LoopyLisa21f: One time me and Craig (he sometimes works there as well) climbed underneath one of those, and pretended to be a turtle! We scuttled around for hours until our supervisor caught us.

PhilPhil69: no i mean naughty as in sex or played with urself

LoopyLisa21f: Oh. Well, no. Not at work. There's nowhere at work to do something like that. There are security cameras everywhere. The only safe place would be the aquarium bit, and the fish creep me out. Every time I go in there I get convinced that I'm drowning.

PhilPhil69: ever had ur ass grabbed at work

LoopyLisa21f: I don't think so. Someone once coughed in my face. Why do you ask? Have you ever "grabbed an ass"?

PhilPhil69: yes, i like dirty girls, plz may i see ur pic hun

LoopyLisa21f: Ok.

LoopyLisa21f: Sent now.

LoopyLisa21f: Tell me when you have it.

<IMAGE SENT – lisa13.jpg>

PhilPhil69: thats a fuckin bloke

LoopyLisa21f: I'm sorry?

PhilPhil69: ur a guy

LoopyLisa21f: Maybe I've sent the wrong thing.

PhilPhil69: thats a guy lyin on the floor

LoopyLisa21f: I'll send another.

PhilPhil69: ok

LoopyLisa21f: How's this one?

<IMAGE SENT – lisa8.jpg>

LoopyLisa21f: Got it?

PhilPhil69: its a guy wot u playin at ????

LoopyLisa21f: I don't know what you mean.

PhilPhil69: who the fuck are they ??

LoopyLisa21f: It's me of course.

PhilPhil69: ur messin me bout its a guy

PhilPhil69: im goin to tell the administrators

LoopyLisa21f: I've sent you my last one. Let's see if that calms you down. Please don't call the Administrators. I wouldn't survive if I received a visit from the Administrators.

<IMAGE SENT – lisa24.jpg>

PhilPhil69: no i no longer wanna chat with u u r a freak

LoopyLisa21f: I had a stalker, you know!

LoopyLisa21f: I can't be that ugly if I had a stalker!

PhilPhil69: thatsa a guy coz he as hair on his face im reportin u nowe

LoopyLisa21f: Well, you could. But bear in mind that you were the one who turned this conversation sexual. You were the one who said that you liked to imagine me having sex with a turtle.

PhilPhil69: wot the fuck r u on????

LoopyLisa21f: Perhaps I should report YOU for harassment.

LoopyLisa21f: I don't think the Administrators are going to care that I sent you photos which you requested, but they might be interested to hear about your curious sexual picadillos.

PhilPhil69: do wot u like

PhilPhil69: but if thats not u in the pics i rather u say so

LoopyLisa21f: That IS me.

LoopyLisa21f: They're not great photos, because they were taken with a waterlogged camera.

PhilPhil69: so ur a transvestite then

LoopyLisa21f: NO!

LoopyLisa21f: I'm a girl just like any other.

PhilPhil69: thats no girl ill get my dad whos a cop to ave a look in a sec

LoopyLisa21f: Will you show your dad the rest of the conversation?

PhilPhil69: he sittin here all the time

LoopyLisa21f: Did he like it when you asked if I played with myself at work?

PhilPhil69: he laughed, and said those pics r no girl

LoopyLisa21f: I'm looking at those photos, and I'm sorry – but I can't see that I look that much like a man. It's just me.

LoopyLisa21f: Why are you being so horrible to me?

PhilPhil69: ok ill send it to my gf and ask her ok

LoopyLisa21f: Your gf? Your grandfather?

PhilPhil69: girlfriend

LoopyLisa21f: Will your girlfriend and/or grandfather like to know that you've been asking internet girls about their naughty work habits? And how you tell them how much you'd like to see them having some sort of strange liason with a turtle?

PhilPhil69: she likes me doin it

LoopyLisa21f: Then she's a broader-minded girl than I am!

PhilPhil69: dnt worry ok

LoopyLisa21f: Don't worry about what?

PhilPhil69: talkin to me

LoopyLisa21f: But I was enjoying it until you got nasty, and started saying I look like a man, and threatening to call in the Administrators.

PhilPhil69: u do luk like a man

LoopyLisa21f: Well, I'm sorry – but I'm not a man.

PhilPhil69: why has the pic got hair on chin n round mouth ?

LoopyLisa21f: Do you have any idea how hurtful that is? I'm actually crying.

LoopyLisa21f: I don't know why it looks like that, but it ISN'T hair.

LoopyLisa21f: It's just shadows, and stuff.

LoopyLisa21f: Do you normally treat women this way?

PhilPhil69: no coz they normally fit n got sense

LoopyLisa21f: What do you mean? So I'm stupid as well as ugly, is that what you're saying?

LoopyLisa21f: Can I ask you something, dear?

PhilPhil69: wot

LoopyLisa21f: When you say I look like a man, you're not actually saying I'm ugly though, are you?

PhilPhil69: no i just dont go for ur type im sorry

LoopyLisa21f: Well, I have one more pic. See if that's any clearer.

PhilPhil69: ok

LoopyLisa21f: Try that one. My hair's a bit different.

<IMAGE SENT – lisa27.jpg>

LoopyLisa21f: Any better?

PhilPhil69: no sorry

LoopyLisa21f: Well, I can't pretend you haven't hurt my feelings. I'm profoundly distressed.

PhilPhil69: cool goodbye

LoopyLisa21f: Are you going?

LoopyLisa21f: Can't we at least be friends? Please.

PhilPhil69: look im goin now

LoopyLisa21f: I'm sorry you don't find me sexually attractive, but I have a nice personality, and quite a round, smooth bottom.

LoopyLisa21f: Is that any help?

LoopyLisa21f: Is it?

PhilPhil69: look i want a girl who dnt look like a guy ok im sorry

LoopyLisa21f: Why do you keep having to say that?

PhilPhil69: accept thats my type

PhilPhil69: thats the girls i like

PhilPhil69: normal girls wit tits and fannies

PhilPhil69: goodbye ok ur nt my type so im off now bye got friends to go see

LoopyLisa21f: Please wait one second …

PhilPhil69: why?

LoopyLisa21f: I'm really lonely tonight.

PhilPhil69: tough find sum1 else

LoopyLisa21f: I don't look like a man in real life. Maybe we could meet up.

LoopyLisa21f: You could show me your tank.

PhilPhil69: if u dnt look like a girl then no sorry

LoopyLisa21f: But they're bad photos, that's all.

LoopyLisa21f: You've really hurt my feelings.

PhilPhil69: well to me its a guy im sorry but

PhilPhil69: dont put the fuckin blame on me now u can forget ever talkin now

LoopyLisa21f: Well it's hardly my fault, is it?

LoopyLisa21f: I'm just as God made me.

LoopyLisa21f: You're the one who threw the insults around.

PhilPhil69: goodbye for the last time

LoopyLisa21f: Phil, wait. It's me.

PhilPhil69: who

LoopyLisa21f: It's me!

PhilPhil69: wot the hell ???

PhilPhil69: its me who ????

LoopyLisa21f: Guess.

PhilPhil69: dont know

LoopyLisa21f: Take a look at the photos and you'll know who it is.

LoopyLisa21f: Take a close look.

PhilPhil69: i dont know

LoopyLisa21f: Look really close ....

LoopyLisa21f: And give them a big kiss!! Ha ha!

PhilPhil69: still dont know

LoopyLisa21f: It's me!

LoopyLisa21f: Lisa!

PhilPhil69: lisa who ????

LoopyLisa21f: Your new friend for life!

LoopyLisa21f: Lisa!

LoopyLisa21f: Who you met on the Internet!

LoopyLisa21f: Tonight!

PhilPhil69: goodbye ur now gonna be blocked from im-ing me now

LoopyLisa21f: Why?

LoopyLisa21f: Why are you blocking me?

LoopyLisa21f: What have I done?

PhilPhil69: coz ur fuckin about n they aint pics of u so bye bye

LoopyLisa21f: They are!

LoopyLisa21f: Of course they are!

LoopyLisa21f: I sent you one … two … three … four pics.

LoopyLisa21f: Who else are they if they aren't me?

LoopyLisa21f: I'm just as God made me.

PhilPhil69: its one of ur m8s ie: craig so bye im not replyin no more

LoopyLisa21f: That isn't Craig. Craig doesn't wear make-up, or have a woman's hairstyle.

LoopyLisa21f: I mean, look at the hair!

LoopyLisa21f: Of course I'm a woman!

PhilPhil69: that is a guys hair style coz my cousin got that so its not u good fuckin bye

LoopyLisa21f: Does your cousin wear make-up?

LoopyLisa21f: Is he in the army too, Phil?

PhilPhil69: yes

LoopyLisa21f: Phil ...

LoopyLisa21f: Phillip ...

LoopyLisa21f: Phil, tell me – what's it like inside a tank?

LoopyLisa21f: Have you ever put anything up the barrel of the gun, like a loaf, or some loafers, and fired it out?

LoopyLisa21f: Philly, I'm sorry. I've obviously done something wrong.

LoopyLisa21f: Please say you forgive me.

LoopyLisa21f: Please. I won't be able to sleep if you don't.

LoopyLisa21f: Please, Phil. I'm really genuinely upset.

LoopyLisa21f: Just give me a little kiss. An "x" and I'll leave you alone.

LoopyLisa21f: I'll give you one, look: xxxx

LoopyLisa21f: You got four!

>>PhilPhil69 SIGNED OFF AT 20:18

LOOPYLISA'S BLOG

Friday, September 15

Yesterday, Craig and I went to watch the town's annual tortoise and hare race. All kinds of people from across the borough bring a tortoise or a hare to enter the race, and the starting line looks just like the starting line of the London Marathon – but with more tortoises and hares.

Unlike the famous fable, a real life tortoise and hare race isn't so cut and dried, and there's no guarantee of who will win. You see, whilst hares are – technically – faster than tortoises, there's no way of getting them do their running in a straight line.

Also, there was a brief altercation before the start of the race, when one of the would-be entrants turned up with a porpoise, having misread his flyer. I'm not entirely sure how he thought a porpoise and a hare race would work.

Maybe he'd done it on "porpoise" (purpose)!!!!!!

POSTED BY LOOPYLISA AT 08:08

<<NEW CHAT SESSION STARTED

DebarresHimself: I thought i'd say hello

LoopyLisa21f: That's very civil of you.

LoopyLisa21f: Are you always this decent?

DebarresHimself: i'm very civil

LoopyLisa21f: Are you a "Civil Cyril", dear?

DebarresHimself: lol

DebarresHimself: may i enquire whereabouts you are?

LoopyLisa21f: North West London. You know: near where that big tornado hit.

DebarresHimself: did it get you?

LoopyLisa21f: No. It just missed me by a couple of feet.

LoopyLisa21f: However, I was quite badly "buffeted" by some "gusts". It blew my trouser legs up over my head, which was quite painful. Also: it destroyed my house.

DebarresHimself: ok, i'm in east london

LoopyLisa21f: Ok. Ever any tornados there?

DebarresHimself: nope.

LoopyLisa21f: Hurricanes?

DebarresHimself: not really

LoopyLisa21f: "Squalls"?

DebarresHimself: just strong winds

LoopyLisa21f: Have you ... snigger ... have you been on the bum beans again? LOL!

DebarresHimself: lol

LoopyLisa21f: So, why are you on here so late? It's practically tomorrow.

DebarresHimself: waiting for someone to talk to

LoopyLisa21f: Well, here I am. What do you want to talk about? We could do a general knowledge quiz, perhaps.

DebarresHimself: could do.

LoopyLisa21f: Or how about we play truth or dare? How's that sound?

DebarresHimself: ok

LoopyLisa21f: You go first.

DebarresHimself: truth

LoopyLisa21f: Ok. Um … when did you last have a bath?

DebarresHimself: last year sometime. we don;t have a bath tub here

LoopyLisa21f: Where are you? A field?! Some kind of arid wasteland?

DebarresHimself: no, we only have a shower

LoopyLisa21f: Ok. That's kind of ok. I'll have truth.

LoopyLisa21f: Please?

LoopyLisa21f: Hello?

DebarresHimself: do u ever go out with no underwear on?

LoopyLisa21f: I have done, but not by choice.

DebarresHimself: How do you mean?

LoopyLisa21f: Well, one time I lost all my knickers.

DebarresHimself: u lost them all???

LoopyLisa21f: I know it sounds unlikely, but we think one of my dad's friends took them.

DebarresHimself: what???? no way

LoopyLisa21f: Yeah. It doesn't matter.

DebarresHimself: yeh it does!!!!!

LoopyLisa21f: My friend Craig said he saw the guy passing them around in the pub.

DebarresHimself: no way!!!!

LoopyLisa21f: Mm-hm. He was sharing them out with his other friends – the drunks.

LoopyLisa21f: Truth or dare?

DebarresHimself: i don;t mid telling u nothing but truths

LoopyLisa21f: Ok then. I suppose dares are a bit tough to do on here.

LoopyLisa21f: I played truth or dare on here with someone one time, and he dared me to eat some raw bacon, and when I did it he didn't believe me, so I ate some more, and he still didn't believe me.

DebarresHimself: were u sick?

LoopyLisa21f: A little bit into my hand.

DebarresHimself: ok so truth again

LoopyLisa21f: Ok. If you had to kiss a dog, would it matter if it was a boy dog, or a girl dog?

DebarresHimself: probably not

LoopyLisa21f: Interesting. I shall note that down in my ledger. What if you had to have "full sauce" with a dog?

DebarresHimself: dunno

LoopyLisa21f: It's important that you answer.

DebarresHimself: girl dog

LoopyLisa21f: I hoped you'd say that. Truth please.

DebarresHimself: whats the baughiest thing u have ever done?

LoopyLisa21f: Naughtiest?

DebarresHimself: yeah, that too

LoopyLisa21f: I broke into a teacher's house once, and had a bath. After I'd finished in the bath I put his bed sheets, and the contents of a fruit bowl, in the bath.

DebarresHimself: ok

DebarresHimself: truth again

LoopyLisa21f: Ok. What do you think happens when you die?

DebarresHimself: u meet the people again who went before u

LoopyLisa21f: Really? What, in Heaven?

DebarresHimself: yeah

LoopyLisa21f: Cool. What are they doing up there?

DebarresHimself: they dead

LoopyLisa21f: What did they die of?

DebarresHimself: allsort of thing

LoopyLisa21f: Your turn to ask!

DebarresHimself: what do u wear to sleep in?

LoopyLisa21f: It depends on how hot it is. If it's very cold I wear this sort of all-in-one wearable sleeping bag, which has separate compartments for the limbs, and an integral balaclava. If it's hot, I just wear cut-off denims, and a tricorn hat.

DebarresHimself: ok

LoopyLisa21f: My turn.

DebarresHimself: ok

LoopyLisa21f: Which would you rather eat: a bee, or a wasp?

DebarresHimself: neither

LoopyLisa21f: You have to eat one. There's a man there with a pointed stick, and he's going to jab you with it if you don't eat one.

DebarresHimself: i don;t know

LoopyLisa21f: You have to answer! Your life depends on it!

LoopyLisa21f: Bee or wasp ... bee or wasp?

DebarresHimself: bee

LoopyLisa21f: Ok. Cool. Your turn to ask.

LoopyLisa21f: Hello?

DebarresHimself: thinking

DebarresHimself: what wouldn;t u do, sex wise

LoopyLisa21f: Hmm …

LoopyLisa21f: I probably wouldn't do it in a hot air balloon, because I'm scared of heights, and balloons. And hot air, and hot air balloonists.

DebarresHimself: ok hun

DebarresHimself: ur turn

LoopyLisa21f: If you could have unlimited coconuts for the rest of your life, or unlimited chocolate for a week, which would you choose?

DebarresHimself: chocolate. i hate coconuts

LoopyLisa21f: Yes, but you could sell the coconuts on eBay, and use the proceeds to buy as much chocolate as you want. Much more than a week's worth.

LoopyLisa21f: Anyway, your turn to ask.

DebarresHimself: what 3 wishes would u ask a genie?

LoopyLisa21f: Ooh, good one.

LoopyLisa21f: 1. I'd like a new pair of shoes. 2. To get a promotion at work one day. 3. To have 50% off my next two haircuts.

LoopyLisa21f: Ok. My turn to ask.

LoopyLisa21f: Who is your favourite member of Genesis?

DebarresHimself: Phil collins

LoopyLisa21f: Hmm. I'd have gone for Mike Rutherford.

DebarresHimself: phil is the only one i know

LoopyLisa21f: Well, that's ok, but really you should know that Genesis isn't just Phil Collins. He wasn't even in the original line-up of the band. The origins of Genesis begin in the late 1960s, when founding members Peter Gabriel and Tony Banks were pupils at the esteemed Charterhouse School. The original five man line-up was comprised of Peter Gabriel (vocals), Anthony Phillips (guitar), Tony Banks (keyboards), Mike Rutherford (bass and guitar), and Chris Stewart (drums). Following the departure of Stewart, and his subsequent replacement John Mayhew, Phil Collins joined Genesis on 4 August 1970 after successfully impressing the other band members with his drumming skills during an audition at Gabriel's parents' house. Collins made his studio debut – alongside guitarist Steve Hackett – on the album Nursery Cryme (released November, 1971), which featured Collins's first lead vocal performance on the sublime "For Absent Friends".

LoopyLisa21f: Your turn to ask.

DebarresHimself: what 2 things would u take to a desert island?

LoopyLisa21f: A mallet (for opening coconuts, killing boars, and digging/thumping holes in the sand), and a couple of DVDs.

DebarresHimself: do u like coconuts?

LoopyLisa21f: Not really, but what else would there be to eat? Sand, I suppose. But that's really gritty. And pebbles don't taste of anything.

LoopyLisa21f: My turn to ask.

DebarresHimself: ok

LoopyLisa21f: If you could mentally control any one pop star to do your bidding – for the rest of their life – and get away with it without anyone knowing, would you do it, and who would it be?

LoopyLisa21f: Bear in mind, they would no longer have free will or a life of their own.

DebarresHimself: britney spears

LoopyLisa21f: So you'd do it?

DebarresHimself: yes, i would make her look after her kids properly

LoopyLisa21f: I'd control the late George Harrison. I'd bring him back to life, and make him chase after a crowd of kids, going "Graaaaah!".

LoopyLisa21f: Your turn.

DebarresHimself: g-string, thong or big pants?

LoopyLisa21f: None of the above. Just regular knickers normally.

LoopyLisa21f: Have you ever given an old man a bed bath?

DebarresHimself: no

LoopyLisa21f: Would you like to?

DebarresHimself: no

LoopyLisa21f: Ok. Are you sure?

DebarresHimself: yes

DebarresHimself: what is ur dream car?

LoopyLisa21f: This is going to sound really odd, but I once had a dream about a car that was shaped like an satsuma, and I'd really like that car for real.

DebarresHimself: i'm off to bed

LoopyLisa21f: Oh, ok. Good. Abrupt.

DebarresHimself: i hope this won;t be a one off

LoopyLisa21f: Me too! It was absolutely brilliant.

DebarresHimself: i hope we can become good friends

LoopyLisa21f: Yes please! Ok. You go then.

DebarresHimself: goodnight sexy

LoopyLisa21f: Bye now! x

>>DebarresHimself HAS SIGNED OFF AT 00:26

LOOPYLISA'S BLOG

Sunday, September 17

I really feel like I've done a lot of growing up this year, and come to terms with who I am. Things really started turning around when I started visiting a personal trainer called Guy Woburn.

Woburn believes that the secret of inner enlightenment can be unlocked by following three basic rules, which he repeats throughout his sessions:

1. Visit Guy Woburn more often.
2. Buy more of Guy Woburn's books.
3. Write to TV producers to try and get Guy Woburn his own TV show.

Sometimes, Guy Woburn likes to make a little joke, and that joke is: "*If you're happy, Woburn Abby (Woburn is happy)*". To be honest, I never really thought it worked very well, either as a joke, or as the slogan on his advert in the Yellow Pages.

POSTED BY LOOPYLISA AT 21:01

<<NEW CHAT SESSION STARTED

PRICEUK2: hi there – hows you? hope im not interruptin ya ...

PRICEUK2: how has ur year been?

LoopyLisa21f: I've had better ones to be honest with you. I've spent most of this year trying to find out who I am.

PRICEUK2: cant ya remember?

LoopyLisa21f: There's no need for that sort of sarcasm.

PRICEUK2: soz

LoopyLisa21f: Earlier this year I spent a couple of months in a commune off the coast of Scotland trying to discover the inner me.

PRICEUK2: nice but not 4 me like

LoopyLisa21f: We didn't have any electricity. We had to live in teepees, wash our clothes in a peat bog, eat raw, live crabs, and feed the real monster who lived in the loch.

PRICEUK2: right lol

LoopyLisa21f: What's the matter?

PRICEUK2: monster right

LoopyLisa21f: You don't believe me about the monster?

PRICEUK2: no

LoopyLisa21f: Nobody ever believes me. I'm not talking the Loch Ness Monster here, dear. This was the real deal. A proper monster.

LoopyLisa21f: Do you not accept that there are things in this world which are beyond our understanding?

PRICEUK2: fuck all surprises me but a monster 2 me is someone that rapes a girl

PRICEUK2: or fucks with kids etc

PRICEUK2: thats a monster

LoopyLisa21f: Well, I have to say I've never heard of rapists living underwater before, but it's possible I suppose. I mean, he'd have to use a snorkel, and probably need to surface every now and then to eat, and rape things. And I did once hear about a paedophile who lived in a tree, and there's a tramp near me who smells like he lives down a drain, so I suppose it's within the realms of possibility.

LoopyLisa21f: Nevertheless, this was an actual monster like you get on Doctor Who, but more real, and less "televisual".

PRICEUK2: did u pay 2 go there?

LoopyLisa21f: I just had to give a donation. I didn't know about the monster before I went, and if I had I might have given a slightly smaller donation.

PRICEUK2: right

LoopyLisa21f: It has really opened my eyes. You know: opened my eyes to the fact that some types of monsters are real.

PRICEUK2: you want 2 kill him now then ?

PRICEUK2: hunt him down ?

LoopyLisa21f: Not really. I mean, at the end of the day a monster is just an animal. It's basically just a really monstrous animal that looks like a monster

PRICEUK2: and kills?

LoopyLisa21f: I never said that it kills. I'd imagine that it does sometimes, but it didn't kill anyone while I was there. It did knock over some bins, and throw a lantern in the loch.

PRICEUK2: you dont want 1 as a pet do u lol

PRICEUK2: you make me laugh i like you

LoopyLisa21f: I'm not trying to be funny.

PRICEUK2: ok lol

LoopyLisa21f: I'm just telling you about the monster, guy.

PRICEUK2: what did it look like ?

PRICEUK2: is there a web site ?

LoopyLisa21f: It was hairy with a green face, and big, yellow eyes. And it had this sort of flesh pipe – like a pink, veiny hose/nozzle – sticking out of its chest. Sometimes stuff would come out of the nozzle – either a thick, sticky froth, or coins. Also, there was a number tattooed on its forehead. We think it might have escaped from somewhere.

PRICEUK2: sounds like some men i work with.

PRICEUK2: woz it maybe a chimp?

LoopyLisa21f: A chimp? Living underwater? With a chest nozzle that disburses froth and change? Don't be ridiculous.

PRICEUK2: is there a pic etc?

LoopyLisa21f: No. I don't have a pic of it.

PRICEUK2: dunno then

LoopyLisa21f: I can't stress this enough. It wasn't a man, or a regular animal – it was a monster.

LoopyLisa21f: It used to climb out of the loch at dawn, and root around for food. One time it ate a tent peg.

PRICEUK2: why?

LoopyLisa21f: I don't know. I'm not a cryptozoologist. Perhaps he thought it was a root. We were watching it through a seam in the wall of our tepee, and it bent down, and just sort of inhaled the peg in one big gasp.

LoopyLisa21f: Given the chance, would you not wish to encounter the monster, dear?

PRICEUK2: ive not time 4it

PRICEUK2: ive got my son and thats all that matters 2me

LoopyLisa21f: You have a son?

LoopyLisa21f: Does he believe in monsters?

PRICEUK2: only on scooby doo

LoopyLisa21f: Will you tell him tonight that monsters exist?

PRICEUK2: i cant he is 3

LoopyLisa21f: It's best you prepare him now.

LoopyLisa21f: I wish someone had been honest with me when I was 3.

PRICEUK2: why? you dont have them were u live

PRICEUK2: and we dont have them in liverpool

PRICEUK2: so unless i take him there he no need 2 worry is head

LoopyLisa21f: No. You're quite right. But what would happen if the monster swam over here one day?

LoopyLisa21f: Do you think it would cause ructions?

PRICEUK2: not bothered

PRICEUK2: u believe in ghost too?

LoopyLisa21f: I've had direct contact with ghosts on four occasions, and indirect contact on seven occasions.

PRICEUK2: indirect?

LoopyLisa21f: Yes. When you can smell the ghost, but not actually see it.

LoopyLisa21f: Do you believe in the supernatural?

PRICEUK2: not sure ...

LoopyLisa21f: Why not?

PRICEUK2: never though about it..

PRICEUK2: no actual beings, more feelings

LoopyLisa21f: When have you had these feelings?

PRICEUK2: cudnt say ...

LoopyLisa21f: Was it when you were drunk? Was it when you were "in the bar"?

PRICEUK2: i honestly cant remember details

LoopyLisa21f: I actually spoke to a ghost once.

PRICEUK2: how was it?

LoopyLisa21f: Unusual. His speech was all sort of out of synch with his lips, and he kept looking around like he was expecting to be caught by a more senior ghost, and all he wanted to talk about was what it was like to be a ghost. He was really self-obsessed, and arrogant.

PRICEUK2: i went to a crystal therapist thingie was a bit cautious before – feelin better now

LoopyLisa21f: What happened? What did the therapist do to you?

PRICEUK2: hypnosis

LoopyLisa21f: Wow! I saw my friend being hypnotised once. The hypnotist made him take off his trousers.

LoopyLisa21f: Not my friend's trousers, you understand; the hypnotist made my friend take off the hypnotist's trousers – and pants.

PRICEUK2: on stage?

LoopyLisa21f: Yes, on stage.

PRICEUK2: right …

LoopyLisa21f: It was a bit weird, to be honest.

LoopyLisa21f: Nothing like that happened to you I hope!

PRICEUK2: not sure!

PRICEUK2: hehehe

LoopyLisa21f: What does it feel like to be hypnotised?

PRICEUK2: relaxin

LoopyLisa21f: My friend Craig said it made him feel a bit gay.

PRICEUK2: ????

LoopyLisa21f: Well, he did remove a man's trousers and pants. And he wasn't even hypnotised at that point. The hypnotist just asked him to do it, and he did.

LoopyLisa21f: Plus, Craig became a bit too excited while he was doing it, so … y'know.

PRICEUK2: oh – opsie!

LoopyLisa21f: Yes. He was very embarrassed.

LoopyLisa21f: Why did you have hypnosis?

PRICEUK2: my head is broken …

LoopyLisa21f: What do you mean?

PRICEUK2: theres a load of things ive been through over the last wee while, messed me up a bit …

LoopyLisa21f: I'm really sorry to hear that. Anything I can do to help?

PRICEUK2: oer the last number of years ive been ill made redundant twice, parents busness closed down and thy nearly lost the house, granpa died, dad got made redundant from his n job after a year, went through 2 relationship splits – second one ju recently … i miss hugs..

LoopyLisa21f: I feel a bit bad now for burdening you with my monster. You've got enough to worry about without worrying that monsters might swim over here and eat your son.

PRICEUK2: least im ready 4 them now

LoopyLisa21f: Yes. And you seem like a good person at heart.

PRICEUK2: thanx

LoopyLisa21f: Anyway, it was nice talking to you. You know: nice and depressing.

PRICEUK2: been really great to natter to ya …

PRICEUK2: have a great day ...

LoopyLisa21f: You too, dear. Bye.x

PRICEUK2: peace and love ...

>>LoopyLisa21f SIGNED OFF AT 17:58 **"**

LOOPYLISA'S BLOG

Wednesday, September 27

You'll be glad to hear that I recently qualified as a teacher, and now that I'm earning some real money I can finally pay off my debts. This couldn't have happened at a better time. I recently had some bailiffs come round to the flat, and I'm fairly confident that they were the strangest bailiffs that I – or anyone else – has ever seen.

One of the bailiffs was a Cyclops, but instead of having one eye in the middle of his face, he had one eye on the back of his head, and another one in a bowl he was carrying. The other bailiff was one half of a pair of Siamese twins. The other twin was still attached, but appeared to have died sometime in the previous couple of weeks.

The living twin was fully clothed, but for some reason the dead twin was wearing nothing but a pair of very skimpy trunks, and cropped t-shirt with a picture of a coffin on it.

POSTED BY LOOPYLISA AT 23:41

<<NEW CHAT SESSION STARTED

Khan78: hi how r u 2nite?

LoopyLisa21f: I'm feeling better than I have in weeks now that the sores have almost healed over. How are you?

Khan78: i'm knackered. r u high on something?

LoopyLisa21f: Why are you knackered? Have you been lifting things?

LoopyLisa21f: You know: lifting things like tumble dryers, and bags of spanners?

Khan78: no just got in from work

LoopyLisa21f: What is your work?

Khan78: i work for a hedge fund as an analyst

LoopyLisa21f: Is "hedge" short for 'hedgehogs'? Do you analyse hedgehogs, and other things?

Khan78: no its relating to financial industry

LoopyLisa21f: I see. You mean the hedgehogs are for sale?

Khan78: trading shares on new york, london stock exchange, comprende?

LoopyLisa21f: Shares in hedgehogs? Is that like when you go to the zoo, and you can sponsor an animal, or part of an animal? Craig was going to sponsor me a red panda for my birthday, but he could only afford the scrotum. It's not very glamorous going to the zoo to visit your scrotum. Plus: you'd have trouble trying to feed a scrotum. The best you could do is rub the food into it, but they won't even let us get close enough to do that. And we asked nicely and everything …

Khan78: ok. so what do u do

LoopyLisa21f: I'm a school teacher.

Khan78: a school teacher. right

LoopyLisa21f: Primary school, if that counts. Something cool happened at school today though. A little boy called Dainty James sung me a song!

Khan78: let me see that thong- was that teh song ha ha

LoopyLisa21f: No. I'll write it down for you.

LoopyLisa21f: Ready?

Khan78: sure as long as its not explicit

LoopyLisa21f: Here it is: "Hello Mrs Teacher, We are here to be taught today, Hello Mrs Teacher, Is it time for our SATs test yet?"

LoopyLisa21f: It didn't really rhyme, but it was a sweet enough tune. Afterwards he did some bodypopping for me. He said he didn't know what bodypopping was, but I insisted he try. It wasn't very good.

Khan78: so don't they know your name?

LoopyLisa21f: Yes they do, and it did indeed feature in the song. But for now? For now I'm keeping it secret.

LoopyLisa21f: You might be a strange man who wants to track me down and ravish me with your hairy, sweaty hands, and filthy fingernails.

Khan78: i guess your name isn't lisa then

LoopyLisa21f: I can't divulge that information.

LoopyLisa21f: What's your name?

Khan78: can't tell u as u might track me down

Khan78: r u always loud?

LoopyLisa21f: Am I being loud? Is the sound of my typing hurting your ears?

Khan78: no its cool

Khan78: i like loud people

LoopyLisa21f: I normally get told off for being too quiet.

Khan78: who by the kids?

LoopyLisa21f: No – by Mrs Palmer, the headmistress. She tried to get me to talk to the class through a cardboard tube once, because she thought it might amplify my voice. She even attached it to my head using some elastic bands, but all it did was scare a couple of the deaf kids. Because they hadn't heard what was going on, they thought I was some sort of deformed, featherless, bird.

LoopyLisa21f: Never mind, eh.

Khan78: so have u overcome your shyness?

LoopyLisa21f: I'm never said I was shy. Just that my voice just doesn't work right.

Khan78: why

LoopyLisa21f: When I was eight years old I inhaled some rice pudding for a dare, and ever since it's been a horrible voice.

Khan78: what squeaky voice?

LoopyLisa21f: No, all sort of bunged up, as if I've still got some rice up there. When I speak it's like I've got a cushion over my mouth. I've had the x-rays done, but the x-rays apparently pass straight through rice and pulses. Craig says I sound like Noo Noo from the Teletubbies.

Khan78: i see

Khan78: so tell me about yourself

LoopyLisa21f: I desperately want to know what it is that you would like to know about me.

Khan78: start from scratch where your from, interests,likes/ dislikes

LoopyLisa21f: I have a strong dislike of nuns.

Khan78: do u dress like a nun

LoopyLisa21f: No.

LoopyLisa21f: Are you deaf in the ears (eyes)? I said I HATE NUNS.

LoopyLisa21f: I call them "No-funs".

Khan78: so whats your dress sense like at work and out of work

LoopyLisa21f: I wear dungarees sometimes. And every other weekend I'm a special constable, so I have to wear the uniform. It's not the one that normal police wear, and it's not very flattering. It's just a baggy, brown, courduroy jumpsuit, with the word "constable" on the back in white lettering. We're so under-funded we have to work in a big wig-wam with 'POLICE' written on the side in felt tip, and they haven't even spelt it right.

Khan78: ok so whats in store for this weekend

LoopyLisa21f: I'm going shooting with Craig tomorrow at his dad's club!

LoopyLisa21f: Craig is bad. He once shot a hen.

Khan78: who's craig

LoopyLisa21f: My friend.

LoopyLisa21f: I've known him since I was 4 years and three months.

Khan78: cool, so r u a pro or something

LoopyLisa21f: No! I just do it for fun. I've never shot a "hen" if that's what you're implying.

LoopyLisa21f: Craig didn't kill the hen, by the way. It was just a low-power air rifle he was using, and he was actually aiming at a farmer's son.

LoopyLisa21f: Consequently, the pellet pinged off the hen's flange.

Khan78: so what do u shoot

LoopyLisa21f: I shoot lightbulbs.

LoopyLisa21f: Lightbulbs with faces painted on them. Sometimes I dress them in doll's clothes too. I call them "The Bright Face Family". They've even got their own theme song!

Khan78: must have a good aim then

LoopyLisa21f: Well, they're different sizes, and they move back and forth on an automated trolley system of my own design. I even give some of them names, like "Dad", and "Uncle Ron". "Uncle Ron is the cheeky one, Little Ellis is the saucy one, Poor old dad is only 50 watts, But he does the best he can with all the watts he's got".

LoopyLisa21f: The trick is to aim for the lights.

LoopyLisa21f: Which is what Sister Wendy said when I was little: "If I lose control and murder you in your sleep tonight, Lisa – aim for the light".

Khan78: i see, where is this shootin place based

LoopyLisa21f: High Wycombe.

Khan78: do u live nearby

LoopyLisa21f: Not too far. We go in Craig's Jeep.

LoopyLisa21f: Actually, I don't know if it's actually a real jeep.

Khan78: is it a big monster

LoopyLisa21f: I dunno. It's green, and has three wheels, and Craig cut photos of Jeeps out of magazines and glued them all over it. There are loads of empty wine bottles in the back.

LoopyLisa21f: So, what's it like working with all those hedgehogs?

Khan78: frantic and fastpaced

Khan78: u could get stinged

LoopyLisa21f: Stung, dear. You mean 'stung'. So, do you just work in the offices? Or do you actually handle the hedgehogs?

Khan78: yes in farringdon

LoopyLisa21f: You go to Farringdon to handle them, but you aren't permanently based in Farringdon?

Khan78: yes i go there to handle them

Khan78: 2day i managed just fine

LoopyLisa21f: Do you wear gloves? In my experience they're sometimes ok to pick up. Oh, but the fleas!

LoopyLisa21f: Oh man, the fleas!

Khan78: oh woman

Khan78: big mama

LoopyLisa21f: What?

Khan78: don't worry

Khan78: so u got anything arranged for 2moz evening

LoopyLisa21f: I might go to the gun club bar.

LoopyLisa21f: Craig's on antibiotics so he won't be drinking. That means it won't be any fun.

Khan78: where is that

LoopyLisa21f: High Wycombe!

LoopyLisa21f: Keep up, Keith.

LoopyLisa21f: It's the gun club bar.

Khan78: moi has never been to that part of the world

LoopyLisa21f: I like it when Craig gets drunk.

Khan78: why is that

LoopyLisa21f: Craig is funny.

LoopyLisa21f: He once did an impression of Nelson Mandela. The bit where he showed everyone Nelson's column nearly got Craig thrown out. It was covered in pigeon muck, and everything.

Khan78: moi heading off to cc club

LoopyLisa21f: What's that? Is something to do with the band 10cc?

Khan78: a classy bar in leicester square

LoopyLisa21f: It sounds classy just from the name.

Khan78: yes by inviation only

LoopyLisa21f: You must be pretty important!

Khan78: not important but i do have good contacts

LoopyLisa21f: Do lots of famous people go there?

Khan78: i've met kate moss and spoken to her, and i've met anastacia

LoopyLisa21f: I met Yorkie Peters once.

Khan78: yorkie peters?

LoopyLisa21f: Yorkie Peters is better than Kate Moss. He has his own equipment, and even writes his own songs.

Khan78: I met laurence fishbourne too

LoopyLisa21f: I love Laurence Lewellyn-Fishbourne! I like it when he designs a room, and the people hate it.

LoopyLisa21f: And I like his hair. It looks like a droopy, black plant perched on his so-called "bonce".

Khan78: so do u have a man

LoopyLisa21f: Not at the moment.

Khan78: why not

Khan78: u seem to have a terrific personality

LoopyLisa21f: My last boyfriend said I was a skank.

Khan78: thats mean

LoopyLisa21f: And he said my food gave him an infection.

LoopyLisa21f: Specifically: an infection in his eye, and his pancreas.

Khan78: r u bad in cooking?

LoopyLisa21f: No, but I had done a beef "stroganoff", and the next day he rolled out of bed, and banged his pancreas on a plug, and his eye also swelled up, and he blamed me.

LoopyLisa21f: I wouldn't mind, but at the time he said it was the best stroganoff he'd ever had. He specifically said it was so tasty it made his ears water.

LoopyLisa21f: I mean, how can beef stroganoff give you a pancreatic eye infection anyway? It's just crazy talk. But then he is a manic depressive, so I shouldn't have been that surprised.

LoopyLisa21f: Anyhow. This has been a whole lot of fun, but I need to get to bed.

Khan78: oh your ditching me?

LoopyLisa21f: Yes. I need to go to bed, and I badly need a poo first.

Khan78: so rude

LoopyLisa21f: Yes. So rude. So brown. Goodnight, Keith. Love you!

LoopyLisa21f: xxxxx

Khan78: ok babe , ciao xx

LoopyLisa21f: Must hurry – it's coming out!

Khan78: ahhhhhh

Khan78: gooooo

LoopyLisa21f: Yes – coming out like goo. Xxxx

>>LoopyLisa21f SIGNED OFF AT 23:10

LOOPYLISA'S BLOG

Monday, November 13

Here is my horoscope for today, according to the local paper:

"VIRGO (Aug 23–Sept 22)

Wdfdlc vdsfdf asfsd kljfsdklfjsdlkjf sflkjsd lfkjsdlfkjsdf sdfsdfk ;lsjdieqw eqw cas,das;l'k asdlkasdpok asdas dasdkjm sdsqweqc,,asploplasd asdasd"

I don't know whether it's meant to be like that or not, or if it's written in Polish, or something, but the more I stared at it as I walked to work, the more I felt like something good was just around the corner.

However, this turned out not to be the case, as just around the corner was a tramp, sprawled in the doorway of Blockbuster, eating a rancid stingray.

POSTED BY LOOPYLISA AT 21:49

<<NEW CHAT SESSION STARTED

DebarresHimself: hello Lisa, remember me?

LoopyLisa21f: No, sorry. Who are you? What do you want?

DebarresHimself: we just chatted a weeks r so ago

LoopyLisa21f: Really? I talk to so many – BRAAAAAAP! – people.

DebarresHimself: I live in East London

LoopyLisa21f: So do loads of people. It's hardly something to get excited about, love.

DebarresHimself: true

DebarresHimself: u don;t live far from where that tornado hit

DebarresHimself: am i right?

LoopyLisa21f: Oh yes! Hello! How are you?

DebarresHimself: i am fine, u remember me now?

LoopyLisa21f: I think so! BRAAAAAAP!

DebarresHimself: what u doing?!?!??

LoopyLisa21f: BRAAAAAAP!

DebarresHimself: ok. So what u been up to ?

DebarresHimself: you said that you wanted us to get to know each other better, and hopefully meet up for a drink one day

LoopyLisa21f: Did I? That doesn't sound much like me. Was I drunk?

DebarresHimself: i don;t know

LoopyLisa21f: What time of day was it?

DebarresHimself: evening

LoopyLisa21f: Hmm. That's weird.

DebarresHimself: why hun?

LoopyLisa21f: Y'know, I feel really strange tonight.

DebarresHimself: why hun, whats up?

LoopyLisa21f: I went to see a tarot reader today.

DebarresHimself: and?

LoopyLisa21f: And he said I was either going to die in the next three months, or get ill in a way that would eventually either kill me, or lead to a protracted illness that would change my life in unforeseen ways.

LoopyLisa21f: It has left me really shaken. I'm a-shakin' and shiverin' with fear.

DebarresHimself: i'm here if u ever need to chat

LoopyLisa21f: Thankyou. Have you ever been to a tarot reader?

DebarresHimself: no

DebarresHimself: being ill can mean many things

LoopyLisa21f: Yeah, but what kind of things? I mean, he looked at the cards, and didn't want to tell me at first, but I insisted. Can "you're probably going to die in the next three months" mean many things too?

DebarresHimself: you can catch a cold and meet the man who u will spend the rest of life with

LoopyLisa21f: How will that happen?

DebarresHimself: u never know

LoopyLisa21f: But it seems like a really unlikely thing to happen, though. I suppose I might have a sniffle on a bus, and ask to borrow a man's handkerchief, and he might ask me out. But what if he's a hankie fetishist? What if he murders me, by forcing me through that little gap at the top of the bus window? Or by making me eat a handkerchief, and I choke on it?

LoopyLisa21f: I'm really scared, love. I don't want to die.

DebarresHimself: u won't die

LoopyLisa21f: He said I would. And then he asked me to pay him 25 pounds.

DebarresHimself: money grabby scuz-bucket

LoopyLisa21f: Do you think he was making it up?

DebarresHimself: yep

LoopyLisa21f: I was crying, and he had some tissues next to him, and I asked for one, and he said I couldn't have one because a ghost lived in the box, and if I took one out it would have disturbed the ghost.

LoopyLisa21f: He rattled the box, and covered his mouth, and made a ghostie sound, but I know it was really him. I thought that was a bit off. I only wanted a tissue to dab my eyes.

DebarresHimself: babe, he just wanted to scam you

LoopyLisa21f: I feel so stupid.

LoopyLisa21f: I went outside, and threw up in a frog's nest.

DebarresHimself: i wish i was there to give u a hug

LoopyLisa21f: You're a very, very, very nice man.

DebarresHimself: and i might even take u out for dinner

LoopyLisa21f: I dunno about that. You might try and scam me too. You might pretend that there's a ghost in the dinner.

DebarresHimself: i would never do that.

LoopyLisa21f: I once stayed at a hotel, which my friend Craig said was the most haunted hotel in the UK. As we were checking in he said: "Even the toast is a ghost, and your daddy is in the toast".

LoopyLisa21f: What do you think he meant?

DebarresHimself: he was just kidding babe

DebaaresHimself: i would pay for dinner for u

LoopyLisa21f: Ok. Thankyou. Could I have chicken kiev?

DebarresHimself: you could have anything u want

LoopyLisa21f: Could I have chicken kiev with Smarties inside instead of garlic butter?

DebarresHimself: sure thing

LoopyLisa21f: But ... what if the food was poisonous, and that's how I die?

DebarresHimself: stop dwelling on it. no-1 know what the future holds

LoopyLisa21f: What is your dream for the future, dear?

DebarresHimself: to get married and have a family

DebarresHimself: i need to find someone special for that

LoopyLisa21f: You seem like a really nice man. I think you deserve someone special.

DebarresHimself: there was some1, but she dumped me

LoopyLisa21f: : -(

DebarresHimself: but thats in the past

LoopyLisa21f: It's only a matter of time until you find someone new.

DebarresHimself: i would like to take u out for a drink one day

LoopyLisa21f: You really wouldn't want to take me out. I'm probably not your sort.

DebarresHimself: i still would like to take u out

LoopyLisa21f: Hang on – do you mean "take me out" in the sense of murdering me in a gangland fashion?

LoopyLisa21f: I'm sorry. I think you're a genuinely really sweet and lovely man, but following today's events I can't take the risk that you're also in the employ of the mob.

DebarresHimself: not at all. u have got a new friend in me

LoopyLisa21f: Gosh. Thanks for that.

LoopyLisa21f: For the record, even if you are a murderer, you're the nicest person I've ever spoken to, and I sincerely hope you find someone soon.

DebarresHimself: thank u kindly

LoopyLisa21f: You know: I hope you find someone to murder who isn't me.

>>LoopyLisa21f SIGNED OFF AT 00:10

Acknowledgements

While I dare say that nobody in their right mind would want to be associated with this grotty pamphlet, I'm afraid that duty and gratitude requires me to thank the following people:

Faye Webber at The Agency for her patience, and being the nicest agent a boy could hope to have; Tim Moore, Adam Keeble and Gavin Lambert for the *Digitiser* years – without them this book simply wouldn't have happened; Robert Popper for Robin Cooper's foreword, and generally being a champion of the cause over the past decade; and everyone at The Friday Project for saying yes so quickly.

I'd especially like to thank my family for putting up with so much, and a special thanks to Mrs Biffo for the make-up session.

Lastly, I'd like to reserve the final thank you for Phillip Barnes, the original inspiration behind the book – whether he knows it or not. No hard feelings.

About the author

Mr Biffo is sometimes better known as BAFTA-nominated screenwriter Paul Rose. He has written for everything from *EastEnders* to *Sooty*, and was a lead writer on cult children's series *My Parents Are Aliens*. He is currently writing funnies for a number of TV comedy shows, including his own projects for BBC1 and BBC3.

He also created, edited and wrote the legendary Teletext videogames magazine *Digitiser*. He owns several wigs.